To Remember the Faces of the Dead

New Directions in Anthropological Writing
History, Poetics, Cultural Criticism

GEORGE E. MARCUS
Rice University

JAMES CLIFFORD
University of California, Santa Cruz

GENERAL EDITORS

To Remember the Faces of the Dead

THE PLENITUDE OF MEMORY
IN SOUTHWESTERN NEW BRITAIN

Thomas Maschio

THE UNIVERSITY OF WISCONSIN PRESS

The University of Wisconsin Press
114 North Murray Street
Madison, Wisconsin 53715

3 Henrietta Street
London WC2E 8LU, England

Printed in the United States of America

An earlier version of chapter 7 appeared in *Ethos*. Copyright © 1992 Society for Psychological Anthropology. Reprinted by permission from *Ethos: Journal of the Society for Psychological Anthropology*, Volume 20, Number 4.

Library of Congress Cataloging-in-Publication Data
Maschio, Thomas.
    To remember the faces of the dead: the plenitude of memory in southwestern New Britain / Thomas Maschio.
        256 p.   cm.—(New directions in anthropological writing)
        Includes bibliographical references and index.
        ISBN 0-299-14090-3 (cloth).   ISBN 0-299-14094-6 (pbk.)
        1. Rauto (Papua New Guinea people)—Rites and ceremonies.   2. Rauto (Papua New Guinea people)—Ethnic identity.   3. Philosophy, Rauto.   4. Anthropological linguistics—Papua New Guinea—West New Britain Province.   5. West New Britain Province (Papua New Guinea)—Social life and customs.   I. Title.
        DU740.42.M373   1994
        306'.089'995—dc20   93-32388

For My Parents

Contents

Illustrations

viii

Acknowledgments

I would like to thank a number of people for helping me to organize my thoughts enough so that I could write this book. I would like to thank Roy Wagner and James Clifford for their helpful criticisms. I would especially like to thank Roy Wagner for his sustained engagement with the issues raised by the ethnography, and James Clifford for the vision and power of his biography of Maurice Leenhardt, *Person and Myth*. The biography convinced me of the value of a Leenhardtian perspective on Melanesian religious phenomenology. Geoffrey White also contributed much in the way of advice during my year at the East-West Center, and I thank him for his efforts here.

I am grateful to Matt Cooper, John Colarusso, and David Counts for their encouragement and support, and I am glad that David Counts suggested that I consider West New Britain as a possible place for field research.

Rick Goulden and Bill Thurston have my heartfelt gratitude for teaching Tok Pisin to my wife Coralie and to me, and for their corrections of, and comments on, my various representations of the Rauto language. I am also grateful to Karen I. Blu for offering helpful suggestions and comments on parts of the book and for supporting me throughout my career. Ellen Badone, Jim Roscoe, and Nancy Lutkehaus also made comments on parts of the manuscript, and I thank them for this.

My father, and while she lived, my mother, made it possible for me to study anthropology by offering understanding and financial and moral support. My father has my love and my thanks for this.

I owe much to my wife Coralie for her steadfastness, her company, her humor, and her good spirits and charm. Her help both in the field and during the period of writing was invaluable. She has shared all the good and the hard times. *Kikalme itau ambip*.

I owe a debt beyond words to the Rauto. I consider the period of my fieldwork to have been the most interesting and personally fulfilling time of my life. I especially wish to thank Vatetio, Tamal, Parak, Kalapua, Brumio, Lumbat,

Rakome, Toliam, and Komosio for their help and friendship, and for sharing the poetry and the power of their lives with me and Coralie.

I am grateful to the Government of Papua New Guinea, and the West New Britain Provincial Government for allowing me to live and work in southwestern New Britain. Funding for my field research during 1985–87 was generously provided by the Fulbright-Hays program, and I am grateful for the program's support. Field support during 1990 was provided by a small grant from the Institute for Intercultural Studies, and I take this opportunity to thank the Institute. Finally, I am deeply grateful to the East-West Center for the postdoctoral fellowship that allowed me the leisure to revise this book.

To Remember the Faces of the Dead

Introduction

After having arrived in New Guinea, one travels to southwestern New Britain by first taking a jet from Port Moresby to Kimbe, a new town that has grown up around a government-sponsored oil palm project. One then takes a small plane over the rugged mountain range that cuts across the center of the island of New Britain to Kandrian, where there is a small government station, a mission, and a hospital. To reach the coastal villages from Kandrian, it is necessary to take a motorboat either up or down the coast. In order to visit the bush villages, one must take a jeep a few miles up into the interior and then walk in. Each stage of this journey has a different character and feel to it. The sight of government officials and expatriate businessmen taking the plane from Moresby up to Lae reminds one of the forces of change that are taking hold of the country of Papua New Guinea. The sight of whole families and of groups of oil palm workers making the trip to Kimbe is a sign of some of the consequences of change. The experience of sharing a small plane with villagers who are carrying taro, sweet potato, and areca nut to their kin on the south coast highlights the tenacity of the traditional lifeways of the south coast in the face of change. Finally, visiting the villages of the south coast for the first time creates a sense that one has entered a world with rather different values and expectations than one's own.

I had not expected to carry out my fieldwork on the south coast. Originally I had planned to live with and to study a group, called the Lamogai, who live near the center of New Britain. On my arrival in Port Moresby, however, I was told that the New Tribes Mission—an American evangelical group—had established itself in Lamogai and would not look kindly on having an anthropologist take up residence in this area. For a young and rather green anthropologist who was about to undertake his first field trip and was not feeling all that confident to begin with, this was rather disconcerting news. I decided not to think about the news too much, and to push on to Kimbe, where I hoped to be able to assess the situation with more precision.

Once there, a government official told me that the provincial government would prefer that I carry out research in southwestern New Britain. He suggested a number of possible research sites to me and my wife Coralie, and we set off with these places in mind. I did not however choose to settle in any of the villages that he suggested. Rather, I decided to work with a group of south coast people who speak a dialect of Lamogai. In the linguistic literature this group is known as the Rauto.

We decided to settle in the village of Wasum. Coralie and I lived there from October of 1985 until December of 1986 and then again from February to June 1990. The village is located on the banks of the Anu River, some thirty kilometers from the government station at Kandrian. Every few weeks we would make field trips to the villages of Ipuk and Giring, which are located some four to five miles inland from Wasum. We would also make weekly visits to the nearby coastal village of Sara.

My first impressions of the place and of the people are not easy to put into words. I remember first how the intense light of hamlet clearings and of the brilliant waters that covered coral reefs set in contrast the darkness that engulfed the interiors of houses, and the interior of the forest. I remember also how the people as well as the place seemed alternately brilliant and dark. Indeed the exuberant demonstrativeness that often characterized my Rauto friends' personal styles set in contrast their occasionally dark, moody, and even frightened reticence. It took Coralie and me years to understand the meaning of the dark and brilliant spaces.

During the first few hours after our arrival at what was to become our major field site, we were not sure whether we would have the opportunity to find out the meaning of all these dark and brilliant places. The people held an impromptu meeting to decide whether or not we would be permitted to live among them and learn their language and customs. One man said that the old people had been waiting a long time to tell the story of their custom to someone "from the outside"; another said that we should only be permitted to stay if we agreed to remain with them for a long time. He said he would have nothing to tell us if we did not agree to do this. And so we did.

Just a few days after our arrival our hosts held a song festival and ceremony to mark the slaughter of a number of tusked pigs. The tuskers had of course first to be rounded up from their hiding places in the bush, and carried down to the ceremonial grounds. I remember people's looks of amazement as I ran off after the tuskers with the men who had been asked to capture the pigs. I remember the laughter as people described again and again how I kept faltering as I helped carry the tuskers back to the ceremonial grounds. Later, after the ceremony was completed, Coralie helped the women cook the pigs in the stone ovens which the Rauto call *silmen*. Getting our hands dirty in these ways made us begin to seem at least somewhat human to these people, an impression we tried to reinforce as often as possible.

Like many first-time field workers, we had a difficult first few months. We made numerous faux pas, and continually felt either put upon, angry, or sorry for ourselves. We were also often quite sick with fever. Yet we were fascinated by what we were finding out about the Rauto, and our piqued curiosity kept us going in the difficult early months of research.

In these initial months we took down genealogies, began compiling a dictionary of Rauto, recorded behavior, and carried out interviews. Initially we worked in Tok Pisin; only after some seven months in the field did we begin to do interviewing in the vernacular. During the early months, Coralie took the initiative by beginning to record Rauto myths in the vernacular. As she worked on the laborious task of transcribing and translating the myths, she began to acquire an understanding of Rauto and an appreciation for the poetry of the language. She then would teach me what she learned of the language and of the myths. Soon, I tried my hand at transcribing and translation. I then began to collect and translate spells and a number of different genres of song. I also took down some life histories in Rauto.

During this period of intensive text collection, I discovered that Rauto elders knew a great number of proverbs and metaphors. I spent a few weeks learning these figures of speech. Learning the tropes was time-consuming and difficult because the process of their translation had at least four different aspects to it. First I had the metaphoric phrase spelled out for me by my informants. Then the reference of the verbal image the metaphor created was described for me. The images described socially and culturally important events and scenes of life, and because I had not seen and was therefore not familiar with some of these, the scenes had to be described in some depth. Finally, the meaning or moral of the metaphor was explained to me.

The metaphors fascinated me. They seemed to resonate with much that we had seen during our field work and with much that we had discovered through our translations of other sorts of texts. It was apparent from the metaphors and from the other texts we had collected that speech and song were extraordinarily important symbols in Rauto culture and were related to concepts of self and person. Yet, I could not put together more than part of the picture that these symbols played in Rauto culture during my first period of time in the field. The initial work of conceiving the thesis on which this book is based and proceeding with the analysis of the texts took place after I got back from this first field trip, when I began to reacquaint myself with a particular tradition of anthropological thought. During the period when I wrote my dissertation, Maurice Leenhardt's work *Do Kamo* (1979), James Clifford's biography of Leenhardt (1982) and the seminal work of Michele Rosaldo (1980), Lakoff and Johnson (1980), Roy Wagner (1978, 1986, 1981) and Edward Schieffelin (1976) provided a steady supply of analogies with my Rauto data, as well as ideas for its interpretation. The works of these authors showed me how to make use of the opportunities afforded to me by the traditions of interpretive anthropology. Partly because of the influence of these works I decided to center my thesis and, later, this book around the Rauto concept of the person.

It was clear that the metaphors I had translated represented Rauto commentary on the relationship between language and person. Having made this elementary observation I began to see that the understandings expressed by the tropes about language could help explain other salient beliefs and practices. Indeed, they provided me with a way of understanding important aspects of ritual and of Rauto religious phenomenology.

When we returned to the field, these metaphors also made me redouble my efforts at trying to understand the range of meanings that the Rauto associate with the concepts of speech, and song. During our efforts at compiling a dictionary we found that the sung and spoken word had a culturally comprehensive significance for this people. Thus, for instance Western concepts such as religion, providence, tradition, law, transgression, and prayer were all translated either as "word," or "speech." More specifically *law* was translated for me as the "boundary" or line created by a leader's speech (*amala leina*), *honor* as "strong" or "hard word" (*ilo kanesngen kairak*), an *evil deed* as an "evil and great word" (*amala alang uate sulu*), *prayer* as "word offered as compensation for word" (*nga uaurum ngado amala pe ngado kanesngen*, "I expunge my deed by my word"). *Religion* was translated for me as the "speech from before" (*amala alingo ino*). As important, a person of knowledge, understanding and power is called by a phrase that translates as "a bearer of skillful speech and song" (*pato ko ilim ogor ino*). For the Rauto, as for the New Caledonians of Leenhardt's day, speech and song are something "more than simple discourse" (Clifford 1982:214, see also Leenhardt 1979:113–52). That "something" is revealed in the particular religious and emotional significance that special speech and song genres have for the Rauto. These genres are the songs of initiation, of death, and of production, and the category of proverbs and metaphors that Rauto call *amala arlem amta*. Both of our field trips consisted primarily of a study of these speech and song genres, genres that to my mind made up a good part of what can be called the formal discourse of Rauto culture.

However, after completing a dissertation based on a study of this formal discourse, I began to see a need to learn more about the informal discourse of the Rauto people, that is, articulated notions of friendship, of interpersonal relationship, and most especially of emotion. I realized that a second stint in the field was necessary and that this field work had to be based on a more re-ciprocal ethnographic conversation with my Rauto friends than the one I had carried out with them during my dissertation research. During most of this re-search, Rauto men and women had *taught* me about their culture, in response to my sometimes awkwardly expressed questions about it. Yet, though one can be taught about the culturally patterned meanings by which people live, the personal character of a life cannot be formally taught or delivered to the ethnographer by an informant. This more personal understanding comes only with time, and with the sharing of deeply held feelings and thoughts. Our sec-ond time in New Britain provided us with greater opportunity to share such thoughts and feelings with our Rauto friends and to learn their language more thoroughly than we had during our first field stay with them.

During this second stint in the field, we tried to understand the character of Rauto life and emotion by identifying and translating the range of mean-ings associated with terms of emotion, and then by asking a number of people to recount times in their lives when they had experienced a number of these emotions. We then collected detailed life histories from these people, and so attempted to get a sense of the way their emotional experiences influenced the interpretations they put on the character of their lives.

We also continued to collect texts, and we were especially interested in collecting and translating expressive forms that had a certain emotional reso-nance: for example, mourning songs, "love songs and spells," myths that the Rauto consider to be poignant. Some of the things we learned by concerning ourselves with these subjects form the gist of this book.

I should include a note about the character of Rauto poetry here. Many of the scenarios that are called to the Rauto mind by this poetry are not described so much as alluded to. As we shall see time and again, often a single word or short phrase serves as a leitmotif of a poetic image or scene. In translating the poetry I have often had to place in brackets a brief description of a scene that was evoked rather than described by a word or short phrase.

THE PEOPLE

The Austronesian-speaking Rauto number about 2,500 people and live along the coast and in the interior rain forest of the southwest portion of New Britain. Their lowland forest environment is crisscrossed by many streams and rivers, and the general topography is quite rugged. Unlike the neighboring Kaulong and Seng Seng, they are intensive horticulturalists, obtaining over 80 percent of their subsistence from the slash-and-burn cultivation of taro, yam, and sweet potato, supplemented by banana and amaranth. Their diet is rounded out by coconut, breadfruit, and occasionally pork and wild game, such as cassowary or wallaby, with fish a frequent addition to the diet of coastal villagers.

The Rauto language is one of a number of dialects of Lamogai. Lamogai languages are widespread in New Britain. They extend from the southwest coast almost all the way up to the north coast and include Lamogai proper, Mok, Ivanga, Aria, and Rauto.

Although both coastal and interior-dwelling groups prefer to live in hamlet settlements, the Rauto have been exhorted to construct and live in villages from the early days of the Australian administration of New Britain. This instruction has been heeded more by coastal than by bush groups. Indeed, with the decline in the frequency of government patrolling since independence in 1975, the people of the interior have given up the village pattern of residence almost entirely. This continues to frustrate both the administration and the various mission groups who proselytize among the Rauto. The missions view the dispersed hamlet-dwelling pattern as indicating a lack of concern for sociality and the ties of community in general. The government, for its part, finds it difficult to administer and count hamlet dwellers.

Traditionally, houses were (and in some cases continue to be) built near garden sites that are under immediate cultivation. In traditional times these small hamlet sites were surrounded by stockades for protection against parties of raiding warriors. Where possible, the stockades were built around giant banyan trees. Fighting platforms were constructed some way up the trunks of the banyan. If the men of the settlement found that they could not hold the stockade from a raiding war party they would scramble to the banyan and man the fighting platforms.

Hamlet residences usually have from twelve to forty inhabitants occupying anywhere from five to ten family houses (*itar*), with one or two large ceremonial houses (*udiep*). The number of residents fluctuates, however, since people frequently leave the hamlet to attend ceremonials or visit and take up temporary residence with trading partners or distant kin.

Exploratory German patrols first visited southwestern New Britain in the waning years of the nineteenth century. Effective government control of some coastal areas was not established, however, until the 1920s, and the bush Rauto were not effectively brought under control until the early 1950s. Tribal fighting of one sort or another continues to this day, although it was markedly curtailed from the mid 1960s onward, especially due to the establishment of the mission station at Sara. At the time of this writing, the Gimi-Rauto census district remained the only noncouncil area in Papua New Guinea, as these people continued to reject the idea of establishing local government councils and thus bringing themselves more directly under the aegis of government. On the eve of our fieldwork, there was little development in southwestern New Britain. People could usually obtain money only by growing and taking to market cash crops, or by traveling to Rabaul or Kimbe and taking up contract plantation labor there. Yet cash cropping was minimally established—in bush villages it was not established at all—and, for most men at least, a stint as a plantation worker was seldom more than a once-in-a-lifetime endeavor.

During my second stint in the field, two Malaysian/Chinese timber-cutting outfits established themselves at various points along the south coast. This certainly promised to change the tenor of life for the Rauto. Whether they will continue to hold fast to the beliefs and practices that I describe in this book I do not know. I would hope, however, that they can find their way to a satisfying future while nevertheless continuing to remember the faces of the dead and thus continuing to remember something of what past generations contributed toward the spiritual shaping of the present.

The Rauto were first visited by missionaries in the 1930s, and permanent missions were established along the southwest coast in 1935 and 1936, when the Catholics built one at Pililo Island, and one at Turuk, which is a bluff overlooking the bay of Kandrian. However, despite a good many years of mission work and government control, the Rauto, as well as the neighboring Gimi and Kaulong, remain committed to traditional lifeways and belief systems. This is no doubt one of the reasons that the New Tribes Mission has targeted southwestern New Britain as fertile new ground for their evangelical efforts. During my time in the field they established themselves among the Seng Seng, Gimi, Rauto, and Kaulong language groups. They have also built a center in Kimbe, where they plan to coordinate their data on the languages and beliefs of the peoples of southwestern New Britain, so that they might begin the process of Bible translation. The new mission, like those that came before, is having its effects. One of these has been the strong reemergence of cargo cult beliefs and practices. Another is the redisruption of the character of mortuary ceremonial, especially of the rites of secondary burial (discussed in the last chapters of the book).

There have been no prior ethnographic studies of the Rauto; indeed, few ethnographers have worked in southwestern New Britain. The first anthropologist to visit the south coast was A. B. Lewis, who spent a little more than a week sailing up and down the coast and visiting various native societies in 1910. Lewis's *New Britain Notebook* ([1910] 1988) describes a number of incidents of first contact with some of the scattered groups living on the coast and a few miles in the interior. Lewis was followed in 1927 by the ethnographer E. W. P. Chinnery, who also spent a few weeks exploring the south coast. From his descriptions and accounts I can see that he visited at least five different language groups (see Chinnery 1927). In 1935–1936 an ethnographer named J. A. Todd lived and worked in Kandrian (then called Mowe-haven). In the 1960s and early 1970s Jane Goodale and Ann Chowning carried out fieldwork among the Kaulong and Seng Seng peoples, groups that live in the foothills of the Whitman Range. I reference and in some cases discuss the works of most of these scholars in the body of the book.

A NOTE ON CEREMONY, KINSHIP, AND PERSON

Rauto social structure, is basically organized around a principle of cognatic descent. Cognatic descent groups, which are usually associated with a particular territory, are called *rip*. Though people can reside with and share in the use of the resources of either paternal or maternal kin, there is a bias toward patrifiliation. Coresident patrikin who claim close association with a particular territory also enjoy a slight political dominance over matrikin living with them. The patrikin of a place are said to derive from, or "be born of men"; their co-resident matrikin are said to be "born of women." The Rauto also distinguish matrikin from patrikin with the phrases "those of the barkcloth" (patrikin), and "those of the grass skirt" (matrikin). Unlike the neighboring Kaulong, the Rauto apply these particular distinctions to all coresident patrikin and matrikin, not only to the children of a sister and the children of a brother (see Goodale 1980:283–86).

I was also told that patrikin share the same blood and bone, whereas the blood and bone of resident matrikin will derive from other men, or from another apical male ancestor. This idea is an extension of the Rauto procreation belief that the father contributes blood and bone to his child. The mother's physical contribution to the developing fetus is said to be "only water"; her biological contribution is thus downplayed. The one-blood distinction, and the recognition of the principle of patrilineal descent that it implies, was invoked most often during my period of fieldwork when disputes arose between the matrikin and patrikin of a residence over the use of resources. During one such dispute I heard the patrikin of the residence say that since the resident matrikin "derived from women," they did not really belong in the residence. Therefore they had no right to make a claim on the group's resources. In contrast, the cognatic model of both descent and resource use was invoked when the patrikin needed the cooperation of or desired the good will of resident matrikin. In such situations I sometimes heard patrikin tell resident matrikin that "we are all brothers here," thus implying that all the occupants of a hamlet residence should share equally in bearing the burden of labor and ceremonial.

Patrikin are also said to share the same totem, or emblem. It is said to be wrong for a man and a woman who share the same blood, bone, and emblem to be married to one another, though I was told that sexual relations occasionally do occur between "one blood" classificatory siblings. Ideally one should marry a distant (not closer than second-generation) cross-cousin. Second-generation cross-cousins will not share substance, yet will be close enough relations so that they will demonstrate concern for and care properly for each other.

Like the Kabana of northwest New Britain (see Scalleta 1985:76), the Rauto practice a form of sister exchange. The preferred marriage strategy is for a woman to marry a man (*mmbss*) of her mother's patrikin who resides "in her mother's natal village" (Scalleta 1985: 76). The Rauto say that this woman has then "come back" to the place of her mother, or that she has come back to her origin place (*sep uate*). Thus the woman's matrikin will receive a replacement for her mother. The Rauto use two phrases to refer to the completion of sister exchange: "the return of the fire" (*aii nondro*), and "the return of a woman" (*ilim nondro*).

Rauto kinship terminology is a variant of a Dravidian-Iroquois system. That is, the system distinguishes "cross from parallel relatives in each of the middle three generations" (Keesing 1975:105). Thus there are separate terms for Mother's brother (*atenme*) and for Father's sister (*ado*), while Mother's sister is classified with mother, and Father's brother is classified with father. Ego distinguishes his or her own cross from parallel cousins. Ego also distinguishes the children of cross-cousins from the children of parallel cousins. Importantly, male ego distinguishes his Sister's son and Sister's daughter with a special kin term (*tuturek*), while female ego calls Brother's son and Brother's daughter by the same term. The term differs from those that are used for either the children of cross or parallel cousins and appears, as I indicate below, to mark the culturally significant relationships between a man and the children of his natal sister on the one hand, and a woman and the children of her natal brother on the other. Ego also "distinguishes a class of cousins (MBC and FZC) from parallel relatives who are equated with siblings" (Keesing 1975:106).

One of the many matters that the terminological distinction of cross from parallel relatives appears to mark is the special set of ceremonial, economic, and ritual duties that the matrikin and the patrikin of a person have to each other. These reciprocal duties and obligations are implicated in the creation of the social identity of persons. Lying at the core of the matrikin/patrikin relationship and partly providing a model for it is the special relationship of nurturance and mutual support that should ideally exist between siblings of the opposite sex. Here I would like briefly to discuss this relationship, especially how it ultimately comes to engage the energies, resources, and ritual acumen of groups. Part of what follows is similar to Goodale's discussion of sibling relations among the Kaulong (see Goodale 1980:279–98).

Apparently unlike the neighboring Kaulong, the Rauto see a double aspect to the opposite-sex sibling relationship. It is characterized both by mutual support and by a degree of avoidance. Indeed, as a sibling pair approaches sexual maturity, an injunction prohibiting the pair from sitting together unaccompanied, or eating in each other's presence comes into effect. This prohibition will extend to the end of the lives of cross-siblings who share one or both parents. However, the prohibition does not disrupt the pattern of aid and assistance that brother and sister provide to each other. Aid consists of reciprocal gifts of food, acts of labor, and offers of economic aid for the entire course of the life of siblings. This behavioral norm also guides the relationships of patrilateral parallel cousins of the opposite sex.

The obligations of siblings to each other become particularly culturally marked when they take spouses and produce children. Before marriage, sibling relationships and duties are of a personal nature. After marriage, siblings' reciprocal duties bring separate kin groups into relationship. One sees this most especially in the reciprocal exchanges that accompany the rituals performed for children. Mother's brother (*atenme*) and his paternal kin are key participants during most of the ceremonies that are performed for sister's children. Indeed the ritual and ceremonial duties of mother's brother and his patrikin to the children of their sisters are greater in number, if not importance, than those that they have to their own children. The atenme and his kindred are key actors in the series of ceremonies that raise a child's name, and thus help establish the child's social identity.

The atenme rather than the child's father usually chooses the name of the child of his sister's son or daughter. The name, which is usually taken from the store of names associated with the maternal uncle's own patrikin, is called out by him in a public naming ceremony—see discussion in chapter 2, p. 47. Through the performance of this action the maternal uncle attempts to augment an aspect of the child's developing identity with the social identity of his group. The atenme, or a man who is classified with him, also bears responsibility for carrying out the circumcision of the male child of either his actual or classificatory sister. The maternal uncle also sometimes sponsors but more often performs the initiation of his sister's male child. It is also the duty of the maternal uncle, or a man classified with him, to teach his actual or classificatory sister's son the names of the different sections of the sacred spirit masks that are kept in the men's ceremonial house. The ceremonial context in which the teaching is done marks part of the formal introduction of male children into the men's house.[1] Finally, mother's brother, or a man classified with him, and a specified group of maternal relatives are responsible for honoring the first born children of their sisters during a series of ceremonies that are performed exclusively for first born.[2]

Through the performance of these ceremonies, the matrikin of children invest something of their spiritual efficacy and agency in them. This honoring of children through ritual and ceremony is meant to enable them to become effective social agents. The children's fathers, along with other patrikin, provide payments of pearl-shell valuables, pigs, and taro to the maternal uncle and the assisting matrikin for honoring their children, and as compensation for the energy that they invest in them. Thus, resources flow as payment to the matriline; affect and spiritual nurturance are given back to the children of sisters. Though the matriline does not share "substance" with the children of its sisters, its continual celebration of and ritual shaping of the social personhood of these children establishes a spiritual connection to them. It would not be an exaggeration to say that the matrikin are the kin of spirit for the Rauto. The patrikin are the kin of power; they provide political and economic wherewithal and position to their children. The culturally significant relationship between a person and his matrikin does not end with the person's death. As I show in the final chapters of this book, rites of secondary burial provide a final opportunity for a person's matrikin to honor him with ceremony and song and to celebrate his past social agency.

I now turn to a brief consideration of the set of ideas and approaches that have been used to interpret cultural constructions of the person and culturally specific concepts of human agency. I also discuss how this set of theoretical ideas has influenced interpretations of the significance of the ritual or ceremonial events that frequently provide a context for the expression of ideas of person and agency.

---

1. Ideally, a man should also teach his sister's son his best magical spells. He is required by custom to do this, whereas he does not have to instruct his own son in ritual and magic.

2. Reciprocally, sister will also be an important cosponsor of and a key performer during the achievement ceremonies and the ceremonies of the life cycle which are held for the children of her brother. Sister is usually assisted in her ritual duties to brother's children by her own and by the children's matrikin. Often these are also sister's affinal relations. That is, they often belong to the group which sister has married into, which is—because of the preferred strategy of MMBSS marriage—often the natal group of her mother.

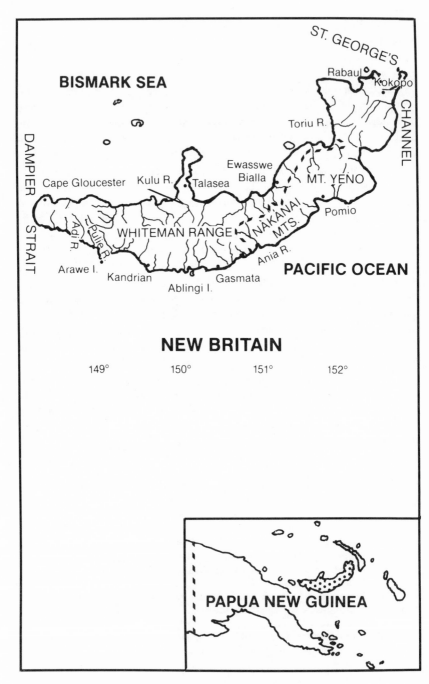

BISMARK SEA

ST. GEORGE'S

CHANNEL

DAMPIER

STRAIT

Rabaul

Kokopo

Toriu R.

Cape Gloucester   Kulu R.   Talasea   Ewasswe
Bialla

MT. YENO

Pomio

Adi R.   Pulie R.   WHITEMAN RANGE   NAKANAI MTS.

Ania R.

PACIFIC OCEAN

Arawe I.   Kandrian   Ablingi I.   Gasmata

NEW BRITAIN

149°   150°   151°   152°

PAPUA NEW GUINEA

New Britain. Map by Robert Melende.

14

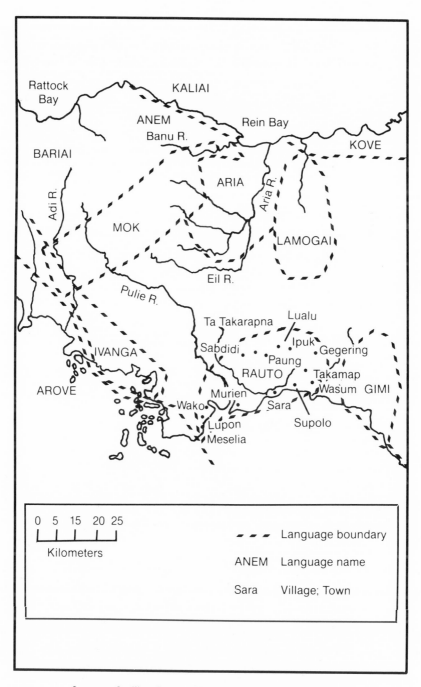

Rattock Bay

KALIAI

ANEM
Banu R.

Rein Bay

KOVE

BARIAI

Adi R.

ARIA

Aria R.

MOK

LAMOGAI

Eil R.

Pulie R.

Ta Takarapna

Lualu

Sabdidi

Ipuk

Gegering

Paung

RAUTO

Takamap

IVANGA

Murien

Wasum

GIMI

AROVE

Wako

Sara

Lupon

Supolo

Meselia

Language families of western New Britain. Map by Robert Melende.

15

Chapter One

Theoretical Considerations

From Mauss to Dumont, the study of ideas of self and person has turned on the distinction between individualism and what has been called holism. Put simply, in many anthropological accounts, non-Western and or preindustrial societies are said to define the person primarily in terms of his relationship to others or to the traditions, offices, and roles that mark out the operation of society (Bourne & Shweder 1982:97–133; Dumont 1986; Fajans 1985:367–95; La Fontaine 1985:123–40—to name but a few). The second implicit, and sometimes explicit assumption of much of this work is that people of modern Western societies entertain "a conception of the person as a bounded, unique, more-or-less integrated motivational and cognitive universe, a dynamic center of awareness, emotion, judgement, and action organized into a distinctive whole and set contrastively both against other such wholes, and against a social and natural background . . ." (Geertz 1983:59).

Mauss (1985:1–25), Durkheim (1965:305–8) and Lévy-Bruhl (1928:196–237) believed the holistic concept of the person to be historically prior to the individualist concept. Durkheim especially believed that the evolution of a more advanced division of labor in the West was directly linked to the rise of individualism and the establishment of the variety of values, beliefs, and viewpoints that distinguish Western societies.

While tending to eschew the evolutionist aspects of Mauss's and Durkheim's thinking about the person, modern writers sometimes argue that traditional people's relational and holistic understanding itself represents a moral stance toward the world. In Bourne and Shweder's view for instance, peoples of non-Western cultural orientation are held to be quite capable of thinking of persons as individual entities with specific character traits, behavioral tendencies, personal histories, and particular passions and attachments (1982:26). They are simply less inclined to express such views of the person because they do not value them as highly as do Westerners. Bourne writes that people such as the Balinese, or the Gahuka-Gama of New Guinea "live by a metaphor and subscribe to a world premise that directs their attention and passions to particular systems, relationally conceived and contextually appraised" (1982:26), because they are morally committed to this metaphor.

The view expressed by Bourne and Shweder that particular conceptions of the person lie at the core of a society's moral system is the key idea to emerge from the cross-cultural study of ideas of the person and of the self. It has provided scholars with a way of focusing their discourse about the range of beliefs and practices that constitute culture while at the same time allowing them to speak about the overarching pattern of meaning that informs various aspects of culture. Yet we now know that the contrast between holistic and individualist moral systems has too often been overstated—so much so that it has taken on the character of ideology. In scholarly writing the opposition of individualism to holism has become part of Western society's discourse about itself, often forming the basis for either critique or self-congratulation. One has only to read a bit of modernization theory to perceive how individualist values are often associated rather exclusively with the dynamism and progressiveness of the West and how Western scholars have associated a relational understanding of the nature of the person with economic and social stagnation. In contrast, in the writing of some Marxist anthropologists, we see how the portrayal of holism can itself serve as a type of moral and economic critique of capitalist society (Taussig 1980).

I find that both individualist and holistic accounts say something about the Rauto understanding of the nature of the person. Both the metaphor that depicts a person as an autonomous entity striving to create a personal and social identity for himself and the metaphor that portrays a person's life as a reflection of and a product of the lives, beliefs, and actions of others are clearly to be found embedded in the discourse and practices of Rauto culture. Yet both metaphors are, in the final analysis, reductions. As such they do not reveal to us the richness of meaning that informs Rauto discourse about persons. Nor do they explain satisfactorily how and why this concept is the reference of so much of both practical and ritual activity.

To account for the centrality of the metaphor of the person in Rauto culture, we should consider not only the discourse and practice of the Rauto, but also the anthropomorphism—*humanism* would perhaps be a more appropriate term—that distinguishes Melanesian expressivity in general. Leenhardt was the first to discuss with sensitivity and thoroughness the conceptual force that the notion of the person frequently has in Melanesian cultures. He was also the first to discuss with both analytic subtlety and power how in Melanesia this concept is itself often a concept of force, or human agency. This is most clearly seen in his discussion of the notion that his informants translated as *parole*, "word."

In writing *Do Kamo* Leenhardt drew much inspiration from the complex and varied meanings his New Caledonian informants associated with the term *no* (word) (see Clifford 1982:194–214). Leenhardt perceived that word was an "innate property" of the New Caledonian person's existence—that it was a manifestation of both personal and social being. That is, he implied that in New Caledonian usage the spoken word was a means by which people distinguished their own identities from those of others and at the same time established relations of participation with others, with created objects, with the landscape. Besides being a means of inventing the self, *word,* or *no,* had connotations that were almost as varied as the world. *Word* was not only to be experienced in speech, it was as well "property, signatures, seals of agreement, exchanges, contracts, songs, sculptures of the habitat." All these objects and activities were "manifestations of creative being in the world" (Leenhardt 1979:151).

In translating the meaning of the New Caledonian experience of and understanding of *word,* Leenhardt sought to portray a state of being, one in which "spiritual content and its sensuous expression were united" (Cassirer 1955: 178). In doing this he portrayed a particular form of creativity as well, one characterized by the energy and immediacy of a "spontaneously created and experienced event" (Clifford 1982:214). Event was represented by *word,* the expression of personal and social efficacy. Yet, in Leenhardt's understanding *word* represented more than simply an expression and externalization of self. *Word* was experienced as an event, as an instantaneous, "fleeting, emerging and vanishing mental content" (Cassirer 1953:17) because it created and represented an indivisible moment of experience for the person. *Word* was the leitmotif of what Leenhardt called mythic consciousness, a mental state that presented the separate elements of the world as part of a whole. Writers and philosophers such as Preuss, Cassirer, and Freud have identified this state with "the religious sentiment" (Cassirer 1953:17), and indeed the New Caledonian objectified it through the creation of a divine image. "On the frames of the houses, on the rooftop spires, on dozens of stakes" he placed that "august figure," the deity of *word.* Its emblem was an oversized representation of the human tongue (Leenhardt 1979:139).

While the New Caledonian experience of *word* represented a profound form of religious experience, the use of the word seemed often an act of faith that represented a belief in the value of a particular way of life. It represented an attempt to enjoy the "plenitude in which the New Caledonian felt himself to be *do kamo,* 'true person' " (Leenhardt 1979:195) because it both actualized and embodied tradition. Thus, *word* was at one and the same time what the Westerner might identify separately as law, politics, religion, kinship, art, creativity, love, evil, power—the list could be extended indefinitely.

Leenhardt's seminal ideas about *word* and *person* imply that the creative impetus of a culture, as well as its religious sense, can be discerned in its attitudes toward language (see also Wagner 1981:107–14). This is one of the insights that I take from his work. Indeed one of my aims is to show how the Rauto understanding of *speech* is also a notion of religious force and of person, "something more than discourse" (Clifford 1982:214). A second aim is to show how the Rauto constitute the person and the series of moral relationships that is called social life through acts of speech and song. Yet what I am ultimately after in this ethnography is the portrayal of a particular form of experiencing the world, one in which the evanescent immediacy of the spoken and sung word itself appears to express a sense of life as an ephemeral plenitude of feelings of loss and communion—the feeling that Leenhardt called "participation." This sense is captured most movingly in Rauto ritual life when adults recall the poignancy of their own pasts and consider their own mortality, at the very time when they invest their spiritual power in the next generation by singing the songs (*aurang*) of initiation to adolescents. Yet, as I show, this special sense of poignancy is evoked for the Rauto by many of their cultural practices, even those as simple as bestowing a name on a child, preparing a garden for planting, or holding a pearl shell. Part of my argument is that these practices can evoke strong emotions because they represent a type of discourse about relationships between persons. They are about treasuring others, or they are about the experience of having lost someone who was dear. A major argument of this ethnography is simply that Rauto people perceive the locus of the sacred to be contained within memories that culturally encode and valorize emotions of loss and of communion or participation. Speech and song evoke the sacred by evoking such emotions, especially the emotion that the Rauto call *makai* (nostalgia, full sadness, plenitude).

Geertz's suggestion that the notion of the person can provide an excellent vehicle for "poking into another people's turn of mind" (1983:59) takes on an added cogency and significance in the Rauto context because of the key metaphor of speech. A question remains, however, as to how one might initially speak about the shifting manifestations of concepts of the person in Rauto expressivity. I feel that the concept of metaphor is the most appropriate idea that we can apply in attempting to speak effectively about Rauto expressivity. There are a number of reasons for my choice. Some of these have to do with Rauto views about the nature of language; others have to do with the relationship between the Rauto's understanding of the nature of metaphor and our own.

METAPHOR AND RAUTO VIEWS OF LANGUAGE

James Fernandez has written that metaphor provides an evaluation of ideas, people, and forms of conduct by placing them in more or less desirable positions "in the quality space of a specific culture" (1974:10). Fernandez has argued that metaphor accomplishes this ranking of phenomena by translating inchoate sentiments and ideas to domains of experience, or to objects and actions, that are clearly understandable to a people. In his view metaphor is part of the living experience of a people; its creation and use is one of the most important ways a people has of imposing meaning on the world.

Wagner has argued that metaphor creates meaning by transforming a people's experience of the world (1986:7). It does this, as both Fernandez and Ricoeur also suggest, by drawing into relation different domains of experience and thus allowing people to see the "similarity in dissimilars" (Ricoeur 1979:143). Wagner considers the establishment of a metaphoric relationship between different realms of experience to signify "the replacement of conventional meaning with innovative meaning." He calls this "symbolic obviation," a phrase that registers the fact that the meaning of a metaphor is more than the meaning of its semantic parts—that this meaning obviates the conventional meaning represented by the separate semantic components of the metaphor. According to Ricoeur and Fernandez, metaphor manages actually to establish innovative meaning through the creation of an image that visually depicts this meaning. As Aristotle writes, "it sets before the eyes the sense that it displays" (quoted in Ricoeur 1979:142). Goodman (1968) and Black (1962), stress that this iconic aspect of metaphor serves as a type of model linguistic description of an aspect of cultural or social reality—a paradigm of understanding. While these scholars focus on the iconic aspect of metaphor, Ricoeur (1979:146), Wagner (1978:32) and Lakoff and Johnson (1980:3–25) stress that metaphor is both a process involved in the formulation of meaning, as well as the structured expression of specific meaning. It is both a way of understanding and a part of understanding itself.

The understanding of metaphor that I have glossed here is derived at least in part from the view of romantic writers, such as Herder, that language is inseparable from thought and from being. For the romantics, as for Ricoeur and Wagner, language is a phenomenon that continually transforms and creates meaning in the world. The romantics also saw figurative speech in general, and metaphor in particular, as the most transformative and meaningful aspect of language.

Enlightenment thinkers such as Locke, in contrast, were unreceptive to the idea that figurative speech represented a locus of profound meaning. Locke considered metaphor to be an "abuse of language," since he thought it could "dismember the text of reality and reassemble it in the most capricious of ways" (de Man 1979:19). Thus to speak figuratively of, for instance, "the legs of a table" or the "face of a mountain" is, in Locke's view, to tell a lie about the nature of reality; it is to mislead. This view is itself derived from the enlightenment notion that language was simply the clothing of thought, rather than its embodiment; that it only existed to convey thought about a tangible, preexisting reality that could and *should* be described accurately. For Locke, the transformative nature of language, most especially figurative language, appeared dangerous or subversive of its primary descriptive function. Thus for him "metaphor was a breakdown in the rule-governed mechanism of language" (Ecco 1986:95).

The most important point raised by modern semioticians in response to this argument is that metaphor is a cognitive instrument that teaches us to see the "subtle network of proportions between cultural units" or aspects of meaning (Ecco 1986:102). Good or suggestive metaphors enable us to see more aspects of this subtle network of proportions than do trivial ones. It is by enhancing the depth of our perception in this way that metaphor transforms our experience of and understanding of reality. In this view, then, metaphor can in no way violate the rules of language and culture, since it both draws meaning from, and modifies an "underlying cultural framework" (102).

As metaphor continually modifies, transforms, and models our understanding of the world, so too does it progressively add depth and resonance to emotion. That is, the Western semiotic of metaphor is in many ways emotion's ontology. We see this most clearly in the many parallels between the classical Western understanding of dramatic art and theories of the semiotic of metaphor. From Aristotle's *Rhetoric* and *Poetics* to the work of Auerbach and down to the present day, the idea of mimesis, or imitation, has modeled Western understanding of both art and metaphor. The classical understandings posit that both forms of representation are imitations of experience. The "imitations" produced by art and metaphor, however, are not so much mere replications of events and experiences as heightened expressions of them. Redfield calls this heightening a "purification of experience" (1975:165). What he means is that art extracts the essential meaning and emotion from an aspect of experience and then represents it in such a way that its wholeness is revealed for the first time (Redfield 1975:219). Art completes experience by circumscribing its meaning through mimesis. In this view dramatic art and enactment also represent experience in a way that draws the audience toward an emotional participation with an event, a character, or an idea. As such, it completes or clarifies the nature and definition of an emotion. It deepens awareness of the life meaning of an emotion by cogently relating it to a particular event or action, or to a particular aspect of personal or social experience.

In the dominant Western understanding, metaphor is described as well as a completion of experience. It represents experience through the creation of images that, though often imitations of experience, heighten its meaning. Also,

both the mimesis of dramatic art and of metaphor seem in the classical understanding to complete experience, to render a representation of its wholeness,
because of what can only be called their character of lucid opacity. When, for
instance, in Shakespeare's *Hamlet* we see the equivocal actions and hear the
convoluted and ambivalent thoughts of Hamlet, we are led to an emotional participation with the complex opacity of his experience. We feel the complexity
of his experience and the opacity of his vision with great lucidity. The play
takes us beyond a mere sympathy with the character's emotional experience by
allowing us to understand the full and complex meaning of Hamlet's emotional
torment.

Poetic metaphor takes these principles of blurring and elaboration to greater
extremes, so much so that the mimesis it creates of an experience can seem far
removed from the actual contexts or commonsense references of that experience. When, for example, in his poem "The Lovers," Rilke invites us to

> See how in their being all becomes spirit;
> into each other they mature and grow.
> Like axles, their forms tremblingly orbit,
> round which it whirls, bewitching and aglow.
> Thirsters, and they receive drink,
> watchers, and see: they receive sight.
> Let them into one another sink
> so as to endure each other outright.
>
> (Rilke 1975)

Rilke invites us to contemplate an image that he has objectified, an image that
both draws the reader to a heightened sense of the experience of love that it pictures and distances the reader from the actual referents of that experience. The
poem is meant to convey the sense of mutual being that love brings, but it does
so indirectly through the creation of an image that appears to have little to do
with the usual scenarios of courtship and lovemaking. This image is precisely
what strikes us as beautiful and meaningful. The paradox of the metaphoric
image is that it creates an identification of a sort with an emotional experience
by placing itself at a distance from the everyday acts and scenarios of love. As
in dramatic art, here experience is rendered complete, whole, and emotionally cogent through the application of a principle of symbolic elaboration and
distancing.

These brief characterizations of metaphor, of art, and of feeling are not
simple digressions. They relate directly to the problem of the ethnographic
representation of cultural forms and of experience. In fact when a recent and
prominent writer in symbolic anthropology states that metaphor is a process

in the continual "constituting of cultural frames" (Wagner 1986:9) and that a primary means of cultural expression, creation, and understanding can be seen in the way metaphor "expands the frame of its self-referentiality by processual extension into a broader range of cultural relevance" (1986:9), we approach the classical understanding of art as an elaboration and heightening of experience. Tropes seem in Wagner's understanding to extend the meaning of an aspect of experience by connecting this meaning to "larger cultural frames." In the process they heighten meaning by *subverting* it through what Wagner calls obviation. I take this idea to mean, in part, that a metaphor can represent many and sometimes contradictory aspects of experience as it "presents the enigma of what Freud called condensation—a richness of potentially elicited analogies all at once" (1986:29). What a single metaphor—I would say a single consummate metaphor—"invariably presents" in a lucid and powerful way, is the opacity, the complexity of experience. Understanding, cultural expression, and invention in this view involve the continual processual substitution of complex opacity for simpler, or perhaps more trite representations of experience. It is in this way that the obviation process can be seen as a heightening and "purification" of experience.

Such a theory of cultural forms resonates with and perhaps even draws some of its obvious explanatory power from cultural systems in which symbolic elaboration seems especially to distinguish the character of art, ritual, myth, and drama. One is reminded of Geertz's description of the Balinese searching out and fashioning meanings in "significant symbols, clusters of significant symbols, and clusters of clusters of significant symbols" (Geertz 1973:408). Confronted with Rauto metaphors and other forms of this people's expressive culture, I have had to consider whether hermeneutics and the classical theories of representation that are subsumed under the label hermeneutic interpretive anthropology can render an adequate ethnographic account. As the analysis shows, in some ways the classical understanding is useful, and in others it is not.

The involute character of Rauto expressive culture often presents a wry face to the elaborate and elaborating Western semiotic. Many of the central metaphors and images of this people seem not so much "purifications" of everyday meanings, emotions, and experiences as restatements of them, "restatements that encourage a total personal reinvolvement in their character" (Wagner, personal communication). Wagner writes that Rauto tropes, and other forms of expressive culture, "seem to acknowledge situations that carry their whole meaningful and emotional force in their familiarity or repetition" (personal communication). In other words their meaning seems to derive from the common events they represent; it is not in some exaggerated and abstract rhetoric. When, for instance, in the Rauto female puberty rite women ritual adepts instruct the initiates—rhythmically and through song performance—in the proper way of planting a croton, one does not see a heightening of woman's experience so much as a repetition of it.

There are the standard ways of explaining this sort of thing. There is the memory and recall theory of Ong and Yates, that is, the idea that oral cultures tend to group material for memory and recall around action in the human world (Ong 1967:84) because, in the absence of writing, the need for preserving cultural memory promotes the continual reinvocation of everyday scenarios and activities. Havelock (1963) and Bourdieu (1986) argue further that the context-dependent forms of expressive culture that we often see in oral cultures are not really examples of cultural invention or creativity at all, but are rather means of both describing and enforcing the overall habits—whether these be political, private, or moral—of society.

There is also the "poetic" or romantic argument of Schiller and, to a lesser extent, of Auerbach that would discern in the concrete imagery that distinguishes the female puberty rite the powerful desire "to identify with the character of existence and to wish nothing more than to be part of the existence and operation of things in accordance with their nature" (Schiller, quoted in Auerbach 1991:5).

Though this last explanation seems consistent with the external character of Rauto religious expression, it falls short as commentary upon the pathos evoked by it. The quality of this style of expression that awakens emotions such as *makai* (plenitude/nostalgia/full sadness) and *kipitngen* (quietly suffered emotional pain) seems as much an attempt to contain or enclose feeling as to externalize it, and it is precisely this muted style of expression that most powerfully elicits a felt understanding of the pathos of experience. As we shall see, the objects, metaphors and acts of religious expression contain meaning and emotion because they are objectifications of personal and cultural memory. Ritual life establishes a quality of emotional relationship between person, object, and image by often picturing the human memories that are embodied, contained, by objects and ritual acts.

Memory itself contains and is characterized by a specific emotional tone, one that Rauto call *makai*. I translated this term as "plenitude," "nostalgia," and "full sadness" in the preceding paragraph. How it is simultaneously all of these feelings will not really become clear until I have described its centrality in Rauto religious life and shown how the Rauto themselves "summarize" its meaning in their songs and rites of death. I can say now, however, that for the Rauto, memory and the mimetics of expressive culture are pathos, a patterned emotional reaction to the experience of living. The particular quality and meaning of the experience of makai show that the Rauto do not simply "wish to be part of the existence and operation of things in accordance with their natures" and therefore do not look beyond the surface of experience; rather, they appear to feel that experience is poignant, powerful, and often painful enough so that representations of it need to be understated. Such representations say enough by seeming to say too little.

The sum of all the meanings of these representations is an actual philosophy of experience, if we can use the word *philosophy* to describe a form of understanding that is not a "purification" or elaboration of experience. What this philosophy does express, however, is a culturally specific understanding of the nature of the person and of emotional experience. I argue that the "semiotics" of Rauto expressive culture parallel an understanding of the person and of the forms of emotional expression proper to the person. That is, the contained yet dramatic tone of Rauto expressive culture and the simple character of its imagery not only elicit and create pathos, they express an ethos—something of the character of the person, of the Rauto people. This book explores the relationship between Rauto ethos and pathos and then argues that indigenous concepts of emotion and person should be taken into account by theories of cultural representation. One of my major objectives, then, is to outline a psychological approach to cultural representation, one that links forms of expression and of expressive culture on the one hand with forms of emotional experience and transformation on the other.

The meaning and character of Rauto expressive culture are interesting not least because they convey the complexity, even opacity, of emotion and experience with a simplicity, a terseness of utterance and expression. As we shall see, examples are legion:

> I leave you now,
> smoke rising; these
> things are yours;
> (no, they go with you.)

The song signals the conclusion of the mourning ceremony that the Rauto call *serpoua;* it is sung just before some objects belonging to the dead and mourned-for person are gathered up and thrown into the sea. Singers represent the lyrics as the words of the dead person's ghost, which the ghost utters as it dissipates into nothingness "like smoke in the wind." As the ghost loses its ties to substantiality—to its body or container—so it seeks to rid itself of the material objects that served as markers of its personal, corporeal identity. It offers its possessions to kin. They refuse the ghost's gift out of grief and anger and rid themselves of these objects by throwing them into the sea.

Somewhat like the Japanese haiku, the song's main image shows a certain "resistance to meaning" (Barthes 1990:32). It has few apparent connotations; it does not seem to symbolize anything. The image seems completely naturalistic, simply picturing a moment of the lived as well as imagined experience of death—the ghost taking leave of its kin and of the world, dissipating like smoke. If we cannot exactly read this image and thereby follow its trail of analogies and meanings into all the different corners of Rauto culture, we can acknowledge that it appears to represent "that which cannot be represented" (Barthes 1990:62), that is, the powerful experience of loss. The image imitates a scenario that should be faced with calm acceptance by the bereaved but which cannot be accepted in such a way. The anger and grief of "letting go" forces the angry destruction of, and the casting out of the dead's possessions. The disjunction between the ought and the is, between the containment of emotion and its eruption at precisely the moment when the ghost separates finally and ultimately from its kin, creates a quality of pathos. In its portrayal of the tragic anger of the kin, it also reveals something of the Melanesian ethos, something of the character of the person. The kin's anger embodies the perception that death is not a gift and should not bring gifts—the ghost's offer of its possessions. In this scenario death seems instead to be an assault on the living. We see the Melanesian ethos in the essential quality or character of anger and strength that requires the return of injury for injury; therefore, the injury caused to the living by the death of their kinsman receives its answer in the destruction of the things of this person.

As in haiku, however, the real or complete meaning of the song's image and of Rauto ethos and pathos is rather more obtuse, in the sense of its being more "blurred," "rounded," persistent, and fleeting (Barthes 1990:61). The song is part of the counternarrative of the mourning ceremony. In fact the point of this ceremony, as we shall see in a later chapter, is not so much to portray and elicit anger—the emotional sign of the Melanesian ethos of strength—as to transform this emotion into the culturally creative form of nostalgia and plenitude that the Rauto call makai. Thus the song image is a signifier without an obvious signified. The opacity of the image, its resistance to meaning, elicits a feeling that the Rauto (and Melanesian) ethos is less obvious, less rigid than the scene the image presents would suggest. After seeing the ceremony during which this song is performed, one comes away with a feeling that loss is not simply an assault on the Rauto self, but that it is, and contains, a plenitude of meanings and feelings.

Not all of the images of Rauto expressive culture have the character of counternarrative, although many do appear to represent ineffable as opposed to obvious meaning. The images of expressive culture also render the meaning of key cultural moments of individuation. Rauto metaphors, figurative usages, and images represent a series of moments in which the person constructs an aspect of his or her own identity. These key or central moments in the life of the person, and in the life of this culture, represent the fuller, more rounded meaning of Rauto ethos and pathos. In the course of the ethnography I shall chart the relationship between ethos and pathos by describing the significance of the individuation process as it is lived and represented in the images of expressive culture.

As we shall see, the complex opacity of ethos, of pathos, and of individuation is often fashioned or culled out of experience by the sung and spoken word. The images that are such an important part of Rauto cultural and religious forms are moments of the word, as well as key emotional moments of what Leenhardt would call a "myth of identity" (1979:17). These forms are often pictured in vivid, concrete imagery—sensuous, rhythmic imagery that seems appropriate to elicit and convey the complex emotional character of the Melanesian religious experience. For instance, the discussion of women's ritual indicates how the images of everyday things and of everyday activities that form the basis of the female puberty rite forcefully convey the emotional value that such activities have for Rauto women by expressing and circumscribing a moment of the individuation process. The seeming naturalism and presentness of these images and of the activities they describe make up only the most obvious meaning of the individuation process, however. They often seem simply women's acted valorizations of their characteristic roles and duties. Something of their full meaning and of the part they play in expressing and creating the identity of the person is felt by the Rauto in their recollective character. They not only establish a felt participation or immersion in the present, in the everyday activity represented, they also create a sense of the past by evoking memories of those who performed the rite in times past. As the songs, images, and acts of the puberty rite create a participation in both past and present, they establish a series of relationships between persons, between the person and the objects manipulated during the rite, between the living and the ancestors, between the person and the natural world. The collective and the recollective aspects of these images and activities together make up the meaning of the rite, of an aspect of the individuation process, and of Rauto ethos and pathos, that is, of character and feeling.

This perspective suggests that Rauto religious and expressive culture is but a series of emotions and moments in which the person finds an aspect of his or her identity. This insight into the character of Melanesian cultural forms is suggested by Leenhardt's seminal work on the character of New Caledonian religious experience. It is an insight that to my mind has neither been applied, or even recognized, save tangentially, by the anthropology of religion.

In the long years of his ethnographic encounter with New Caledonian culture, Leenhardt was faced with the problem of understanding and representing involute cultural forms and immanent forms of religious experience—forms of experience that did not seem to exist outside of "concretely experienced events" (Clifford 1982:214). The suggestive final chapter of *Do Kamo* indicates that he came to view such forms of experience, which he called "mythic experience," as a necessary part of the individuation process, the process of attaining authentic personhood. Mythic experience carried great moral and emotional resonance; in its complex opacity it defined the spirit of a culture and the gist of the Melanesian person's spiritual life. Here I should like to consider briefly Leenhardt's understanding of the nature of the Melanesian person, of the Melanesian self, and of the relationship between individuation and mythic experience.

At first glance Leenhardt's understanding of the Melanesian self seems to be an expression of the sensationalist vision that perceives the self as simply a bundle of perceptions, with no true center or ego. In this view the phenomenon that can be called a self consists of an "association of impressions" (Cassirer 1955:102), as if the whole that is the self originates in a series of temporal moments that have the character of impressions. Leenhardt called such moments "participations." But even the Melanesian person was not completely awash in the immediacy of the moment of sense perception and impression. Leenhardt balanced the sensationalist character of his theory with his particular understanding of mythic authenticity. The series of temporal moments, or participations, that constituted the New Caledonian person were themselves given meaning by the person's attachment to and experience of a particular sociomythic ensemble. Leenhardt's notion of mythic place, which consisted of both an actual geographical and a spiritual landscape, essentially the habitat of the person's social group and its series of altars, seemed to provide a diffuse center for the self (see Clifford 1982:182–88). Sociomythic space gave a certain emotional unity to the person by giving his life a general moral value and meaning. In fact, Leenhardt positively valued the fact of the Melanesian person's mooring to a general sociomythic space, seeing it as the basis of positive communal social experience and thus, in his view, of moral life.

A participation then was not simply an immediate impression of relationship; it was an experience that was part of a configuration toward being or identity. The participation took meaning from a diffuse whole, which was the socio- or spatiomythic domain of the self. But what was this true domain of the self, and how did it figure in the creation of identity?

Clifford notes the importance of duality and parity in Leenhardt's thinking about Melanesian identity. Each relation, each object, each utterance had, Leenhardt argued, two aspects which were "complementary, corresponding, symmetrical" (Leenhardt 1979:102). These aspects were reflected in the very structure of language, as well as in village architecture, sculpture, kin terms, and marriage arrangements (184). There was hardly ever the experience of I, of the one; the New Caledonian self was composed of two. The nephew and the maternal uncle, the son and the father, were both in Leenhardt's interpretations "dual entities," and each aspect of the entity only came to know itself through its relation to the other. This fact was reflected in all forms of cultural (Leenhardt would have said "mythic") representation. The sociomythic space of the group is what constituted this experience of the dual. Thus the nephew and maternal uncle pair was perceived as an entity because uncle and nephew shared the same totem, the same ancestral gods, the same clan, the same altar, the same men's house, and the same mythical attachment to their matriclan's land. All these shared objects, beings, presences, and places together made up the mythic geography of the nephew/maternal uncle pair. This sociomythic space circumscribed the two beings, making each the other's "habitat," making each the other's identity. Each perception or experience of *le duel* such as this already encompassed the notion of sociomythic space and of identity.

This space seemed to be experienced more as a series of images than of ideas. The image of the ancestor, god, or totem was realized and perceived with each sacrifice or request to one of these entities for assistance. These images contained the mythic experience of participation and somehow existed at the "onset" of purely discursive language and conceptual thought (Clifford 1982:210). They also preceded the formation of the authentic integrated self; they possessed an archetypal intuitive character rather than a symbolic discursive character. The mythic image always portrayed an event of self-construction, a moment in which identity was realized, as in the example of the traditional healer Jopaipi, who wrestled with his ancestor god at an altar in order to participate in its healing power. While the mythic image of the traditional healer entering into the temporal space of his ancestor, wrestling with it, and taking power from it is portrayed as an augmentation of the self, the image does not represent a sharp formation of the individuated or individual self, of the I. Again we have an example of identity being constructed as part of a duality (see Leenhardt 1979:159).

While Leenhardt's work is concerned with the workings of "intuitive" archetypal intellect and image, his notion of *do kamo*, of the authentic or individuated person, at the same time points beyond the sphere of immediate intuitive experience and participation to something less obscure, more tangible. In the suggestive final chapter of the work *Do Kamo*, he attempts to balance his portrait of the Melanesian person as deriving identity solely from his participation with a sociomythic domain with a portrait of a being that recognizes its distinctive body and possesses a distinctive consciousness, a consciousness that "opposes itself to the simple receptivity of the senses" (Cassirer 1955:193). Yet in Leenhardt's view the consciousness of the individuated person could not only oppose itself to the intuitive realm of mythic experience but could also continue to use it as a mode of support and self-construction. The construction of the centered and individuated self could proceed apace with a conscious recognition of the emotional, moral, and spiritual value of mythic participatory experience and thus of the intuitive, mythic image.

Leenhardt's insight about the link between individuation and the conscious use of mythic modes of experience and perception—as these are represented by the images of mythic experience—resonates with certain Jungian ideas about the character of the individuation process. Both Leenhardt and Jung dealt with the old philosophical problem of formulating an understanding of representation and of experience that could account for the richness of intuitive primary forms of sense experience while taking account of consciousness and the intellect. Mythic experience and the mythic image seemed to both men to be archetypal representations of intuitive experience. For Jung, especially, the mythic image seemed to be a sort of pictured emotional experience that was somehow basic to human existence. Yet such images could be subject to interpretation and valuation. That is, they could contain and convey moral value once their meaning was comprehended rather than simply experienced.

The mythic image could objectify emotional experience to a degree, thus giving it a sensible form and putting it at the disposal or use of the person. Still, the image would always retain an archaic "primary" form and thus retain its power to evoke the concrete richness of intuitive, sensuous experience. In Roland Barthes's terms the mythic image would particularly retain and convey the "obtuse" and sometimes obscure meaning of primary intuitive experience. The Latin "obtusus means that which is blunted, rounded in form . . . like the blunting of a meaning that is too clear" (Barthes 1990:55). This blunting and obscuring of meaning and message "seems to open up the field of meaning", so much that discursive language becomes inadequate for the task of representing it. In fact the "obtuse meaning is not within the language-system" (Barthes 1990:60). In other words "it is not situated structurally, a semantologist would not agree as to its objective existence" (Barthes 1990:60). It has the "enigmatic voice of anagram, unoriginated and obsessive" (Barthes 1990:61). "It is outside articulated language, while nevertheless within interlocution" (Barthes 1990:61). That is, it is a way of knowing that eschews clear conceptual thought and language.

These remarks describe important aspects of Leenhardt's understanding of mythic experience. Certainly *la pensée obscure et confuse* of mythic experience communicated something of the nature of Melanesian being without recourse to discursive, conceptual language. One of the key insights to be derived from Leenhardt's work is that the realization of Melanesian being, of personal authenticity, is actually accomplished through both "mythic" and "discursive" or symbolic thinking—that the images and acts of Melanesian expressive life have both discursive and "obtuse" mythic significance and, further, that the gist of Melanesian culture and expressive forms is contained in the participation or interplay between these aspects of person and of being.

As I have suggested, the philosophy of symbolic forms that gives thematic structure to modern symbolic anthropology does not resonate with this idea. Interpretive anthropology has always been primarily concerned with that aspect of the mythic, artistic, or ritual image, and of the linguistic sign that "points beyond the whole sensory sphere" (Cassirer 1955:106). It eschews the idea of the intuitive archetypal intellect as simply another cultural construction, one that has its roots in a suspect stream of Romantic thought. In its view cultural form is part of a constant process of configuration, and it often concerns itself with revealing the social practices and beliefs that are the formative principles behind the process of cultural configuration. This idea of configuration has often been expressed through the use of metaphors of reading, writing, and (even more distant from the sort of phenomenology that Leenhardt tried to understand) of editing. Thus we are told that representation should be viewed as an act of "writing on the landscape of culture" or as a "displacement of meaning onto different perceived markings" (Battaglia 1990:2). We are also told that material images (Leenhardt would perhaps have called them mythic images) "are ascribed the weight of a vehicle of a past or potential truth . . . and are endowed with the status of public record" (Battaglia 1990:6) through an act of "reading." That is, people read significance into images, thereby making them socially significant. This writing, reading, and editing amount to a way of placing feeling, remembrance, and significance into the "public record." Here the Melanesian native appears to take on the ethnographer's concern with "writing it all down" and creating a public record, like an ethnography perhaps.

Cassirer saw the difficulty with this sort of formulation clearly when he wrote that everything the discursive intellect of culture "creates in its constant process of configuration removes us more and more from the originality of life" (Cassirer 1955:112). The idea that cultural representation and meaning can be spoken of as forms of writing, reading, and editing does seem to distance the actor from his creation, or from something that can be called the "originality of life." These metaphors seem part of the language of theoretical thought, the sort of thought and language that seeks to represent "structure and systematic connection" (Cassirer 1953:56). Mythic thinking, in contrast, "comes to rest in immediate experience; it does not dispose freely over the data of intuition in order to relate and compare them to one another, but is captivated and enthralled by the intuition that suddenly confronts it" (Cassirer 1953:32).

If the metaphors of reading and editing appear to distance the actor from *la pensée obscure et confuse* of mythic experience, the metaphor of the "social" image or symbol appears to eschew the question of the "use" or sense of the mythic or the intuitive as obscurantism. We are told again and again by those who favor this view of symbol and image that these phenomena mediate, represent, and even realign social relationships, or that mythic and artistic images are primarily "tools that enable the recall of socially relevant information" (Kuechler 1987:244). Thus, one Melanesianist asserts that we mainly see the historical panorama of shifting social alliances and relationships in the mythic images of Malangan sculptures (see Kuechler 1987).

This is far removed from how thinkers in the Romantic tradition such as Leenhardt, Jung, and Vico thought about image, memory, and experience. Their work particularly concerns me here because it hints at a way of understanding the relationship between mythic image, memory, and the invention of personal authenticity—the invention of person and self. The ideas of participation and of individuation in the work of Leenhardt and Jung and the treatment of the development of consciousness in the work of Vico seem part of a form of discourse about both memory and the primary poetic forms and images out of which consciousness, cultural form, and the concept of person are born. For Leenhardt and Jung in particular, participation and individuation seem to be functions of memory and image. They seem part of a continuous attempt by the person to reestablish a feeling of plenitude, a feeling that is somehow simultaneously a sense of loss and of relationship.

If the tropes of loss and of memory figure prominently in the work of these thinkers, this is perhaps because, as Crapanzano (1979) suggests in his review of Leenhardt's *Do Kamo,* this work is itself a refraction of a myth—the myth of the fall, of the person's separation from nature and thus from the originality of life. Yet the power of myth, or of a particular myth, to circumscribe important aspects of feeling and experience should lead us to be cautious about rejecting the notions of plenitude, loss, and memory as inadequate grounding for a theory of cultural representation. Certainly imagination and value have been viewed as being born of memory and loss in traditions other than our own, and often it is the poetic, mythic, or religious image that appears to circumscribe the plenitude of a people's cultural memory and imagination. The famous Hindu and Buddhist images of the unenlightened life as a sort of forgetful sleep, and of enlightenment as a form of achieved remembering come to mind here, as does the ancient Greek belief that the poet is given the gift of invention by being granted the facility of memory by Mnemosyne, the goddess of memory, inspiration, and creativity. In professor Eliade's terms the remembering of the ancient bard and of the Yogi represent attempts to participate in "primordial memory" (Eliade 1968:114–38). He also argues that in the rituals that circumscribe the experience of the "eternal return" and that are practiced most especially by "archaic cultures," we see how the primordial memory becomes an actual spatiotemporal domain that provides a central mythic axis, or place of centering, for the person. We can certainly hear echoes of this notion in our own intellectual life, for instance, in the importance accorded remembering by analytic psychology and psychoanalysis. The idea that the primordial memory figures in the construction of self and the world is not so very distant from the modern psychoanalytic idea that the images of dreams and myth circumscribe "archaic," "primary" "feeling/tone complexes" that often play a major role in the formation of personality and emotion. Integrating the meaning and power of these images into consciousness is a major goal of analytic psychology in particular. In this integration of image and person we can perceive something of what Leenhardt attempted to describe with the term *plenitude,* which meant the fullness of relationship that was experienced by the authentic, individuated person. But this integration, which was simultaneously an aspect of individuation and of participation, was a function of memory and of recovery.

The New Caledonian felt such moments of mythic experience and of plenitude to be moments of the word. In fact the New Caledonian simply called them *words.* Not simple discourse, *word* to this way of feeling was all forms of expressive action that circumscribed the event of feeling oneself to be *do kamo* (true person).

One cannot help asking if it was because the act of speaking seemed so powerful and expressive of human creativity to the New Caledonians that they experienced all forms of human power and creation as words. We may ask as well then if the act of speaking appeared to offer the New Caledonian a way of understanding the subtle network of relationships and forms of meaning that we call culture, and thus if primordial feelings and images of mythic participation were the original antecedents of ideas and understanding. Certainly in the philosophy of language of the Rauto, speech, song, and word appear both as ways of understanding the subtle series of relationships that we call culture and as dynamic and transformative forms of participatory experience, experience that transforms persons. Rauto ritual events, song festivals, and oratory provide evidence for this assertion. Yet, perhaps not surprisingly, Rauto metaphors also provide clear indications that for this people language is inseparable from being, from meaning, from power and person.

A disproportionate number of Rauto metaphors allude to speech. Many describe occasions during which people use their voices in song or in the performance of magic. Still others describe the use and character of the personal voice when it is used to direct men in battle. Speech, song, the character of the personal voice, and the social contexts in which speech, song, and by extension, the voice, are used constitute realms of experience that seem readily understandable to Rauto and that circumscribe important aspects of their cultural life. In this form of life, character is judged, sustenance and peace are secured, moral life regulated, and personal and social identity are fashioned, through the use of speech and song.

The genre of speech that expresses these ideas is called *amala arlem amta* by the Rauto. *Arlem amta* refers to something that is slightly hidden from view. It may also mean something that appears to be something else when first perceived. Speech called *amala arlem amta* is speech that appears to have multiple meanings. In the Rauto view this makes such speech initially elusive to understanding. However, its character of mystery intimates profundity, thus inviting the listener to try to determine the true meaning of the speech. Like our own word *metaphor* then, the Rauto phrase *amala arlem amta* suggests that tropes effect a transformation of the meaning and form of language, thereby transforming or creating aspects of a people's understanding of the world. But in contrast to our own understanding of metaphor, the Rauto amala arlem amta, as well as the images of song genres such as the *aurang,* the *serpoua,* and the *agreske,* appear also to circumscribe meanings in such a way that they provide metaphoric language with limited opportunity for symbolic elaboration— the images also contain something of the originality of life, something of primordial cultural memory. The argument of this book, and the metaphor that organizes the perspective it expresses, has been influenced by Rauto understanding of the nature of language in general and of metaphor in particular. In fact I have chosen to view concepts of person, time, and agency, as well as Rauto understanding of the nature of ritual activity, through the lens provided by metaphor. It is true that I could have chosen some other vehicle for discussing the centrality of the notion of the person in Rauto culture. For instance, an analysis of sorcery beliefs or exchange practices might have provided an adequate rendering of Rauto symbolic forms. However, my analysis begins with a discussion of metaphor at least in part because the phenomenon encompasses a variety of other symbolic forms. It does this by providing a comment on them that is also, as the work of many suggests, an evaluation or interpretation. Most importantly, it provides us with an initial understanding of what I can only call a different philosophy of "symbolic" forms, such as metaphor specifically and language more generally.

The form of the book has also been influenced by the meaning of Rauto metaphors. The first two ethnographic chapters of the book consist of an analysis of the meanings of these metaphors. They show how amala arlem amta refer to notions of self and person, and to language and human agency. In those chapters I establish the notion that in Rauto understanding, speech and song shape experience by both expressing and shaping the nature of the person.

The next two chapters discuss a category of ritual and of song that the Rauto call *aurang*. Aurang is performed during female and male puberty rituals, during the collective planting of large gardens of taro, and as an essential part of rain magic. The rituals and songs are said to promote the growth of young men and women, as well as to enhance the growth of the taro crop. During these ritual events the notion that speech and song both express and affect the physical and moral nature of human beings is literally performed. The songs and ritual acts express ideas about the moral nature, duties, and privileges of men and women. They constitute a type of mythic discourse about such matters.

My analysis of the aurang and the metaphors the Rauto call amala arlem amta is guided by the premise that the speech and song of men and women are often used to secure rather different ends. I discuss this point in order to portray Rauto understanding of ideals of male and female identity and to chart some of the culture-wide ramifications of these ideals. Subsequent chapters discuss how concepts of human agency and of person color aspects of the Rauto experience of time, place, and death. The book concludes with chapters on the songs and rites of death and on cultural memory and mythic thought. Another part of the conclusion is a discussion of the notion of participation, a notion I also consider in the preceding chapters on ritual.

One of the general theoretical points I make is that an approach that focuses on discourse and that "backgrounds the institutional implications of ethnographic facts" (Marcus and Fischer 1986:45) can be an effective way of talking about participation, a concept Leenhardt defined in part as "a felt relation between the self and an interior or exterior object, immanent or transcendent" (quoted in Clifford 1982:222). This is especially the case when considering questions of the relationship between ritual activity and concepts of the person. As I discuss in the pages that follow, stereotypical events such as ritual seem amenable to a style of interpretation that presents a holistic portrayal of society and a relational understanding of the nature of the person. An approach that is based on the premise that ritual is, among other things, simply one of many kinds of discourse about meaning might provide us with a cogent way of considering the meaning of participation and of holism for the Rauto. This is important because these people have many different ways of speaking about the world and themselves. As Wittgenstein might say, their culture is composed of many different language games. An approach that is based on the analogy of discourse can enable us to hear and understand these different ways of speaking and to place notions of participation, holism, and individualism in relation to them.

Here I feel it would be useful to flesh out these assertions and to see how these ideas have been discussed in work that most especially considers the problem of ritual and person in Melanesia. This overview will necessarily force me to consider problems of the relationship between systems of meaning on the one hand and notions of society and individuality on the other. This will provide a basic background for the ethnography that follows.

RITUAL, PERSON, AND SOCIETY

Work on ritual is well advanced in Melanesian studies. For work on rituals of production see Malinowski 1978 [1935], Fortune 1963 [1932], and Kahn 1986; for work on children's ceremonies see Lewis 1980, Allen 1967, and Scalletta 1985; for treatment of the relationship between the two see Barth 1975:232–38; Herdt 1982; Gell 1975:277). Many different theoretical concerns are represented in work on these ritual processes. Herdt (1982:ix–xxii) provides a skillful analysis of a number of these, ranging from the concern of the old culture and personality school with showing how rituals performed for children play an important part in shaping sexual and social identity, to the present interest of symbolic anthropology in describing the relationship between world view and ritual process. I will not repeat Herdt's discussion here. The purpose of this brief gloss on theoretical matters is to identify certain themes of recent ethnographic work on ritual in Melanesia that at least identifies a relationship between person and ritual event or process. I will suggest that much recent work on ritual and personhood is guided by a new synthesis of theoretical assumptions. Here and in the course of my presentation of ethnographic data, I intend to indicate how this new synthesis of ideas might be useful in explaining certain aspects of Rauto ritual and ideas about the person, and to indicate how it does not account adequately for other aspects.

Much recent work on rites of production and on children's ceremonies especially is concerned with explaining the dynamics of what has come to be called "sociocultural reproduction." This popular phrase serves as shorthand for actions or processes that reproduce a culturally specific relationship between belief and social or institutional forms. Of course, one could say that the study of these processes has been a traditional concern of anthropologists, especially those influenced by the work of Durkheim. One of the things that distinguishes more recent analysis of this problem from earlier work, however, is the current emphasis on describing how ritual action expresses values and sentiments that structure or maintain forms of social inequality. These concerns are implicit or underplayed in more traditionally Durkheimian or Turnerian works on ritual, such as Gell's analysis of the *Ida* ritual of the Umeda, an east Sepik people. They are primary concerns, however, for scholars such as Keesing (1982a, 1982b) and Herdt (1982). Gell is primarily interested in the social effects that the dramatic enactment of ritual scripts has on Umeda social life. In his analysis of the Ida ceremonial he shows (1) that the battery of symbols revealed in the rite essentially derives its meaning from the Umeda system of social relationships, and (2) that the manipulation of symbols through ritual action is a way of both dramatically recreating the Umeda system of social relations and of expressing the system of ideas that informs social relationships. The Ida ritual described by Gell is particularly interesting because it is both a fertility ritual meant to regenerate forces thought to aid horticultural and human reproduction, and it is a "children's ceremony," in which young men are symbolically provided with a new social identity.

One of Gell's points is that the Ida ritual symbolizes the metamorphosis of asocial energies and tendencies into productive social energies. This change is dramatically represented when on the final night of the ritual, masked dancers who are supposed to represent wild cassowary are replaced by young men who have assumed the role of the *Ipele* bowmen, or the hunters of the cassowary. Gell makes it clear that when Umeda bachelors assume the role of the Ipele bowmen, they also symbolically affirm ideals that stress the importance of sociality as opposed to individual autonomy and the importance of restrained sexual conduct as opposed to licentiousness (Gell 1975:277). Importantly, the dramatic enactment of these ideals of conduct is at the same time "an enactment of reproductive processes" (161). Symbols of fertility abound in this ritual process, and the dance itself is said to prompt the regeneration of the stands of village sago palm. The cassowary dancers especially represent "nature in a generalized way" (244). Gell writes that the cassowary mask is a symbolic representation of the "total society" of the Umeda people and that since the mask represents as well a quality of "florescence," like a tree that is "at the apogee of its development cycle" (244), it characterizes Umeda society as being fully "developed," or fully reproduced.

Besides being one of the most sensitive analyses of a New Guinea ritual system that has been done, Gell's work is important in a theoretical sense partly because it shows how the creation of social identity, at least for the Umeda, depends on the proper manipulation of "natural processes" through ritual action. Gell thus restates the Durkheimian idea that culture "appropriates" nature or natural processes through ritual and ultimately gives meaning to these processes by using them for its own schemes, which in this instance involve the expression of an ideal of social conduct. Indeed, in his monograph Gell shows how the classification of objects and processes of nature is related to the Umeda conception of society. This is especially apparent in a chapter that deals with the symbolism of the Umeda language. Here Gell suggests that the Umeda see an identity between the social and the natural. He then goes on to argue that this identity can be perceived in the resemblance between words that describe the processes and things of the two realms (1975:119–55). This relationship between society and nature is invoked and manipulated in the Ida ritual.

Gell's analysis also suggests that the direction of ritual scripts by adult men is a way for them to assert control over processes that shape personal identity and that "reproduce" social forms. He does not stress this point, however, as he is not fundamentally concerned with the political economy of ritual. Nor does he relate the Ida ritual to Umeda folk accounts or to verbal metaphors about the nature of self and person. As Gell does not delve into Umeda ethnopsychology, we do not come to see the Ida ceremony as one sort of discourse about person and society among many. The ritual thus becomes reified as the central cultural process and form of symbolic discourse of this people.

A number of contributors to the Herdt (1982) volume specifically consider how sociocultural reproduction may be linked to the actual shaping of the psychological and sexual dispositions of children, in Highland ritual especially. Thus, in the introduction to the volume, Keesing (1982b:20–32) argues that because of this relationship, such ritual processes facilitate the reproduction of systems in which adult men dominate youths and women. Interestingly, a number of the contributors to this volume write that in many Highland and Sepik initiation ceremonies, adult men literally "forge" an identity for young men that is distinct from and in some cases the symbolic opposite of what is taken to be the nature of women. For instance, the weaning of Sambia, Awa, and Bimin-Kuskusmin initiates away from foods that are perceived to symbolize the nature of women is interpreted to be a part of the symbolic "forging" of a specifically masculine identity by Herdt (1982:56), Boyd and Newman (1982:249), and Poole (1982:106), respectively.

Perhaps paradoxically, in many of the cults described by these ethnographers men seem to claim that they possess powers that are analogous to the abilities of adult women to nurture children. Thus, an idea which informs a number of homosexual cults in the Highlands is that adult men can nurture boys and sustain their physical growth through homosexual acts. Analogously, adult Bimin-Kuskusmin men "aid" the growth of taro by burying bamboo canes holding amounts of semen in gardens (Poole 1982:106). Here I must note that men are considered responsible in a symbolic sense for both the production of food as well as for the shaping of the identity of boys in a number of New Guinea societies (Poole 1982; Williams 1940). This "pseudo procreative" metaphor or "male emulation of women's reproductive and nurturing powers" (Keesing 1982:8) appears even to inform New Guinea ritual systems in which sexuality plays no overt part. Thus, Kahn writes that for the Wamirans of the Massim, taro is symbolically classified as men's children, and that in the practices of garden ritual men "become symbolic masters of reproduction and procreation" (1986:92).

In explaining this politicized cosmological assertion of New Guinea men that they control powers of physical and social regeneration, Keesing notes an overriding concern of men to assert their superiority over and their distinctiveness from women (1982b:8). Thus, he and others such as Kahn (1986:75) imply that a tangible sexual and political antagonism lies at the core of ritual symbolism. He also suggests, like many other writers on ritual, that the cosmological schemes and systems of classification that are revealed in ritual processes are themselves shaped to a large degree by male political interests (1982b:27).[1] This point brings us to the question of the relationship between knowledge systems on the one hand and ideas about gender on the other.

All of the authors whose work I have cited, with the exception of Gell, have implied that in New Guinea adult men are aided in their attempt to assert control over women, over the moral and physical development of children, and over food production by the very form or character of the knowledge that they express and manipulate in ritual processes. That is, they suggest that the character of this knowledge is such that it inhibits the creation of alternative interpretive schemes that could perhaps lead to different and more reciprocal forms of relationship between the sexes. Thus, because New Guinean cosmological schemes so frequently exalt "male" qualities and denigrate "female" qualities, ethnographers argue that in ritual men reproduce a cosmology which is consistent with their political interest in social control. The authors of the Herdt collection take this point one step further and argue that in the Highlands and in parts of the Sepik, cosmologies or abstract classifications of foods, plants, fauna, and human characteristics are consistent with certain sorts of psychological dispositions. Thus, they argue that the teaching of cosmological knowledge and the formation of social and sexual identity and ideas about the nature of the person are different aspects of a single, unified process. Also, the accounts of these authors imply that sociocultural reproduction is partly a

1. Jorgensen (1987) points out that the conception of ritual symbolism and knowledge as political ideology loses force when we take into consideration the secrecy and paradox which often distinguishes knowledge and ritual systems in New Guinea.

product of the performance of a set of formalized acts meant to manipulate the emotions of initiates in specific ways.

The approaches to ritual I have alluded to here appear to be an amalgam of analytical ideas that derive from a number of intellectual traditions. For instance, the social philosopher George Herbert Mead's influence can be seen in the assertion that the self is formed or engaged most completely through forms of symbolic action (Cohen 1977:118). Freud's influence is apparent in the parallel noted between individual sexual identity and abstract cultural ideas. Durkheim's influence can be seen in the concern with accounting for the social effects rendered by the manipulation of symbols in ritual. The influence of Marx can be perceived in the concern for indicating the relationship between the maintenance of social inequality and the maintenance of a "dominant ideology" or a dominant interpretive scheme. Finally, there is another element which, though not stressed by any of the authors of the Herdt collection, has figured prominently in a few discussions of ritual and personhood in Melanesia and has been seen to facilitate "sociocultural" reproduction by a number of scholars working outside of Melanesian studies. I would call this element the *aesthetics* of ritual performance. In New Guinea studies, this element is discussed in most depth by Steven Feld (1982) and by Gilbert Lewis (1980) in his work on the initiation ritual of the Gnau of the West Sepik Province.

Lewis argues that ritual, like theatre, is essentially "expressive performance" (1980:10). His major concern in putting forth this argument is to demonstrate that the aesthetic elements of ritual, "the decorations, singing, the aromatic plants, the formality, stiffness or strangeness of gesture" affect the way that meaning is apprehended by both the spectators and participants in a ritual event (1980:20). Indeed, according to Lewis it is primarily the "emotional and aesthetic coloring of ritual" that creates the feeling that it expresses significant meaning (1980:146). It is important that Lewis argues that ritual events do not communicate meaning in a clear or rational way, as does a written message. Rather, ritual stimulates the emotions and the mind in such a way that it "evokes a response" from participants and spectators. Lewis believes that the nature of this response produces dissonance between the intellectual understanding that the rite conveys meaning symbolically and the feeling or emotional conviction that it actually produces the reality represented by this meaning. In the phrase of literary critics, the ritual performance "suspends the disbelief" of participants and spectators. Borrowing a number of ideas about representation and symbolism from the art critic E. H. Gombrich, Lewis writes that in ritual "people are prone to take the symbolic objects or actions" of the rite "for the reality they stand for." "In other words, they mistake the concreteness and substantial nature of the objects or actions for the reality of the sentiments and ideas they feel" (1980:198). He here implies that the ritual situation is one in which the line between person and the meaning of a ritual symbol has become blurred. His interpretation implies that people "participate" in the ideas and values represented by ritual acts and symbols. Thus, ritual establishes an identity between meaning and person. Following the literary critic Auerbach, we would perhaps call this type of identification *mimesis*.

What most interests me about a number of the works I have mentioned here is the understanding of the person they express. The idea that character is forcefully shaped when the social order is exhibited to people during ritual occasions, the notion that ritual symbolism, while shaping mind and self, limits intellectual speculation—these notions imply that in a traditional society like that of the Rauto or the Gnau, individual consciousness is easily overwhelmed by the ritual process; thus, they imply that the person lacks a center of consciousness distinct from the social ideas and values expressed during this process.

I feel that such understandings of religious phenomenology, and of "participation" say only a little about Rauto understanding of the nature of the person. I find that Leenhardt's idea of "plenitude" complements these approaches, while saying as much about the character of Rauto life and experience. Leenhardt felt that "the person was capable of enriching itself through a more or less indefinite assimilation of exterior elements. It takes its life from the elements it absorbs, in a wealth of communion. The person is capable of superabundance" (Leenhardt 1979:169). The idea that experiential enrichment was made possible by events such as ritual, ceremonial, or speech making, lay at the core of Leenhardt's evangelical project in New Caledonia. He perceived the social usefulness of such events. He recognized that they represented living modes of thought and experience, and he tried for this reason to co-opt aspects of them to the Christian tradition (Clifford 1982:74–91).

The idea that individual enrichment came through participation in the lives and natures of others and in the meanings expressed by ritual events and exchanges implied an element of self-direction and thus self-consciousness on the part of the individual, rather than its absence. Indeed, Leenhardt perceived a desire and an individual need for self-renewal and social renewal in the long planning and staging of such events. The events were forms of social and self-creation, and as such they could not, in Leenhardt's view, be eliminated without dire consequences for the soul of the New Caledonian. Their loss meant the loss of Melanesian consciousness.

Ritual songs such as the aurang and the serpoua, exchange events, moments of oratory, ceremonies, and song festivals are also forms of social and self-creation for the Rauto. Their metaphors and proverbs express an awareness of this, and so I begin the ethnography with a discussion of these. One of the points that emerges is that the Rauto have more than one way of thinking about the nature of their own lives. One of the central ideas of the book is that these different ways of viewing the world are represented by Rauto "theories and constructions of the person" (Marcus and Fischer 1986:45). I follow White and Kirkpatrick here in considering persons to be first "cultural elements, topics of knowledge and discourse. Persons are constructs deemed capable of experience, will, action, identity and the like. . . . Persons are cultural bases for formulating and exploring subjective experience" (1985:9).

A sketch of the spirit being (kamotmot). Drawing by Coralie Cooper.

Chapter Two

Structures of the Person, Ethos, Pathos, and Memory

When a canaque says of a man, "he has no words in his heart," we understand that he thinks nothing or that he is without efficacy, and empty.

Maurice Leenhardt (1979)

Wittgenstein once remarked that human beings think and act through the use of many different forms of language, or discourse (1967:30). This chapter is an extended commentary on this remark. In it I describe some of the many different ways the Rauto have of speaking about persons. The terms and metaphors this people use to provide comment on various aspects of self and person are numerous and convey a sensitive and profound understanding of the range of qualities and characteristics of human beings. However, these terms and metaphors draw meaning from two conceptual structures that possess their own rules for what Crick (1976:135) has called *signification*—the designation of objects, acts, or utterances as meaningful. Chapter 3 discusses one of these structures, which consists of beliefs about and metaphoric evaluations of the "public face" or persona of individuals. Here, in contrast, I note some of the ways in which the Rauto conceptualize and speak about the relationship between person, or public persona and the self: the individual qualities, characteristics, and emotions of people.

This chapter begins with a discussion of Rauto understanding of what can be called the formal aspects of the human personality: name, or social reputation and identity (*anine*), mind and thought (*amta nal*), and heart, or sentience (*momso*). By eliciting the meanings associated with each of these concepts, I outline what can be called the Rauto experience of the human personality. When experience and emotion are talked about, they are always considered in relation to these aspects of the personality. I also discuss the character of Rauto models of mind, emotion, and personality. Unlike some Western psychoanalytic models of these phenomena, Rauto models do not divide the soul into categories that themselves seem to be "structured like a person" (de Sousa 1990:25–28). This is due at least in part to the fact that the Rauto, unlike many Western peoples, do not articulate a view of the person as being subject to a host of conflicting desires and passions, some of which they consider higher than and thus necessarily in conflict with other less worthy tendencies. Rather, Rauto discourse about person and self uses bodily metaphors to outline a series of complex but nonhierarchically arranged capacities for feeling or sensation, thinking, and for different emotional states.

The second section of the chapter considers the Rauto concept of *lai*, which can be translated as the "character" of a person. A person's character is represented by his personal habits and characteristics as well as by his characteristic way of dealing with others. Through a consideration of talk about the character of persons, we can begin to discuss aspects of the ethos of men and women in Rauto culture. In this section I also discuss how Rauto moral philosophy is related to this people's particular understanding of the nature of the human personality. The concluding section of the chapter turns to a consideration of the central Rauto metaphor of the human voice. I suggest here and in the following chapters that the use of the voice in song during the performance of aurang and other rituals of the life cycle symbolizes the relationship between self and person. It is also an expression of an idea that the individual powers of both men and women can be directed toward the realization of positive social ends.

IDEAS ABOUT THE STRUCTURES OF THE PERSON

Anine: *Name, Identity, Reputation, Spirit*

Anine is the Rauto word for "name." [1] In speech referring to persons, the word is most often used when reference is made to someone's social reputation. Thus, to say that a man or woman "has name" is one of the most powerful verbal expressions of status distinction that the Rauto make. A person who "has name" is in some sense perceived as conforming to ideal patterns of "cultural behavior and well-known social routines" (White and Kirkpatrick 1985:10). These especially involve the sponsoring of song festivals, feasts and ceremonies, the settlement of disputes, the successful management of both operational and interpretive knowledge, and the successful production of foodstuffs. By performing all these activities and by cultivating the socially valued

---

1. In religious discourse *anine* has a number of different meanings. First, it is the Rauto word for ghost. *Anine* is also the word for "shade," an aspect of the person that is thought to be capable of leaving the body during sleep. The Rauto sometimes say that dreaming results from the anine leaving the body and walking about on a round of adventures.

personal qualities described in this chapter, a person is said to raise his or her name (*pane anine*). The concept of anine in one sense, then, refers to what Mauss would have called the social persona—the person considered in relation to the roles and requirements of his society (1985:14).

Yet anine has a meaning that extends beyond the individual and thus describes more than simply his or her rank and status. It is also the word for "personal name," and a person's name is itself a statement about the relationship of that individual to the cultural tradition of the Rauto. This is perhaps most clearly seen in the Rauto naming ceremony. A name is given to a child a few years after its birth during the ceremony. A feast is prepared to mark the occasion, and a number of kinsmen are invited to witness the naming. During the course of the feast, the child's father or maternal uncle walks to the front doors of the men's ceremonial house of the child's ramage and then publicly calls out the name that he or his own father or uncle has chosen for the child. All those invited to the ceremony then clasp each other's hands in approval of the child's name. I was told that this sign of approval is shown at least partly because the child's name will remind people of an aspect of their cultural tradition; it might be the name of an important cultural object, such as a part of a sacred spirit mask (*uakuakio*), or a section of the men's ceremonial house (*molokio*). A name can be taken as well from a character in Rauto mythology or from one of the colorful and aromatic plants that the Rauto use for personal decoration or magic.

I was told that because people's names had the meanings that they did, the cultural traditions of southwestern New Britain would be "kept in people's minds." That is, as long as people were given formal names, the meanings and things represented by these names would survive.[2] Names, then, are carriers of memory just as much as minds are. Indeed, the Rauto naming system is an "art of memory" that is based on an understanding of identity or felt participation between person and world. It is because of this felt identity that all the important items of the cultural and natural world have a pair of names, one masculine and the other feminine. Informants told me that the things of the world and their constituent parts had each to have two names so that "both boys and girls could be given names." The things of the world were then named, and thus conceptually grasped, by being brought into relationship with persons. The world was named with the person in mind.[3]

2. The two men who made this statement to me were, however, concerned that their culture (*lai;* in Tok Pisin, *kastom*) was "being lost." They were both middle-aged and had seen a good deal of the outside world. They perceived that the values of that world were incompatible with some of the values of traditional Rauto life.

3. The names associated with an important cultural object are called the object's *ikit*. A good deal of Rauto ritual life consists of teaching children ikit.

When this particular meaning of the concept anine was explained to me, I began to understand the sense of reverence with which Rauto men and women treated the objects, the foods, the aromatic plants, and the clothing of both everyday use and ceremonial occasion. The Rauto treat these things in this way because they see the human metaphor in them. Infused with meaning by everyday use, these things also symbolize belief and confidence in the essential correctness of a way of life, because they allude to a culturally specific metaphysic that extends the provenance of the person to the entire world. It is not surprising then that the Rauto often celebrate these things in song, myth, and ritual. As I make clear in later chapters, these ritual celebrations of important cultural objects convey something of the poetry of Rauto existence. The Rauto's belief in the essential correctness of their way of life and their celebration of the poetry or the aesthetics of that felt correctness are then alluded to by the name of a person. By being given a name, one is being given part of a culture; one is being informed of the Rauto belief in and aesthetic appreciation of a way of life.

The fact that one's name is an important part of one's identity is formally confirmed by the belief that a person should not touch or go near someone who shares his name. A person who takes the same name as a fellow village or hamlet resident is thought to be taking something away from that person. Thus, a time should be arranged for the person who has taken the name to offer some valuable to the original possessor of the name. Usually a small pig and some pearl shell valuables are handed over. A smaller token of wealth is then given back to the name taker as a sign that he can now engage in a reciprocal relationship with his namesake. The two will then clasp each others hands for the first time. Henceforth, they will be able to interact with one another. These beliefs and practices indicate that the Rauto, like the Melanesians of New Caledonia, perceive that life is "lived plurally" (Clifford:1982:x). That is, the Rauto perceive that one's identity can be shared with others, that people participate in each others' lives. A namesake can, however, be a threat to one's sense of identity or individuality. By sharing his name, a person loses a bit of himself; he must be repaid for this loss.

A person also has a number of informal names that describe his personal skills and habits or allude to the events of his life. Thus, if someone is a good fisherman, huntsman, or food producer, he will acquire names that celebrate his practice of these skills. A person accumulates a series of these informal names over the course of a lifetime. After someone's death his various names serve as reminiscences of his life. The names convey a partial image of the person.

Name, reputation, and identity cannot be considered apart from personal experience, emotion, and personal power. Rauto conversation about such matters often refers to what they call *momso,* the "heart." Here I will outline the Rauto concept of heart in order to indicate how its development allows for the construction of identity and also to reveal something of the texture of Rauto emotional life.

Momso: *Heart, Sentience, Conscience*

The term *momso* represents a number of rather complex concepts. In Rauto speech as in English speech, the heart is a metonym for sentience. Indeed, like English speakers, the Rauto use the idiom of the heart to talk about profound and powerful emotional experience. Such experience is spoken of either in terms of its felt immediacy or in terms of long-lasting moods and dispositions. In general, idioms that identify the former kind of experience describe the heart as feeling hot, or as being in a state of agitated movement "upward." Idioms that identify long-lasting moods and dispositions describe the heart as feeling cool and as being either in a movement downward or as already fallen. Let me give a few examples.

In describing feelings associated with the initial reception of unexpected, tragic news, a Rauto person will say that his heart jumps up and then races, making him breathless (*momsoingong ngagnas*) and desiring to move. In contrast, in describing deep and long-lasting sorrow, he will say that his heart has fallen (*momsoingong kai*) and has died (*momsoingong uren*). Many people speak of this state as a type of emotional numbness. While in it, they feel themselves to be unable to carry out the normal tasks of life. It is as if they are stuck in sand.

Idioms that describe aspects of the experiences of anger and of love draw meaning from these same contrasts between hot and cold, up and down, and movement and immobility. A person in lust for another will say that his heart rises for this person, and is inflamed by him or her (*momsoingong pane iei nimbir*). People whose relationship has deepened into love will say that their hearts have fallen down together and thus work reciprocally (*momsoinmi kai ti pulu*). In the initial phase of strong anger, the Rauto will say that the heart, or as often the stomach, rises and burns with anger (*pele pane ye nimbir*). When anger has subsided, they will say that the stomach or heart has cooled and fallen.

Much of this talk about the heart appears at least somewhat reminiscent of emotional states described by English idioms. Yet it was while I was trying to understand the nuances of meaning associated with idioms about the heart that I first began to acquire a sense for an important characteristic of Rauto emotional life. In listening to people use these idioms to speak of their feelings, I noticed that the objects of particular emotional states were often different than what I would have expected given the character of the emotions described. More specifically, in emotional discourse, persons and things are frequently the objects of similar emotions. Here for instance is the speech of a few people whom I asked to describe experiences of loss, sorrow, and tenderness.

First, the words of an elder man:

> I gave my pearlshell [to a man from Wako] for him to hold for me. I thought he would return it quickly, but I waited in vain. My heart was tender toward my pearlshell (*momsoingong manamanaine pe lugu klingen*); this man carried it away. Neither was something given to me to take its place. This man took my heart away when he took my pearlshell (*pat uru tan momsoingong pe lugu klingen*).

Another man with whom I spoke a few days later used phrases identical to these to describe what I took to be a more elemental and authentic experience of loss: the death of his son. The boy had been troubled and mentally unbalanced for years, and this had caused his father great pain. The boy would wander off from work and family for days at a time, making it necessary time and again for his father to follow after him to try to bring him back. One day the boy wandered off and did not return. After a week of searching, his body was found. It was assumed that he was a suicide:

> My heart was tender toward this child; he was truly dear to me. I would always search after him [when he ran away] because my heart was tender for him. Then he ran away [for good]. I neither ate nor drank for days; I only looked for him. I would have been so grateful had he come back to me. And then I heard [the news of his death]. It took my heart away.

Often people specifically equated the loss of a valued thing with the loss of a person:

> When my friend R. died, his death took my heart away. Then I lost all my treasure for him [during the exchanges of death]. This drove me mad (*iang iango*). I gave my shells to those strangers. They took my heart away. I looked in my box and nothing remained, my possessions were gone. Neither did something of equal value come to take their place. It is as if your child had died. Nothing can take the place of this child; it is unique.

These examples indicate that the emotional nexus that joins person to person is similar to that which joins person to possession. Indeed, a loved person is said to be a dear possession and, like such a possession, is said to carry one's name (*aningong ma pe ilim ko angan ko imi*). Yet people and possessions have many names. Another way of putting this would be to say that persons and objects consist of a composite of identities. The first speaker quoted above clarified this matter for me when I asked him why his heart felt tenderly toward his lost pearlshell and why losing it was like losing his heart. He told me that the shell "was the face of his father" and that when he looked at it he saw not the shell "but the eyes of his father." He felt tenderly toward the object because it was a vehicle of memory.

The metaphors that the Rauto use to describe memory evocatively express the sense of longing for persons that objects can engender. In remembering someone who has died for instance, the Rauto say that the mind's eye best follows the "trail of remembrance" (*amta nes*) by viewing, handling, and desiring—literally "coveting"—the things of that person. The phrase for this type of remembering (*amta sisire*) describes a kind of grief as well as a form of nostalgia. *Amta sisire* itself means "the desire to possess something that belongs to another." Yet in remembering in this way, by handling and viewing another's possessions, one's desire for the things of the lost and loved person is transformed into a desire to see that person again, and to "possess" the person in the same way that one possesses his things by holding and viewing them. Yet this desire can never be fulfilled, and the realization of this fact is both a form of grief and a type of helpless longing.

The culturally patterned and stereotypical behavior of mourning is consistent with, indeed confirms, the experiential truth and accuracy of Rauto discourse about loss and memory. Thus, during the formally marked period of grieving that follows upon the death of a person, his or her closest kin will wear some of the dead's clothing, or will carry around some of the dead's most treasured possessions. This betokens a constant state of remembrance and thus of grief. Another Rauto metaphor about the heart expresses the experienced identity between object and person eloquently and economically. When speaking of a treasured object, or a treasured person, a Rauto person will say "this is my heart itself" (*momsoingong kai ine*).

The idioms about the heart that I have described so far explore the phenomenology of the self and thus of personal experience. Yet there is another aspect to the Rauto understanding of the heart and of the person, one that Leenhardt might perceive as having a "mythic character." It is encapsulated by the belief that the inner strength and vitality of a person stems from the heart.[4] The heart

4. In his 1982 work Clifford notes how Leenhardt objected to the use of the word *mystical* in Lévy-Bruhl's descriptions of the mentality of traditional peoples (see pp. 202–7). Leenhardt preferred to use the word *mythic*. For Leenhardt, mythic consciousness "circumscribed immediate emotional experiences" in ways "that discursive language could not express" (Clifford 1982:202). This type of consciousness "grasps complex emotional states through juxtaposed image" (204). These images "form a language of emotions" (204). Where Leenhardt came to perceive mythic consciousness as representing a type of discourse about and understanding of the world which was

is said to give strength to the body by providing an essential heat or warmth to it. As persons mature, their hearts are said to grow stronger and their bodies warmer. This makes it possible for people to engage in an increasing number of social and economic activities. The strengthening of the heart is also thought to be related to the development of certain physical characteristics, for instance taut skin and bright eyes.[5] Still, the major indication that someone's heart is powerful will be the ability to produce an abundance of foodstuffs. Leading men and women are thought to be particularly distinguished by this ability. This idea about the nature and power of the heart was distilled from my many conversations with elders about taro magic and productive ability. The elders pointed out a three-way relationship between "strength of heart," productive ability, and the power of a leader's taro magic. This relationship emerged particularly clearly in discussions about the magical power of the breath of a taro magician and of how the power of the breath and magic of persons inevitably lessened with old age. Here I would like to summarize the gist of some of these conversations in order to explore some of the social implications that the Rauto perceive to accompany the strengthening and weakening of a person's heart.

For the Rauto much of the power of magic is thought to be carried on the breath of the magician. When a leading magician begins to age, people will sometimes say that the magician's breath has gone (*sanger ino, ino ingos la*) or that the breath has lost heat and has become "cold" and "light," and thus no longer laden with power (*sanger ino, ino ingos imbrip konong, ino ingos markan konong*). This will especially be noted after a few poor taro harvests. When the breath of a headman becomes cold and weak, he should no longer perform the garden magic for the people of his hamlet, though his knowledge of the verbal component of his garden spells might be perfectly intact. Thus, one could say that in Rauto perception, as persons age and weaken their magic

---

held in certain contexts by Western peoples as well as by Melanesians, Lévy-Bruhl emphasized that the "primitive" and the "modern" mentality were separated by a vast divide. Neither did he perceive, as did Leenhardt, the positive emotional and social benefits which accrued to the individual who lived within and through what Leenhardt came to call mythic consciousness. Lévy-Bruhl often spoke as if the "primitive mentality" simply confused various concepts and categories.

I use the term *mythic* in my own description in order to emphasize that the Rauto concept of momso is given meaning by a language of emotion which describes experience according to the assumptions of a different system of belief. Also, I use the term because the experience of participation which takes place during initiation rites and during Rauto rituals of production is partly explained by beliefs about the heart. This experience is primarily an emotional experience, during which a person invests his being in others.

5. Goodale notes that for the neighboring Kaulong, the development of the *enu* is thought to be related to the development of certain physical characteristics (1986:127). She translates *enu* as "self."

(*uirim*) weakens along with them. When I asked my older informants why this was so, they told me that as a person ages, his heart becomes weak and is no longer able to warm and convey strength and heat to the body and breath. Thus, his garden magic will lack potency. At this point (or ideally, at some time before it), the aging garden magician is to hand over his duties of magical performance either to his eldest son or to his eldest sister's firstborn son. If, as is almost always the case, the head garden magician is also a headman, he should formally abdicate from this position as well. He is now to direct those with pressing political or economic concerns to take these matters up with his heir. Also, henceforth all the gifts of food made to a headman to secure his favor and solicitude or to enmesh him in the political plans of others are to be redirected to his heir. It will now be the heir's duty to redistribute these gifts and to begin to build upon and extend the social influence given to him by the headman. In order to lessen the difficulty of this transition of social power, the headman may even move his house away from the area of the main hamlet settlement.[6] As the Rauto say, "Father and son have now changed places" (*imi vakase la pe ivo*). I would say here that older people's diminished ability to work and to produce foodstuffs is explained in part by Rauto perceptions of the role played by the heart in promoting the physical and social development and the senescence of the person.

Shame and Idioms that Refer to the Skin (Tandra)

Idioms that refer to the heart are metaphors for the inner being and for the strength of persons. In a way they convey a sense of people as individuals who possess varying degrees of power, capability, and sentience. These idioms stress the differences between and the separateness of persons. Another type of idiom stresses the way in which the person is influenced or affected by the actions of others. This altogether different emphasis is conveyed by idioms that refer to the skin (*tandra*).

First, these idioms are often used to convey fears of personal vulnerability. Thus, to be afraid is to feel fear on the skin (*tandra ulo*). To feel uneasy or threatened is to feel somehow that one's skin is not altogether right (*tandra sulu*). To feel absolutely terrified is to feel that one's skin has literally "come off" (*tandra naura*), thus leaving one unprotected—the Rauto describe this by saying that a spirit is "consuming their skin." Conversely one of the ways of saying that one feels at ease is to say that one has good skin (*tandra itau*).

Rauto often use this last idiom in conjunction with another that means, among other things, relief, satisfaction, and contentment (*tandra plo*). Trans-

---

6. Todd (1935:94) also notes that this was a common practice of the Kaul.

lated literally, the idiom means that one has "smooth" and "open" skin, a metaphor that often implies sympathetic communication with another, or with others. Appropriately, then, the phrase that is used to describe what an English speaker would refer to as loneliness, the feeling of undesired separation from others, is "closed" skin (*tandra tung*). The fact that *tandra tung* is used as well to speak of the type of sadness and frustration that a person feels when he or she has not received word from a far-off friend or relative is consistent with the understanding that contentment consists in reciprocal communication and interaction.

The ultimate rupture of reciprocal good will and social interaction is caused by acts that bring a feeling of shame upon the Rauto person. Feeling shame involves having a sense of social vulnerability. Like a number of other New Guinea peoples, the Rauto say that they have this feeling on their skins: *tandra maing*. [7]

The person who is shamed feels the speech and the gaze of others to be at once a reproach and a violation. Since the idioms that describe this feeling refer to the skin—the external covering of the body—they are consistent with the idea that the cause of the feeling is external to the person. There is thus a certain logic to the character of the idioms.

In the many explanations that were offered to me of the concept of shame (*maing*) almost all identified the speech and thought of others as the cause of the feeling, as in the following explanation:

Maing pe oduk tirie amtasek
Tikanes pe ilo asap kaden.
Timaing pe tiklokopas kai oduk
amtasek. Tikin sulu pe taulip la
solo liki kaden. Osaiye, tikanes "ai
imi ogo ko sulu dok." La kanes
ligo taulip, kanes ilo asap kaden ye
la lia gamgam. Oduk tiwur amala.
Osaiye maing, la kaine kare. Pane
kamut. De apasrong. Me simel
kai kamut. Mela de sep krim-
krim aune. Ye kaine kai kare uren
kano. Ye tilele la ko ta ousine.
Osaiye pat oru la sep "la ko kino
ei?" elim la oduk sep pe amala pe
tikele gamgam ye tikele tikanes ilo

People feel shame when dancing
before the gaze of others or if they
speak to their sisters-in-law. They
will be shamed if their barkcloths
fall and others see. If someone
calls out [sexual innuendo] to his
sister-in-law. Afterward people
will say "this child has committed
a great wrong." People then gossip that this person has spoken
to his sister-in-law and that the
two have stolen away [slept with
each other]. The gossip will rage.
Afterward this person will tie his
barkcloth to the branch of a tree
and hang himself, and thus he will

7. See A. Strathern (1975:347–56) for a discussion of Melpa ideas of shame and skin. See also Read (1955:232–82).

kaden la tikarkar amala. Tir la ko wowrum ye imi ogo la kaine kare isa la ko ous oduk tious la ko, la ko, la ko tarike nangar tir, me oduk tikanes "ooei!" Kaine kare tan tir, uren. Osaiye ous ti songsong tila tirike wala ye mata sep oru pe pat o kaine kare pe oduk ye wala tibulbul pe ina mala. Ye takanes pe ianmala. Ye la kaine kare.

die. People will gather together to talk [about the person's whereabouts]; then they will look for him. Many people will say he has stolen away with his sister-in-law. Meanwhile this child will have hung himself. They will look for him and eventually find him hanging dead. The people will call out, "He has hung himself!" The whole village will run to come and see him. They will then speak about their gossip [how it was wrong for them to gossip so].

The main scenario that is recounted in this passage, which was offered to me as an explanation of the concept of maing (shame), is a familiar one to the Rauto. In it a young man who is accused of sleeping with a woman (brother's wife) whom he is forbidden by custom even to speak to or to look at is overwhelmed by the social opprobrium that this accusation brings with it. The feeling one gets from the passage, and indeed from most Rauto talk about shame, is that the emotion makes a person feel socially exposed in a way that is intolerable. One of the culturally patterned responses to this feeling is to attempt suicide, as I witnessed a number of times during my period of fieldwork.

In the passage the speaker shows by way of anecdote the power that the gossip and the opinions of others have over the life of the person; in effect he shows that these thoughts and opinions are a major part of Rauto moral life. The speaker also indirectly questions the justice of this reality by expressing the idea that gossip and the social opprobrium that it represents can literally kill a person. The last line of the passage conveys a sense of tragic contrition about this social reality and thus a veiled criticism of what can be called the social relations of Rauto moral life.

Though the Rauto most often say that they feel shame "on the skin," they do also speak of a kind of shame that is felt "deep inside people's souls" (maing amto ino). Informants described this feeling as involving a sense of regret as well as a sense of shame, and because of this I thought at first that the emotion was similar to what a Westerner would call guilt. I was wrong. In questioning people, I discovered that, unlike the Western concept of guilt, the feeling did not by definition involve or imply the activation of conscience. It was simply a more intensely felt shame. The following conversation is identical in substance to many others I had while searching for a Rauto sense of guilt:

Q: If you had done a terrible deed, and if no one had seen this act that
you committed, would you have this feeling of deep shame—*maing
amto ino?*

A: If I had done this thing and no one saw it, and talk linking it to me did
not surface, then I would not have this feeling. If people saw me commit
this great wrong and then spoke about it, then I would feel regret and
shame. I would carry this feeling with me for a long time. I would look
sorrowful, I would hardly eat. I would try to hide from others' gaze by
remaining in the forest until nightfall.

In this conversation, as in many others that I recorded, a person expresses a
recognition of the distinction between right and wrong action yet implies that
he would only feel the full significance of acting immorally if others discovered his deed and blamed him for it. The venerable anthropological practice
of invoking a distinction between shame and guilt cultures would perhaps be
appropriate here. It appeared that for the Rauto, as for the Pacific island people
that Levy (1973:341–42) writes about, "feelings related to shame and embar-
rassment have undergone" more cultural definition and elaboration than those
involving a sense of guilt. But this is not the whole of the story. I discovered
the significance that concepts like guilt and conscience have for the Rauto when
I explored the moral nexus that links their idea of tradition to their concept of
person. For this people, conscience consists in part of a proper understanding
of the moral dimension of tradition, or custom (*lai*). Guilt is contained in a
type of regret, felt perhaps more keenly by some than by others, that one has
ignored or violated the spirit of tradition in one's dealings with others.

Informants told me that certain kinds of people carried within themselves
and lived their lives by the meaning and law of tradition. A Rauto metaphor
economically expresses this idea in saying that the "mind's eye" of such a person follows the laws and meanings of tradition as he or she goes about the
business of life (*kamngenngen amta nes*, or *amta nes amala*). It was explained
to me that keeping custom in one's mind's eye in this way allows one to enjoy
a long life, since a life lived in accord with the meaning of custom will not give
others reason for anger or envy, emotions that might lead them to attempt sorcery attacks upon another. One informant endeavored to explain the longevity
of his grandfather by considering the man's adherence to the laws of tradition:

Look at the example of my grandfather. He knew every aspect of our tradition, and he followed all its laws. He lived long enough so that all of my
own children saw him before he died. He died only now. And do you see the
example of A. and L., always fighting and talking badly about others. That is
not keeping tradition. See how both died while they were still young?

A bit later on in the course of this conversation, this man, who was my host during our second period of fieldwork, said,

> If I behaved like A. and L. with you and did not show good way (*lai itau*) in dealing with you, my heart would be sorrowful (momsoingngong ulong). Do you see the way I treat you? I am just following the laws of our tradition.

The person's description of this feeling of sorrow constitutes the closest translation of the concept of guilt that I was able to collect during my period of fieldwork. The fact that the sorrowful feeling the speaker describes is said to arise when and if the character of a personal relationship is violated, regardless of whether or not the violation is witnessed by others, is one of the things that distinguishes the emotion from shame. The speaker's words reveal a sense of personal responsibility for another, as well as a sense of personal responsibility for observing what I know he regarded to be the finest aspects of his people's tradition, or custom. For the Rauto as for Europeans, the personal sense of having violated an internal "law" is guilt (*momso ulong*). We call this internal law *conscience;* the Rauto refer to it as an understanding of the meaning of custom.

In the passages that we have discussed so far, we see that the Rauto tend to explain the nature of specific emotions such as anger, guilt and shame by relating them to incidents of either proper or improper conduct in life. Thus, we could say that descriptions of emotions such as these represent "perceptions" about right and wrong action as much as they represent powerful feelings that may tend to blur perception and understanding. That is, these emotions have a rational component to them (de Sousa 1990:45). We can see a linkage in Rauto discourse about emotion between notions of the proper conduct of life on the one hand, and knowledge of tradition, or custom, on the other. In an ideal sense the "good person" is someone who can live the meaning of tradition because he carries an understanding of it in his mind. Perhaps appropriately, then, one of the Rauto words for tradition—tradition considered as a people's characteristic conduct of life, the sum total of inherited beliefs and practices— is the same as that used to describe personal character: *lai.* Before we go on to explore the meaning of this semantic identity, we need to discuss, albeit briefly, the aspect of the Rauto understanding of mind which enables a person to conduct his or her life in accordance with tradition.

MIND AND THOUGHT: *AMTA NAL*

Rauto understanding of the nature of mind and thought is complex and multi-layered. There is first a social dimension to mind; the acquisition of culturally valued "objective" knowledge marks what can be called the social development of mind. For instance, in learning an important myth, or the names of the different sections of the men's ceremonial house, or those of the different sections of a sacred spirit mask, a young person is introduced to a socially recognized store of knowledge. This development of the social dimension of mind is often formally noted with the performance of ceremonies and the giving of certain types of feasts. Achievement ceremonies are also performed for young men and women to celebrate their first attempts at the management of socially useful knowledge. For instance, a small feast may be held in honor of a young person who has made a first attempt to perform taro magic.

Since the development of mind allows for the development of self, there is also a personal dimension to mind. One of the ways in which the development of this aspect of mind is thought about is in terms of a person's increasing ability to invest energy and self in objects and in relationships. Another way of stating this would be to say that in Rauto thought, the mind allows for the application of will, thought, and self to a realm that is external to the person. Thus, a Rauto person will say that the things and people that he has invested something of himself in "carry his name" and identity: *aningnong mana pe angan ogo*. The expenditure of knowledge and energy in securing the development of things and people (i.e., crops and children) during the performance of various aurang is one form of the investment of self in the external world; performing the labor of planting and harvesting trees and crops is another; cultivating trade partnerships is yet another way. It is through the investment of energy and self in things and people that strength of heart (*momso*) and body develop, and a person begins to raise his name (*anine*). Thus, the person begins to differentiate himself from others by consciously directing his spiritual power outward toward others, and toward the world.

This thought takes on greater religious significance when considered in relationship to the spiritual character of childhood. The Rauto feel, for instance, that young children lack will and thought—and hence lack the ability to direct their spiritual power outward, toward others and toward objects—because they are at the mercy of various spiritual forces of the external world. More specifically, the thought is that children are easily possessed by these forces and thus are not, strictly speaking, differentiated from them. These forces are the spirits, or souls, of animals, plants, the dead, and of various sacred places of the land. To protect their children from possession by these forces, Rauto parents make them observe a series of taboos, many of which are food taboos. For example, children are not fed cassowary in order to ensure that the spirit of this entity should not become angry with them and deform them in such a way that they come to move as awkwardly as cassowaries. The great number of prohibitions that parents place upon children are enforced until the children begin to develop consciousness and will—usually, in this people's view, at about three years of age. The development of these capacities is taken as indication that the child's spirit (*anine*) no longer mingles with the spirits of the dead and with other spiritual forces of the world. It is also an indication that the child's mind has begun to direct, or guide, its own physical and spiritual development.

The directing function that the mind carries out in the development of self is perhaps appropriately revealed in idioms that use the eye (*amta*) as a metaphor for individual thought and will. Metaphoric discourse attributes active perceptive functions to the eye that we would consider appropriate to the mind. Thus, a person who possesses both knowledge and understanding is said to have a thoughtful and knowledgeable eye (*tu ogo amta nal ino*). A discerning mind, one that is able to sense the true character of a person, thing, or situation is called *amta te ino*. The type of knowledge an English speaker would call wisdom is described through the use of an idiom that translates as "firm" or "strong eye" (*amta kairak*). Creative thought, the bringing into existence of a new custom or idea, is *amta totole*, "the mind's eye creates."

The greatest number of Rauto idioms that describe kinds of understanding or knowledge are about practical expertise. More specifically, they refer to how the mind's eye guides a person through the practice of a craft, or through difficult physical labor. A number of these idioms describe what both we and the Rauto call an experienced eye, one that has a thorough understanding of the work with which it is engaged (*amta mlok kototong, mlok amta konong*). For the Rauto, however, one of the most practical of all forms of knowledge is knowledge of custom, or tradition: an understanding of the proper conduct of life. As I have noted, this type of knowledge is referred to by the phrase *amta nes kamngenngen:* the mind's eye understands and follows the meaning of tradition.

Learning about the proper conduct of life, learning practical skills and crafts, learning the names of the things of both the cultural and natural worlds, and demonstrating such knowledge in the course of ritual and song festival are all part of what it means to acquire custom (*lai*) and personality (*lai*)—a characteristic way of behaving and of being. In what follows I consider the meaning of this term by considering Rauto discourse about socially recognized personality traits of men and women. I then consider what this discourse reveals about the ethos of Rauto culture.

THE WAY OF A PERSON, THE WAY OF CUSTOM

Rauto concepts of self can be discerned in images conjured by talk about the way (*lai*) of people. This talk and these images both reflect and shape the style of personal interaction that constitutes the social life of this people. The images that inform Rauto speech about the ways of people are thoroughly Melanesian. They reflect a strong concern with giving and with receiving, with strength and personal fortitude, with personal and social vulnerability. Yet they also show a lively appreciation of personal eccentricity and a lyrical appreciation of the disorderliness that is often wrought by personal interaction.

The first set of distinctions I discuss concerns personal bearing and generosity, perhaps the most lauded of all the virtues. As with everything else, the Rauto hold a number of thoughts both about generosity and the generous person. A generous woman or man is referred to by the phrase *mela amto*. The phrase translates as the "palm of the hand" and refers specifically to someone who is known to honor his debts and social obligations or to show his appreciation of others by giving away things that are highly valued, such as large and beautiful pearlshells. Such a person is said to show the inside, or palm, of his hand to people. This is one of a number of phrases that use the hand as a metaphor for generosity, for instance, *mela kra*—a person whose hand is able "to find." Penuriousness is referred to by the phrase *elel mela*—one whose hand finds something that is insignificant.

Ideally generosity should be tempered with an ability to husband resources carefully. The ability to gauge the amount of resources in one's possession carefully enough to make possible a dramatic giveaway is a skill that is especially valued. The eventuality of falling short, of not being able to provide either sufficient food or payment, especially for ritual services or ceremonial occasions, is a very real worry for people. It finds expression in a number of traditional sayings, such as the following:

> Ngatongoi nangon   I distribute the food, but
> mulgu la ket.   my hand falls short.

> Amol klipo auna mara   The mouth of the rope
> mara la ko alangdok   [used for ascending trees]
> tang ma.   is too large.

The first trope provides another example of how the hand serves as a symbol of generosity. It also conveys in an understated yet powerful manner the anxiety and disappointment felt by someone who has been unable to provide for his guests or adequately to satisfy his ceremonial obligations. The second trope contains a subtle allusion to the social shame that such an occasion can cause for a person. The rope (*klipo*) referred to in the metaphor is a piece of hemp. When people wish to ascend a tree to gather areca, coconut, or fruit, they first tie the hemp around their ankles in order to keep their feet fitted snugly around the trunk of the tree. If the hemp is fitted tightly enough about the ankles, the climber will be able to ascend the tree easily and quickly. If too much rope is used, or it is not tied tightly enough around the ankles, the person will have a difficult time climbing the tree and may fall. The metaphor refers specifically to the resource demands made on people by ceremonial work. By sponsoring ceremonial events that are too ambitious in scale, that is, cutting too large a length of rope, one invites failure. Though trying to appear generous, one appears instead to be niggardly, or at best incapable and foolish.

While ceremonials provide a major opportunity for people to give things away publicly, the casual visiting and informal meetings of everyday life provide opportunity for the demonstration of one's "good way" (*lai itau*) in less spectacular or less socially visible settings. In these settings gifts of food will usually be offered to people by women out of their own domestic larders. Indeed, one could say that women are most responsible for enacting the Rauto ethic of generosity. This point is made explicitly to a woman just prior to her marriage. Before a woman is brought to her husband, an elder kinsman, usually a maternal uncle, will sit her down and formally instruct her in the proper way of giving, among other things:

> My friend Kienget told his niece Uaulopme that she should never attempt to hide food from the sight of others or to prepare it secretly. Kienget also told her that she should offer food to all who came to her house, that she could not give it simply to those whom she liked. She was counseled against "holding out" when visitors came, hoping that they would leave before it became obvious that she was hiding food. Uaulopme was then told that she would be responsible for giving a portion of her family's food to visitors who came to stay in the hamlet's men's house, and also how she would be expected to prepare food when the community of men met.

Though meant to be a lesson in the ethic of generosity, this litany of do's and don'ts also says a good deal about how the Rauto often find ways to circumvent rules of sharing. To this list can be added a number of other practices. One of these is remaining in one's garden house until late in the evening in order not to have to contribute food to the men's house and to its visitors. Another is preparing and eating food in one's garden house in order to circumvent the rules of sharing that hold sway in the hamlet or village. A somewhat more extreme variation on this theme would be the stashing of a cache of food in the rainforest, where it can be eaten privately. There are also more subtle ways of avoiding the onus of demonstrating lai itau, or "good way." One of these is to understate the amount of food resources or valuables in one's possession. People will use this ploy when they are asked to make a large contribution to ceremonial and do not wish to do so.

These practices and strategies exist alongside of formally articulated beliefs about sharing and generosity. They are as much a part of everyone's life as are the more lauded ways of behaving. They represent some of the ways in which people try to look after their own interests and wants and are an obvious expression of a desire to keep one's food and possessions to oneself. Because the Rauto recognize and respond to this desire, their interactions with each other often appear to reveal that there is a certain complicity between them. For instance, people know when and why their neighbors prepare food in their garden houses. They know if others are lying when they say that they have little spare food or shell money to contribute to a ceremonial. Yet most often people will "wink" at these duplicitous words and actions. By doing this they tacitly consent to giving others a degree of leeway in observing ideals of generosity. The person who shows truly "bad way" (lai sulu) is not always someone who refuses to give, but is one who forces himself on others; it is someone who appears at the family house at the moment at which the food is being brought out, or who makes a habit of visiting families while they are "away" in their garden houses. The Rauto say that such persons lack shame and are avaricious. They are deviant at least in part because they either will not or cannot take part in the complicitous and necessary game of protecting other selves from ideals that can sometimes exact too high a price.[8]

The Rauto possess a complex of proverbs that denigrate avariciousness and link this character trait to a socially recognized style of personal comportment. A greedy person is called either pat amta parom, or pat amta palup, phrases that translate something like "his eye wishes everything." The implication of the trope is that a person will empty your house of its goods if his eye happens to see them. The Rauto compare the eyes of such a person to those of a wild pig, as in the following trope:

Pat ogo nes me pane   The person walks into our
iglano re kai ma adai,   place. He does not sit

8. The requests of overly importunate people were only rarely turned down by their kinsmen. I frequently saw people give away some very valuable things simply because they were asked for them by kin. It was rather frustrating for me to see the gifts which I had given to friends and key informants being taken from them in this way. It became apparent to me rather quickly that Rauto concepts of giving and receiving were rather different from my own. People often said that they were ashamed to turn down a direct request, especially for food. In order to avoid such requests, people would most often try to keep their possessions out of the sight of others.

mela tir ye mela tir,	down at all. He stands
la nak amta langono	and stands, as his eyes shift
kanem keuena.	like those of a wild pig.

The restlessness and the quick movement of the eyes of such a person are said to be signs that he is on the lookout for something and is not really willing to observe the proper social formalities in order to get it. The bearing of a person called *amta parom* or *amta palup* indicates that he has no wish to restrain personal desire with a concern to comport himself with lai itau.

The tension that exists between individual desire and the need to comport oneself with lai itau assumes many forms among the Rauto. This seems most to reflect a series of currents and crosscurrents of belief about the self rather than a unified and consistent philosophy of selfhood. I would argue that a set of culturally patterned reactions to expression and assertion generates this tension and shapes to some degree Rauto ideas about lai itau and lai sulu. Indeed, the Rauto concept of lai consists to a degree of a set of moral judgments about different forms of self-assertion. Another way of putting this is to say that Rauto ethics are not based solely on a conception of the person as an embodiment of moral will; in many ways the Rauto define the person as much in terms of specific criteria of "proper" self-assertion.[9] For instance, the investment of personal power and force in people during aurang is a form of assertive excellence. The way in which moral claims are made on the property, food, or time of others also involves assertion and appeal, or in effect social performance. Frequently one makes such claims by asserting the worth of one's person and thus one's right as an equal to have one's wishes considered.[10] One invests personal power in people during the song rituals called aurang by symbolically

9. In considering this, I recalled the distinction between Kant's and Aristotle's notion of the good man. Kant himself pointed out (1969:13) that for the Greeks a primary moral question was, What is human excellence (*arete*)? Kant's primary question, in contrast, was, What quality makes an action or a person good in an absolute moral sense? His answer to this question was a good will. "The good will is not good because of what it effects or accomplishes. . . . it is good only because of its willing, i.e., it is good of itself" (1969:12). The Rauto certainly understand the concept of good will. However, in their metaphors, rituals, and everyday actions, they celebrate agency or effectiveness more than they celebrate the concept of good will. The value of effectiveness is a more integral part of their definition of the person and of the excellent man than is the concept of good will.

10. Schieffelin notes how assertiveness is also a highly valued personal quality and defining aspect of Kaluli male identity (1976:118). For the Rauto, it is also an important aspect of female identity. Indeed, women are encouraged from an early age to act aggressively toward boys and men. They generally take the initiative in courtship, often pursuing their chosen men with sticks (called *rege*) if the men initially prove to be unwilling. Women's ceremonial and economic life is also marked by a certain assertiveness (see Chapter 4.)

asserting the power of one's personality during the performance of song. In this latter example self-assertion becomes a form of creativity for the Rauto; it is a means by which a person directs his or her strength of personality outward and in so doing creates and recreates the moral fabric of social life and, as I make clear in later chapters, of persons. Ideally, personal power should be asserted in a way that does not harm or offend people and thus tear the moral fabric of society. If it is not done in this way, self-assertion is considered to be a reflection of lai sulu, as it is, for instance, when a person performs sorcery to secure his own interests, or to take revenge on another.

The Rauto ethic of performative assertion has created a belief that strength, magical charisma, or any other unique capacity should be demonstrated and thus actualized and not talked or boasted about. Yet perhaps because many Rauto see nothing wrong with being assertive and frequently are so, boasting, though socially frowned on, is not uncommon. The Rauto recognize this contradiction, and their culture provides a specific way of dealing with it. Ideally, a person wishing to speak about an accomplishment should do so in an allusive manner that downplays its significance and difficulty. A lone huntsman who has managed to track down and spear a wild boar, or one who has successfully wrestled a boar to the ground after it has been driven into his section of the net might, when speaking of his triumph, refer to his prey as a small wallaby (*ngarap keneng sading ino pe isaru*).

This allusive style of speaking is referred to as the "speech of the people of Sara" (*amala Sara ino*), because it is said to have been used first by the people of the Rauto hamlet of Sara. Regardless of its origin, all Rauto recognize it when they hear it, and they know that those who use it are referring to what they consider to be a major accomplishment. The use of *amala Sara ino* allows people to communicate their own sense of pride and importance to others without appearing overly haughty.

A person who consistently speaks in this way is referred to as *pat ko apu amala ogor ino,* a phrase that translates in part as "someone whose speech is sweet, praiseworthy, skillful, and persuasive. The phrase implies that a person's speech somehow conveys a sense of his worthiness and strength and yet is not braggadocio or obviously conceited. The obvious self-control of people referred to as *amala ogor ino* is greatly respected. It is contrasted with the lack of control shown by conceited and boisterous persons who are euphemistically called *oduk adang adang ino,* "joyful people." This less-esteemed character type is spoken of as a laughing jokester who brags outrageously and generally enjoys hearing himself speak.

One of the more obvious points that emerges from this brief discussion of the concept of lai is that, for the Rauto, self-assertion requires a good deal of social skill and consideration for others. The proverbs and metaphors that express this notion resonate with my own feelings and observations about the character of personal interaction in southwest New Britain. In this vein I remember the humility and selflessness shown by even the most prominent men and women when I asked them about their knowledge of custom and of their social accomplishments. I remember the effort people would make to avoid direct confrontation and defiance of others in debate, and their effort not to intrude on others as they went about their daily tasks. I remember the gifts of food that were graciously given to visitors without fanfare and yet with the hope that accounts of such generous acts would be told and thus serve as proof of the giver's lai itau. I have memories that are just as vivid, however, of lai sulu, of overassertiveness, of people deliberately intruding on the space of others and taking what was perhaps too keen an interest in others' possessions. These different forms of human action as well as the terms and metaphors that are used to describe them indicate that social ideals are thought by the Rauto to be realized or undermined by different forms of self-assertion.

In the chapters that follow I show that this insight about the relationship between individual personality and overall cultural pattern lies at the heart of both the religious and the secular aspects of Rauto life. That is, this moral insight links the stereotypical action of ritual to the performative interaction of everyday life and explains why there is a degree of complementarity between these two forms of human action. Another way to say this is that the Rauto ethic of performative assertion gives a culturally patterned meaning to both the desire to secure one's own interests and the social need to reaffirm the structure of moral life in ritual. Indeed, the most powerful and dramatic assertions of individual power and identity I witnessed took place during ritual events that clearly were meant to achieve social, or collective, as well as individual goals. This seeming paradox indicated to me that these ritual events were about the relationship between individual power and social (moral) ideals. They were a symbolic statement about the complementarity of self and what we would perhaps call society. The core symbols of these events are song and speech. In the songs and speech of ritual occasions, individual power is temporarily co-opted for social ends. In this way song performance and speech become examples of lai itau.

SONG AND THE WAY OF A PERSON

In myth and in ordinary discourse, song is a leitmotif of the self—of personal concern, desire, and accomplishment. The singing of song during ritual and ceremonial events, during the telling of myth, and during the performance of everyday tasks is perhaps the most lyrical form of self-assertion and expression that the Rauto people practice. It is also primarily through song that the Rauto celebrate the phases in the life and development of the person. Thus, there are songs that celebrate the birth of a child (*segeingen*). There are categories of song that celebrate circumcision (*aiumete*). The aurang are special songs to celebrate the onset of adulthood in young men and women. There are categories of song that celebrate personal accomplishment and ascendancy (*atauro*). Finally there are the songs that celebrate death and secondary burial (*luungong, serpoua, igle vangna, igle rine*). The acquisition of this large repertoire of songs is a crucial part of the cultivation of social identity. In acquiring it one learns a way of understanding and celebrating the nature of the person, and one learns the most essential aspects of ritual and ceremonial life. Song is therefore perfectly suited to symbolize the particular interrelationship of individual and social concerns that characterizes ritual life.

The two aspects of song, the personal and the social, are discussed in different ways by the Rauto. Myths and personal accounts that show how song is related to personal triumph and concern have an informal, lyrical, and sometimes humorous quality to them. The metaphors and proverbs that convey a sense of the social power of song when it is performed collectively during ritual have a formal quality to them. The former way of speaking about song is best conveyed by the following two accounts. One is a myth; the other is a story that was related to me as an accurate telling of the events surrounding the courtship of the narrator's father. I will recount the latter story first.

> Once the woman [who was to be my mother] came to Ipuk to attend a song festival. My father saw her and liked her immediately. He thought long and hard about how he would win her. On the day of the song festival, he had some betel charmed for him by a magician, and he placed this in his coconut-frond basket, setting the betel nut aside for the song festival. He then chewed charmed ginger and areca, so that he would be able to sing strongly at the festival, and so that he wouldn't tire during the night. When the song festival began, he hid himself well in the midst of the dancers so that my mother could not see him. He kept his head down and did not sing the verses of the *agreske* (warrior's chant) with the other men. He made sure that my mother received some of the betel that he had charmed that day. Toward the end of the night, when the sky began to lighten and the men gathered together to sing the *augosang,* my father hid himself really well right in the middle of the singers. He then began to sing for the first time that night. He sang at the top of his lungs until the sun rose. Everyone was taken by his singing. When the song festival finished, he quietly left the ceremonial grounds and went to rest in his garden house. My mother followed close behind him and caught up with him when he was going into his house. He told her he didn't like her

and to go away. She picked up a heavy tree branch (*rege*) and said she would hit him with it if he didn't sleep with her. He then took her.

Abbreviated Version of the Myth of the Origins of Taro Magic
Once a man called Tuktuk left his hamlet at Gasmata and began to walk westward with his sister. As they walked through the forest together, people would call out to them, "Hey, you two over there come here and sit down with us, you and your wife come and sit down with us." The people thought that Tuktuk's sister was his wife; the two were angry at this, so they just walked on. [Scenario repeated a number of times.]

The two then came upon a young boy and his mother. The boy called out to Tuktuk, saying, "Hey you two over there, you and your sister come and sit down with us." They all then sat down together, and Tuktuk spoke. "Your habits and manners are very good little child; others shamed us with their speech, but you did not." Tuktuk then decided to tell the boy about his taro magic. He told the boy to go into the forest and then carry back ginger and ginger grass, coleus, lemon grass, banana leaves, and many other things, and to separate them into small bundles. When the boy came back, he and Tuktuk passed in front of all the men and women who were making gardens, with their bundles. In front of everyone Tuktuk began to sing the aurang for the taro, and while he did this he sang out his name as well. As he sang, all the people gathered around him. Hearing him sing, these people then realized who Tuktuk was, and they called out to him and the little boy: "We know you now, Tuktuk, now the taro will grow well." Tuktuk and the boy continued to perform song magic until the garden plots of all the people were charmed. Tuktuk then said that the work was finished and that he would now leave the young boy to perform magic in his stead. He told the men to follow the lead of the boy and not to become angry with him because he possessed the taro magic and they did not. He and his sister then walked northward toward Molo, all the while singing the aurang for the taro and placing their magical bundles in the garden plots of many people. When the two reached a place called *ayi omta,* they climbed to the top to an ironwood tree. They turned into a clump of ginger grass that now hangs down from a top tree branch . . . they remain there to this day.

Though the courtship story was said to be an accurate telling of an actual event, there is a literary quality to it. Indeed, the major themes of the story appear time and time again in Rauto mythology. Perhaps the most common of these mythological themes or motifs has to do with the relationship that the Rauto perceive to exist between identity and song. In both the courtship story and the myth of the origins of taro magic, before the protagonist or hero sings, he is essentially an anonymous figure. In the courtship story the hero remains hidden in the midst of a group of dancers and has no identity for the woman he

A boy carried on the shoulders of his maternal uncle during the song festival called *aiumete*, which precedes a child's circumcision.

wishes to win. In the story the protagonist reveals his identity and exhibits his personal and magical power by singing. Similarly, in the taro myth the culture hero Tuktuk reveals his name and also demonstrates his magical power and knowledge through song.

The myth makes a number of other points about song. The most salient of these is that magical knowledge is taught to people and power is passed on to them through the teaching of song: the culture hero passes on his knowledge and power to the young boy by teaching him song magic. The boy then publicly demonstrates his newly acquired power to aid the growth of taro by singing the aurang along with Tuktuk in the presence of a crowd of men and women. The myth specifies that this act has a political dimension to it—that because the young boy can perform the aurang, he should be considered a leader of men and women. The myth then also makes the point that song can serve as a social marker, and that one of the ways in which leadership is achieved and maintained is through the learning and performance of song magic. This point reflects an aspect of the reality of Rauto social life, since people, most especially hamlet leaders, acquire prestige by coming to possess a large repertoire of songs and song magic. Indeed, being a ritual leader in southwest New Britain does not mean, as it does elsewhere in New Guinea (see Jorgensen 1987; Barth 1975), that one possesses a secret body of esoteric knowledge. Being a ritual leader means being a performer and a teacher of song. Thus, the Rauto say that leading men and women "hold" (*tingokop sakul*) the songs that celebrate the person, that serve as the leitmotif of the identity of the characters of myth, that are said to promote the development of children and of crops. This does not mean that they are necessarily the only ones who know them, but that it is thought appropriate that only they should lead others in the performance of these songs. This demonstrates that song and song magic are not thought of in isolation from the person, from his or her personal capability and social influence. Song magic is not thought of as an objective and abstract body of knowledge that is managed by leaders; rather it is thought to be a symbol of personal and social being. Not surprisingly, then, for the Rauto the least noteworthy of human beings is the person who is disinclined to sing at song festival and ritual events and to speak during moot or debate. Such a person is disparagingly called either *akoie* or *auna kip*, "closed mouth." The personality, or lai, of the person so labeled is considered to be weak, while he himself is considered to be ineffectual.

THE SOCIAL POWER OF SONG

A number of metaphors show that the Rauto feel the moment of the song festival—the moment of collective song performance—to be one of singularly concentrated power. A number of these metaphors refer to the power of singing and of the moment of the song festival through reference to forces and events in nature:

Osua ogo alia la ko gel	The shields [men] arrive
lut re kamsek kai	at the song festival,

talelek re ma manikikik	their feet stamp the
langono maululukluk.	ground, which shakes as during
	an earthquake.

Milol ye oduk tide munuk	We softly sing, and people
oduk osua ogo tigel	imitate song doves;
ye terpen uon.	the shields [men]
	appear, and the dancing ground
	overflows with them.

Both tropes derive their power partly from the contrast that exists between day-to-day life and the occasion of the song festival. Activities of everyday life, such as food gathering or garden work, are usually carried out without much fanfare or chatter and only occasionally with song. People either tend to their tasks alone, or they work with members of their immediate family. Frequently they will leave the gardens to search the forest for areca nut or perhaps to follow the trail of game. At about one o'clock (*oklo amto*), they will take cover from the burning heat of the sun in small shade houses that they have built from tree saplings, vines, and wild banana leaves. At this time both the taro gardens and the hamlet residences are dead quiet (*ano reprep*) and seemingly empty (*ano ueue*). Indeed, throughout the day human activity seems intermittent and without focus. As people disperse to pursue their own goals and activities, social life appears to be without focus, center, or concentrated energy. During song festival, however, people gather together and in so doing concentrate their power. They decorate themselves with aromatic and magical plants and leaves, they paint themselves with red ocher, and they "arm" themselves with magically charmed areca nut and sometimes also with spears and shields. When the dancing ground is full, and men and women are singing at the top of their lungs, their voices break the silence of the surrounding forest and are heard for miles in all directions. According to the first trope, during these occasions the power of people seems equal to that of nature itself; the metaphor states that during song festival the earth rumbles from the stamping feet of men and women, as if an earthquake were taking place.

The second metaphor, "We softly sing, and people imitate song doves . . . the shields appear and the dancing ground overflows," refers to the scenario of the song festival itself. Initially, in the early evening, a few adolescent boys and girls appear at the dancing ground (*terpen*) and begin to sing the *segeingen*. This is a category of song that is meant to alert those who will be the main performers at the song festival that people are now waiting for them to appear. I was told that this singing acts to draw others to the dancing ground. Soon a group of singers appears at the edge of the song plaza. Out of shame, they cover their faces with fan-shaped leaves, so that in the fading light of dusk people will be hard put to distinguish their faces. The singers sing softly at the edge of the forest. After a few minutes they enter the dancing ground singing as powerfully as they can. This signals that the song festival has begun in earnest. Soon other groups appear, and the song plaza overflows with people. The metaphor refers to this scenario by comparing the singers to flocking song doves. It relates how initially only a single or a few song doves land on the branches of a fruit tree in order to feed on its fruit. Their cries then attract other birds, and soon the branches of the tree are filled with birds.

ETHOS, PATHOS, AND MEMORY

The preceding discussion of lai and of song is a brief attempt to characterize an aspect of Rauto ethos, an aspect of the essential character of the person. But character is in essence a type of feeling—a feeling for a way of life that is expressed through a patterned way of acting within life. As we have seen, song performance is an example of Rauto ethos; that is, it is a form of action that forms and expresses character by eliciting and creating feeling, and it is feeling—the feeling elicited by numberless acts of custom, songs, and mythic and metaphoric images that constitutes the Rauto person. The images and acts of expressive culture reveal a life of feeling as they create it, and this life of feeling is the life of the person.

I have argued that song is an aspect of custom, or lai, and part of the way of a person. Its expressiveness and mythic power to move the world, to convey moral, physical, and spiritual essence to others, and to transform experience reflect the Melanesian ethos of assertiveness, especially the need to extend the power of one's person outward into the life world. This is the culturally valorized significance of song, of the human voice, of the person. It is song's obvious meaning. Yet though part of custom and put to custom's use, song points somehow beyond custom. Song is also a part of mythic experience:

Avel moro moro	[I place this feather on
uo agila,	Kamotmot's body]. It
palemlem	waves farewell, as the fishing net
	I see shudders and waves in
	the wind.

The song is one of the *olo,* a song genre that is performed for the masked spirit beings that are called *kamotmot.* That it is categorized as an olo indicates that the Rauto do perceive it to convey a coded message of feeling. The olo are meant to express dolefulness. They are sung during the middle of the night and are performed between more energetic, quickly paced genres.

The song expresses its message through the representation of simple gestures that juxtapose rather than describe emotions. In the song's image, a man dancing and singing the olo approaches the dancing spirit mask owned by someone who has just died. He places a feather on the back of the spirit being's costume and sees the feather move with the swaying, rhythmic movement of the dance—seeming, to his mind, to wave farewell. He then glances away toward the fishing net that hangs suspended in front of the men's ceremonial house and watches it sway in the wind, seeming also to wave farewell. What would be the emotional message of the song? A man has died; his spirit mask dances, though he no longer lives. This thought heightens the bereaved's sense of loss. The spirit being's swaying movements are gestures of farewell, as are the movements of the fishing net, which was once used by the dead man and was, as the Rauto say, part of his life (*ino togowong*). The obvious meaning of the image speaks of separation and loss.

The obtuse meaning of the image, its body rather than its voice or coded message, expresses a deeper significance, while containing rather than giving full dramatic expression to sorrow. The image hints at the continuing presence of the dead man rather than speaking of his absence. It alludes to the fact that the dancing mask will always belong to this man and will be called his visage (*amta ino*). Its continued use in song festival will reinvoke memories of this man's life, as will the continued use of his fishing net and the continued singing of this olo, which was composed for his death.

Whenever the mask is brought out and danced with, the dancer will be given a token payment for bringing the dead man's visage back to life and thus allowing others to feel the man's presence once again. The song image reveals the presence of a participation, then, at the same time that it suggests separation. The man, his mask, his fishing net, his absence, his presence *in* the objects, and in the memories and emotions evoked by the objects as they are animated by the dance—this plenitude of memory, of participation, and of separation is called *makai* by the Rauto. It is a feeling that is more than simple sorrow and nostalgia; it is a feeling of emotional fullness. It is the feeling that comes from being composed of others, and of having another's lost presence once again touch one's own. Makai is the feeling that comes from sensing presence in an absence. As we shall see, it is also a sort of triumph over sorrow, a way of transforming sorrow into significance.

This emotion, or way of expressing an emotion, is also a sort of triumph over the more superficial aspects of the Melanesian ethos of strength and performative effectiveness—the personal character and ways of acting that are valorized by the tropes discussed in the first part of this chapter. Makai is an authentic form of gratitude felt toward a lost person who once was a part of the fabric of one's own life. As we shall see, it is the counternarrative of strength, assertiveness, and self-absorption:

Naulungo, o sauro Naulongo.   Naulungo, my child, Naulungo.

This olo is another gesture of makai. Its image represents a man's ghost watching his and his family's spirit mask dance in the midst of a festival. As he watches, he cries out its name, and in that moment recognizes and gives expression to his sense of loss—loss of the things of his life and of everything that he holds dear. Again, sentiment and meaning are contained by a series of juxtaposed moments. The ghost participates in the life of the present once again, yet remains apart from life and from the living. His yearning for his spirit mask is really his own kin's wish to possess his person again; this sentiment of yearning is turned into the song's image, which contains the felt tensions of desire and loss in the gesture of the dance. Makai is that spirit being which in its materiality embodies the person's presence and absence. When the spirit being dances, it dances the memory of the lost presence.

It is significant that the feeling of makai seems here to be part of a dialogue with the lost person, whose name was Sakani. The spirit being must be addressed by Sakani's kin as his ghost addresses it—as a presence, a thing that yet contains something of his life. The address happens quickly, without drama, almost casually, but this should not lead us to think that it is not a significant gesture. The song images of the olo are all like this:

Uo uaiko   Alas, [Uaik sings;]
alei aleio   my child has gone.
imi la rup ailo,   I see the spirit being's finery
paileleo, saleuai o   retreat.

Sulei, uailuke   This spoiled [betel]
ye sulei Uaiuaike.   [belongs to] Uaiuaike,
                                      alas.

A woman at song festival hears Uaik's mournful song as the sun begins to rise. The song pierces her heart as she watches the spirit masks retreat to the men's ceremonial house. Her child has died, and its ghost takes leave of her as the spirit masks disappear. The seemingly empty ritual gesture of the *mesekngen* when at dawn the spirit masks are chased back to their respective ceremonial houses by their fathers or owners becomes an event and image of loss and sorrow.

The play of the image's associations can be "read." The fleeing spirit beings are children chased back to the safety of their homes (the ceremonial houses) by their fathers, the owners of the masks' designs. These spirit children leave the ceremonial grounds but remain with their parents. The child's ghost meanwhile, and in contrast, leaves its parent behind forever. The emotional meaning of the image, however, is simply the fleeting moment of experience that it portrays. It is the moment when Uaik's song is juxtaposed to the image of the fleeing spirit beings and of the departing ghost.

The moment of the experience of makai is also portrayed by the simple image of a man at a song festival who, while beginning to chew some betel, remembers that he had harvested the spoiled betel from the tree of a man who had recently died. Such a tree and its fruit would be considered to embody something of its planter's soul stuff. It would also be called the mark or imprint of the man's visage (*amta mune*). In the song image, the simple act of chewing the other's betel becomes an act of remembrance that bring's an image of the lost person's visage to the singer's mind.

The olo that to my mind best conveys something of the meaningful body of both pathos and ethos is this archaic song; it is a song image that portrays a widow's grief:

> La lassio   I call, [but no one hears.]
> tida lala   I have only my sorrow now.
> iei alei
> uo alei
> na lia uala.

We begin to read the image by picturing a scenario that took place after the death of a man. The man's widow was to await the arrival of her "brothers"— her patrilateral cousins—and then be strangled by them. Her death was rendered as compensation to her husband's kin, by her own primary kin, for the gifts of food, the honor, and prestige which came to the woman as a result of her husband's labor and reputation. The sham of this way of reasoning was not infrequently noticed by the Rauto, as this song image suggests. The image refers to an event that occurred sometime in the early 1940s, well before pacification.

After her husband's death, the widow referred to in the song had to travel back to her native hamlet in order to cajole her brothers to carry out their customary duty and murder her. As the widow screamed for her death, her brothers fled the hamlet. She then insulted them by intimating that they wished to keep her alive in order to possess her sexually and incestuously. The widow's *lassi,* her call for her own death, represented an angry grieving. As she stormed through the hamlet of her kin angrily demanding her own murder, she was seen to strike anyone and anything that crossed her path. The song alludes to her tirade and to a certain transformation of the widow's feeling. As her brothers fled from her anger and violence, she was heard to remark how the only possession and feeling left to her was sorrow. The image suggests that the widow realized she had to endure her situation and in order to do so had to contain her wish for self-obliteration and for violence.

What is interesting about the image is the way it empties out the customary meaning of the practice of widow immolation. The widow was not killed—her anger, grief, and desire for death repulsed her male kin rather than valorizing their supposed ideals. They apparently suppressed their desire to show themselves as men of strength, men who could make good on the laws of custom by rendering the appropriate "compensation" to their affines. They contained their desire to show strength, and would not be shamed by the widow's insinuations.

The widow's remark, that she now possessed only sorrow, is culturally resonant. As we shall see most clearly in the final chapters, Rauto ceremonial life often evokes a contained feeling of sorrow such as that ultimately experienced by the widow. The Rauto call the feeling *kipitngen*. The verb *kipit* means "to endure severe physical and/or emotional pain quietly," seemingly casually. The verb has, of course, a less obvious meaning. Like makai, it is actually a means of heightening the power of emotional experience through understated expressive gesture. An important aspect of the ethos of Rauto culture is conveyed by this particular emotional attitude and tone, by this particular form of pathos. The quality of experience that awakens emotions such as makai and kipitngen is felt in the tension that exists between two aspects of the Rauto (and Melanesian) ethos. These aspects are the need for self-assertion, for the strong expression of strong if simple emotions, and the countertendency to contain or curtail dramatic emotional display partly in order to feel and to express more complex, subtle and culturally resonant emotions. The tension between these two ways of being evokes a quality of pathos. Thus, Rauto ethos and pathos are intertwined in complex and culturally significant ways. There is perhaps nothing surprising in this, since ethos, the essential character and quality of a person, always implies a certain emotional attitude, and qualities of feeling are influenced by ethos or character. In southwestern New Britain, ethos and pathos lie at the core of both emotional life and expressive culture.

In order to support this idea, and to set the stage for the ethnography that follows, I will recount some examples of emotional experience drawn from the life of a Rauto man named Kienget. He was and as far as I know still is one of the preeminent sorcerers and taro magicians of southwest New Britain. He was born in the years before the establishment of the first mission station on the south coast in 1936. The accounts of his that I will discuss here are portions of the life history that I took down from him during my second field trip. What is striking about the accounts is their many similarities to the emotional meanings and countermeanings expressed in the song images we have just discussed. Like those images, these representations of experience seem understated and stereotypical rather than overtly dramatic and personal. Like the song images, they speak of participations of feeling that juxtapose the events and feelings of a life in such a way that they seem more mythic than autobiographical. These representations are distinguished by a persistent animating theme. Kienget's talk about the beginning of his life, for instance, is not so much about the development of his own person as it is a series of remembrances of the part played by others in the fashioning of his identity. Kienget's accounts seem to indicate that people's memories have a decidedly social character and seem as much commemorations of lost others as evocations of the past.

The emotional ethos that corresponds to this habit of commemoration is the same as that which distinguishes the memories contained in the song images of the olo. Memories of the everyday events of childhood, courtship, the birth of children, the loss of parents and other loved ones, as well as memories of the ceremonies that punctuate the course of the person's life cycle seem to be commemorations suffused with the emotions called kipitngen and makai. Memory itself seems as much an emotional pattern and a patterning of experience as a resurrection of the past. That is, the words that resurrect the personalized past describe the events and incidents of experience in order to place a specific emotional mark on experience. It is important to note, then that memory is called a remembered mark by Rauto. More specifically *amta mune* is the mark left by a lost or absent but remembered person. It translates as "the mark or imprint that is the person's visage." For instance objects or places or even persons associated with a lost kinsman or friend are often referred to as the mark and image of the lost person's visage. *Amta mune* is also a phrase that sometimes alludes to the emotion that often accompanies remembering. That is, seeing the mark of a lost other often evokes the feeling of makai. As we shall see, many of the objects of custom are objects of memory; the objects and acts of custom contain a remembered emotional life and evoke a lived ethos of emotional expression.

> These things of custom—Lekrek, Gultul, kamotmot—my vision wanders
> back by them to the faces and acts of my parents. They gave me knowledge
> of these things. I see these things, and I see the faces of my parents. I hear
> and yearn for their talk when I see these things. I remember how they worked
> for me, how they gave me taro. This is why I sometimes cry when I see these
> things.

There is no self-emphasis apparent in this brief account of the memories that are evoked by important cultural objects. The objects have meaning because they are marks of memory. They contain memories of simple everyday acts—people working in their taro gardens, people giving food to their children.

Kienget's account of the personal meaning of the objects of custom is consistent with the creative uses to which the objects are put during ceremonial.
For instance, the olo we have just discussed use images of the spirit masks to
convey memories of loss, memories tinged with the emotions that Rauto call
makai and kipitngen. But as we have begun to see, these objects are not simple
vehicles for permitting the evocation of memories. They are experienced as
possessing something of the lost person's being and therefore something of his
or her efficacy and power. Lekrek, the taro effigy, is really the mother of the
garden. She gives gifts of food to her children the taro corms, just as a mother
feeds her children. As she does this, as she suffuses her magic through the
garden, she evokes memories of parental care and nurturing. She evokes the
visages of mothers and fathers. Gultul, the rain effigy, is a great man bedecked
with *paidela* and other marks of status and power. He is the objectification of
the power of the rain sorcerer, and he evokes memories, images of the ancestral
magicians. The kamotmot, the powerful spirit children, are not really children at all but are "the ambulatory figure of the ancestor or god" (Leenhardt
1979:124) that contains the power of custom and authority. Cultural creativity
or invention seems to consist, then, in making the personal memory into an
object of custom, such as the mask, or the rain or taro effigy. Speech and song
seem also to be objectified by the Rauto; they are made into objects that contain
the power of the being.

Making custom out of memory objectifies custom, making it into an object
of belief that has a personal significance for each person. Making custom out of
memory dedramatizes feelings of loss while subtly emphasizing the poignancy
and cultural resonance of such feeling. We see both an ethos of emotional style
and a form of expressive culture in the remembering that gives meaning to
customary ceremonial:

> My mother, she would give food to everyone, and would not keep it for
> herself. Everyone spoke of her good custom. She was a woman who had a
> name. When she died we honored her with the *luguong* and the *serpoua*. As
> the ceremony went forward during her night, my pain and sorrow grew and
> became heavy. I did not weep; I took my place with the other singers. My
> insides were filled with pain, and I sang with this pain until dawn, though I
> felt that I would die myself. At dawn they slaughtered and cooked her *ipil*. I
> felt sick when I smelled the pork flesh as it was cooking in the stone ovens. I
> remember smelling the ovens as we carried the body to the grave. And then
> the distributions and exchanges of food were made, my family exchanged its
> food with the line of my maternal uncle; all the women placed a portion of
> my mother's pig on the top of their baskets of cooked taro and sweet potato,
> and they then exchanged the baskets. Each family was given the other's

food. I held my pain inside as I saw these things. I tried to ensure that the
distributions of pork were made fairly.

Like the images of the olo (and also of the aurang), the passage seems simply
to present a moment of experience—the lived experience of one of the ceremonials performed for the newly dead. Unlike the olo, the passage provides a
thorough listing of the characteristic activities and feelings that define an event.
Yet the acts of custom that Kienget describes, the singing from dusk to dawn,
the slaughter and butchering of the pigs, the ceremonial distribution of pork
and exchange of food, do not seem individualized. There is no real narrative
explaining the events that preceded the death or that followed it, though I tried
to collect such information. There is simply the naturalistic image of the event
itself.

What gives the image significance however is not to be seen so much in its
simple reiteration of the typical scenarios of death as in the person's emotional
response to these events. Kienget's words convey a sense of how he felt himself to stand apart from the event, how his grief made the ceremoniousness of
death seem somehow unnatural, or inappropriate to his emotional state. Yet
he permitted the event to contain his feelings, thus making his gesture of joining the other singers and participating in the ceremony all the more resonant
with significance and feeling. This event becomes in its retelling a statement
of an ethos of feeling; this is the value that is represented by kipitngen, by the
containment of emotion. Kienget's words also resonate with a view of custom
as a series of events that circumscribe and contain or dedramatize feeling and
memory.

What we discern in a passage such as this is a form of representation that
seems to externalize phenomena—emotions, memories, actions in the human
life world—so that they are visible, almost tangible, and seem to express a
simple and natural meaning. At the same time, this style of representation
seems to use naturalistic meaning as a foil. It actually concentrates and drama-
tizes feeling and meaning by suggesting aspects of experience that cannot be
contained or conveyed by a flat naturalistic representation. It seems, then, that a
way of representing expressive forms—metaphors, songs, figurative usages—
extends to the description of lives, or to the description of the events of a life.

There is something else about Kienget's personal representation that we
need to stress here: its relative absence of narrative. Kienget told me his life
in a way that was similar to the way he told me myths. Neither his life nor
the myths he recounted for me were told as if they were part of a whole. His
life description consisted of descriptions of discrete, seemingly unrelated moments of experience, which gave them the character of myth. Frequently, all

that joined these moments into a story was the emotional tone that they shared, the feeling that accompanies remembering, the feeling of makai.

> Kaiagre was the name of my initiator. He cooked the taro for me and for the rest of us boys during our initiation. As we lay in the ceremonial house, they gave us a bit of the *tavoi* and uttered a spell so that it would adhere to our teeth. They spoke it again and again: *tavoi antim, keto antim, tavoi antim, keto antim* [the tavoi adheres, the tavoi adheres]. Then they asked us if we had hidden a catch of fish somewhere, and I said no; they asked if I had hidden a cache of bananas in the forest, and I said no; They asked if I had not followed proper custom with some woman; I said no. And they continued reciting their spells. And so it went. For ten days we lay shut up in the ceremonial house, where they gave us only a little water. Kaiagre would place a bamboo tube at the back of my mouth and drip the water from his coconut water container on it so that the water did not touch my teeth. We were so weak after a few days of this. When we emerged they had prepared some roasted taro for us; I had just a little. And then we ran to the forest to hide. We hid from the young women, not the old or the married women. We were afraid that the tavoi would fall and adhere to the breasts of the young women, and so we hid from them. When we returned from our time of hiding in the forest, Kaiagre butchered the pig that my father had given him for his work, and he distributed it to all his kin, and then the exchanges took place. My father gave this man seven large pearlshells and ten meters of *tili*. And he had given him our black and white pig. For a long time after the tavoi was put on, we would squeeze the sap from the areca tree and swish it in our mouths to make the tavoi adhere and to glisten. And Kaiagre showed me how to make the tavoi glisten by putting lime powder on it and rubbing the powder in with the skin of the areca. This is magic to attract a woman, and we thought that if the young women saw our glistening black teeth they would like us. Kaiagre told me not to laugh or giggle when the girls would try to make me talk to them so that I would have to open my mouth, and then they could see my teeth. He would tell me to cover my mouth when I had to talk to them. I felt shame in their presence. Because Kaiagre showed and taught me all these things, I was able to grow tall and strong and to marry quickly. If you drink the water of this substance (tavoi) you will grow quickly and strongly and women will want you, their hearts will soften for you. Within a few years of my initiation, I was married. My atenme Kaiagre did this for me. And he and my father gave me the knowledge of all the other aspects of our custom—the story and *ikit* for the canoe, for the taro, for the coconut magic, for the rain, for the hunting and fishing nets, for the spirit masks, for the men's house.

There follows a series of detailed descriptions of the ritual scripts of all the ceremonies that Kienget has just mentioned. Again, the descriptions are generalized rather than personalized, seemingly drawn more from present-day observations of and involvement in ritual performances than from the events that Kienget refers to. We see this same general descriptive style in the remembering of initiation. It seems that the structure that is placed on experience in the course of this personal narrative reflects something of the form of customary religious experience. The most personal element is the gesture of thankfulness that is particularly conveyed by mention of the feeling of makai. The rest consists of the stereotypical reiteration of events "that seem to carry their whole emotional and meaningful force in their familiarity or repetition" (Wagner, personal communication). Kienget went through or endured his initiation; it went without a hitch. He experienced the expected discomforts but also attained the expected gains: greater physical beauty, greater size and strength, an enhanced attractiveness to women, and finally, because of these gains, a woman. The stereotypical scenes described also convey a sense of and embody the emotions appropriate to them. There is the initial fear and apprehensiveness of the ordeal and then the pride of the moment of reemergence, especially indicated by the exclamations of how black and gleaming Kienget's teeth were. There is the shame and yet delight with the effect Kienget felt his new physical appearance would have on women. There is the mythic worry that the tavoi would be lost because of his desire for the girls, that the substance would adhere to their breasts—a veiled recognition of Kienget's sexual desire. All of this is understated, contained by simple gestures, that (as Leenhardt might say) fill the being with a sense of personal authenticity.

This feeling is precisely what renders Kienget's descriptions of ceremonial life meaningful. We see this as well in his descriptions of the Rauto *ikit,* the names and meanings that are recited and taught to children during ritual events.

> They carved the great canoe out of the tree we call Sumi. And then they
> fastened the mast to the canoe, carved the prowboard, and they showed us
> how this was done. The women took the taro out of the stone ovens and
> piled some inside the canoe; they danced as they carried the taro inside the
> hull. Some of the men and women ate the gift of taro on the beach by the
> nose of the canoe. And then the men boarded the canoe, and the women
> threw shell money and pandanus mats into it as they splashed water on the
> men. Afterward the canoe was garlanded all around, and they called for the
> firstborn boys and girls. There must have been ten or twelve of us, and we
> boarded the canoe. Some of us sat in the hull, others on the prowboard. Then
> my atenme taught us the ikit. The canoe, its pontoon (*nisiue*), its paddle
> (*puei*), its punting pole (*to*); and this is the place for the fighting spears, it
> is called the *endeng.* This is the canoe's prowboard, (*vatetio*), this its bailer
> (*aimang*). And the two sticks that connect the pontoon to the canoe, these

are the *nuknuk*. The inside of the hull, this is the *ngutngut*. This is the canoe's bed (*ket*), this its mast (*perero*); the great canoe's tiller (*destia*) etc. I have this knowledge now; I can speak of the canoe and of all the other aspects of our custom. This is why I can speak of these things.

This last sentence was uttered with some conviction and not without some degree of pride. In such feelings we begin to see that the objects of custom, the objects that have ikit—the canoe, the taro and the other objects of exchange and production, the spirit masks, the ceremonial house—"are the person's gesture manifesting some myth from which he draws his life" (Leenhardt, quoted in Clifford 1982:211). The myth is the story that attaches to the object and that renders its use meaningful. The myths as well as the ceremonies that celebrate customary objects show the objects to be meaningful by naming them. In the myth of the origin of the canoe, for instance, a culture hero named Tarauit tells the story and teaches the use of the canoe mainly by revealing the names that distinguish its various parts. The object, its myth, and the uses of the object are things that lend significance to the person's life. The confirmation of this is the fact that learning the ikit confers an aspect of identity to the person. Thus, the rituals of the life cycle wherein the social identities of children are fashioned primarily involve the learning of the ikit. Learning the names of things means acquiring cultural identity. This is one of the reasons why people take their personal names from important cultural objects.

What is important about the ceremonial contexts in which ikit are taught is that these contexts collapse two aspects and functions of memory. In the course of the ethnography we shall see time and again how lost others are remembered through the use and celebrations of objects of custom. The uses of customary objects and of the myths and ceremonies associated with them thereby become valorized by being associated with aspects of the person's personal memory and emotional life. Collective cultural memory is thereby juxtaposed to personal memory, and the qualities, aspects, powers, and names of things become part of the person's own life. While these objects literally give the person a name and identity, they reveal that personal identity comes as a gift from others. In being entrusted with the names and things of custom, which often were once part of other possessors' lives, the person is entrusted with something of the being of these others. We shall see how this creates a sense of personal authenticity, a sense that is colored and accompanied by the emotion called makai.

In the chapters that follow I discuss how song, speech, and makai outline the different parts men and women play in shaping social and moral life; that is, how speech and song are also metaphors for gender. I show how this is so

Kienget in one of his gardens.

in part by discussing the various ritual events that provide a public opportunity for men and women to exhibit their personal power through speech and song. Thus, in the chapters on ritual I consider the moral significance that the expressive uses of singing have for the Rauto. Before considering ritual and song, however, I must discuss some of the more obvious meanings of the Rauto concept of speech, as well as its relationship to ideals of male social identity.

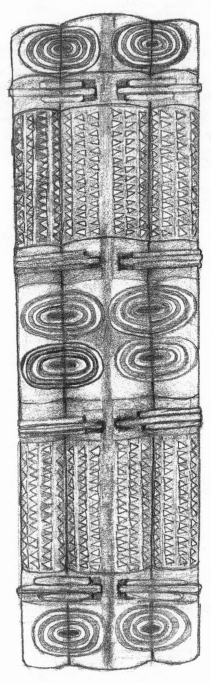

A sketch of a shield (osua). Drawing by Coralie Cooper.

Chapter Three

Speech, Person, and Community

In the construction of personality it (the word) plays the same role as the design of an edifice.

Maurice Leenhardt (1979)

His word is made up of fixed stories, mythic or not, of images which evoke moments of valor; it has a dynamic content, it is the wisdom and brilliance of the ages. It has symbolic value. It lends significance to tradition and actualizes it. It situates men in the time in which they live; it raises them to a higher plane; it calls them to existence.

Maurice Leenhardt (1979)

The figures of speech that Rauto call *amala arlem amta* represent a series of insights about the nature of human power. The tropes express these insights by commenting on how the person provides evidence of his moral efficacy through the use of his word. In gauging the value and power that different uses of speech have, the tropes evaluate the moral worth of people. Moreover, the tropes show how in Rauto thinking law, politics, and religion are different refractions of the word; indeed that these and other aspects of culture are often conceived to be simply different kinds of speech events. Like the song genres that I discuss in subsequent chapters, these simple and seemingly naturalistic metaphors also provide support for the idea that mental or "spiritual content and its sensuous expression" are united in language (Cassirer 1955:178). They do so because they express their abstractions through the use of sensuous, concrete images of everyday life. Thus, in this speech genre the human body and other forms of the natural world serve as springboards for thought and comparison.

The metaphors provide support for Cassirer's understanding of language in yet another way. In showing that the spiritual power of speech and song serves in certain contexts as a spur to reflection, they reveal that, for the Rauto, meaning exists outside of the direct experience of speech events. Speech and

song, then, are not simply—as Leenhardt argued they were for the New Caledonian—"ideas that command" and, by commanding, create an indivisible
moment of experience for the person. They serve as well as the core symbols
of a philosophy of social life. In the metaphoric images considered as a whole,
"there comes to the surface an implicit collective understanding of what things
and actions of the social world are of most significance" (Redfield 1975:187).
Some of the most significant things for the Rauto are of course people, as well
as the many ways in which people fashion their own social and personal identities. Amala arlem amta can be considered to be an extended commentary on
these matters. One of the most interesting aspects of this commentary has to
do with a central problem of Rauto social life. This is summarized by the belief that when men, especially, engage in the range of traditional activities that
bring social prominence, they can sometimes also subvert a number of social
ideals, most especially the value of equivalence. In southwest New Britain
beliefs and discourse that reveal a culture-wide concern with political and economic status and power are balanced by an egalitarian ethic. As in many other
Melanesian societies, the "trick" for prominent men and women is, as White
writes, "to demonstrate strength" and ability "without being cast as overly aggressive, and thus socially disruptive" (1985:346). This delicate balance is not
easily achieved; its maintenance and its loss are central concerns in the lives
of Rauto people, and therefore it is a central topic of speech. The concern is
one of the main subjects of tropes that note a relationship between speech and
ideals of character.

ORDER, SPEECH, AND PERSON

In southwestern New Britain, hamlet leaders (*adepdep*) who direct the affairs
of their own communities, and who have much influence in communities other
than their own, are thought to embody certain ideals of personhood.[1] In political and in economic life the Rauto certainly recognize differences in status
among themselves. They possess a developed system of "big man" status and
of "big woman" status, and people are "measured," or evaluated, in part
according to their place within this system.

   In the first few metaphors that I discuss, speech serves as a shorthand for
conduct and understanding.

_____

   1. The word *adepdep* means "preeminent," or "leading big man." A hamlet, or a kin group
leader with less influence is called in contrast simply "elder brother" (*toro*). Men of influence who
are not, however, leaders, are called *aieng amto ino*. The phrase translates as "the adolescents
belonging to the inside of a place." The phrase is usually used as a euphemism for "elder." It can,
however, be used to describe a middle-aged man who aspires to leadership, yet who is clearly
subordinate to other men.

Ungup ogo anona	The tall coconut tree
de tirkek amles.	[twists and turns] in the
	wind to avoid sorcery.

In this complex metaphor the swaying coconut tree symbolizes a Rauto hamlet leader, or "big man" (*adepdep*). The trope alludes to the stance of a leader as he speaks at a village moot. With his hands clasped behind his back, he twists his torso slightly and continuously as he speaks, just as a tall coconut tree twists and turns in a strong breeze, seemingly avoiding the main force of the wind. In the metaphor the mention of the orator attempting to avoid sorcery is an allusion to the traditional belief that sorcery attacks are often made on a headman at a village moot. I was told that during these occasions a leader's rivals will chew bespelled betel nut (areca) and then direct their spittle at the adepdep as he speaks. The orator's swaying movement represents his attempt to dodge the sorcery of his rivals. Yet, in a wider sense, this movement is a metaphor for a culturally valued style of personal conduct. My older informants told me that this metaphor meant that an elder or big man should try to sidestep confrontations with other men through the skillful use of persuasive speech. In the trope, "sorcery" therefore serves as a symbol of disputes in general.

While discussing the meaning of this metaphor with informants, I was told that in potentially volatile situations where recourse to violence is a possibility, speech should be used to balance claims and arrive at a compromise that ensures fighting does not take place. One of the most important and valued skills of a traditional leader is just this ability to settle claims and to stop fighting. In fact, an important definition of what the Rauto call "firm speech," *amala kairak,* is speech that ends violent dispute or that inhibits it from coming about in the first place. The Rauto say that when people are angry, speech of this kind "clears their eyes," *amala kairak de amta uin,* and "makes the heart fall and cool," *amala kairak de momsoine kai la ma.* A person might also say that speech of this kind has brought him out of a dense tangle of rainforest and has led him to a forest clearing (*amala kairak tanengong pe ano palaga*). I interpret this last trope to refer to relative clarity of perception. The imagery of this set of tropes is interesting. It implies that the Rauto correlate anger with the confusion of being lost. The strong speech of a leader brings them out of their confusion by calming their anger, thereby letting them perceive the proper course of action to take. Here the voice appears as a symbol of domestication and instruction. The imagery of these few tropes and proverbs appeared to me also to express a view of social life as an arena of frequent contention and dispute. As I observed the unfolding and sometimes the culmination of numerous feuds in the hamlet in which I lived, I acquired a visceral understanding of this

view. I also acquired a similar understanding of a proverb that explained anger
and dispute by comparing them to a dense tangle of bush:

Oduk tikarpan;	The men are angry; the
ano mlok arar.	hamlet is like a place of
	tangled bush.

Becoming caught in a tangle of bush means that one's physical movement,
sight, and sometimes even one's breathing become restricted. In Rauto social
life anger and dispute often have the consequence of restricting people in ways
that might seem comparable. They restrict the range of people's social relationships; sometimes they restrict the physical movement of people between
separate hamlets or between sections of a single hamlet. They also sometimes
place restrictions on verbal interaction. In Rauto understanding, firm speech
appears as the primary means for the amelioration of this division of social
space and social relationships. I was told that when the headman of a place
died, feuds would erupt, simmering resentments would come to a head, and the
village of hamlet would no longer be *kadu* (heavy). I interpreted this last phrase
to mean that the village would no longer have significance, a significance that
was created and maintained through the firm speech of a headman.

While the effective voice of a prominent man or woman serves as a symbol of a productive and peaceful social life, the ability to generate and use
firm speech is also a sign of personal power and good character (*lai itau*).
Conversely, tropes that express a negative judgment about types of behavior
or about the character of people do so by alluding to socially disruptive and
destructive uses of speech:

Pat ogo ilo amala	The speech of this
uauia.	person is weak.

Pat ogo kroine	This man's voice is like
langono	the cry of the *ramal*
munuk ramal ko	bird; his voice changes as
kroine	does the voice of the bird.
mlok nekekek	
langono.	

Takanes sokol pe	Let us not speak of this
oduk ogo, auna	person, [he of the biting
ngen la ko uren.	mouth] his own mouth has
	devoured him, and so he has
	died.

Tide omon la ko   They send word; the
la tide   others imitate [the voice]
munuk   of the crow.
leline.

The first trope can be understood to be the antithesis of the phrase *amala kairak,* or "strong speech." The phrase "weak speech" is a metaphor for a person who is not able to halt the fighting and feuding of other people. Indeed, it is a metaphor for a person who is not inclined to try to direct the course of social life in any way. When such a person does venture to speak, his words do not penetrate to the core of the matter that he has discussed, and thus he fails to persuade. The difference between people who are distinguished by the use of either firm or weak speech was also explained to me by allusion to a journey through the landscape. The speech of wise and persuasive people is said to "go around the landscape" visiting all the named places of the land and then to return to its source or base (*uate*). The speech of a person without knowledge is said to go only a short way into the landscape and to miss stopping off at many essential places. In this figure of speech understanding is symbolized by the relative length of a journey. The many places of the landscape mentioned in the allusion refer to the essential points of a person's speech or argument. The reference to "the return to the source of the journey" is an allusion to the basic premise of the person's speech and to how well the various points of the speech confirm this premise. Speech that strikes people as being weak is said "not to bear fruit" or not to have substance, or "meat" (*ilo amala keneine adai*). This idiom indicates an essential connection between perceptive and therefore effective speech and accomplished action.

The trope "this man's voice is the cry of the *ramal;* his voice turns as does the voice of the bird" conveys its message by alluding to the cry of a large sea-bird, called a *ramal* in Rauto. I was told that the bird often flies in the middle of a flock of smaller seabirds, such as terns (*atroi*), crying out in a voice that—unlike that of the surrounding terns—constantly changes in pitch, volume, and duration. The bird's inconstant voice is a metonym for people who constantly change their plans. The speech of such people is said to turn (*nekekek*) constantly. Turning one's speech is often perceived as an attempt to put people off verbally. It is seen as a self-serving and insincere way of acting, and it is also categorized as weak speech. People who turn their speech will not be trusted to act on their word to satisfy creditors or, more generally, to live up to the obligations that others perceive them to have incurred.

In the third trope, *Takanes sokol pe oduk ogo, auna ngen kano la ko uren* (Let us not speak of this person, he of the biting mouth; his own mouth has devoured him and thus he has died), speech serves as a metaphor for the harmful and eventually self-destructive force of anger. The trope specifically refers to the death of a person who was quick to anger and who habitually denigrated other men and women. The trope alludes to an event that almost always follows upon the death of a person. After someone has died, most of the kin who reside within walking distance of the person's hamlet meet and discuss the possible causes for the death. The possibility that the person died as a result of a sorcery attack is always considered at these meetings. People then review the personal history of the deceased and try to find in it evidence of unresolved past disagreements. They also try to consider the person's past "transgressions" (*sulu,* or *amala sulu*) in order to determine who might have had reason to initiate the sorcery attack. When the close kin of the dead person agree on a likely candidate, they will sometimes bring an accusation against this person and will demand compensation payment (*ulu*) for the death. The trope alludes to a meeting of this type; however, as people begin to speculate on the reasons for the death, they are told that these are apparent, that the person caused his own ruin by antagonizing so many other people through his or her speech and actions. He is said to have been devoured by his own mouth.

In the next trope, speech serves as a symbol of social conflict. The trope *Tide omon la ko la tide munuk leline* (They send word; the others give the cry of the crow) is an allusion to a public challenge. The trope describes a group of people making an accusation and then requesting compensation from another group. This second group then openly mocks the speech and requests of the first group. Their defiance is expressed in the trope by mention of the mocking cry of the crow. The trope serves as a particularly apt description of social conflict because of the sensitivity that the Rauto show when their speech is questioned, cut short, or in this case openly mocked. It was explained to me that making sport of another person's speech was traditionally a signal for the beginning of a spear fight.

THE SYSTEMATIC NATURE OF RAUTO METAPHORICAL CONCEPTS OF SPEECH AND OF THE PERSON

The few metaphors that I have discussed express a number of concepts that are part of a systematic style of discourse about the relationship between speech and the person. In this metaphoric discourse and, I argue, in Rauto perception, speech is given a number of anthropomorphic qualities. Thus, like a person, speech or the voice of specific individuals is said to be either firm (*kairak*) or weak (*uauia*). Further, the voice is perceived to be active; that is it shapes the character of social life, and its effects are felt to be immediate and compelling, as are the actions of a human being. A related idea conveyed by the tropes is that speech is a type of body that has a surface as well as depth and volume. Thus, strong speech is said to have depth and heaviness, while weak speech is shallow, and has a quality of lightness.

The attribution of the qualities of a person and of a body to speech is consistent with metaphorical concepts that suggest that the achievement of prominence and the development of personhood are the result of a slow, almost physical or organic process. In the Rauto view the power of the voice increases as a person goes through the long process of constructing his or her own identity or name (*anine*). The training of the voice in song, in the skills of debate, in the recitation of myth and metaphor, and in the performance of magic itself serves as a metaphor for this process. A fully cultivated or skilled voice is a person's main tool as he attempts to build alliances, sponsor and arrange ceremonies, and generally "build a name" (*pane anine*). There are no shortcuts either in the cultivation of the voice or the achievement of influence. One must, figuratively speaking, "grow into" prominence, as the following metaphor suggests:

Pat uru taker taker	The man imitates and
la kele ma adepdep ye	thinks he is the headman,
ko de arol pat ma.	yet he is the *arol* plant
	that sits in the middle
	of a tree.

The metaphor has a number of different aspects of meaning. First, it suggests that a person who too quickly or at too young an age attempts to act the part of a headman must somehow really be without true influence. In the trope such a person is compared to a type of fast-growing fern or air plant (*arol*) that will grow from a crevice or small hole in the branch of a large tree. The arol is not really part of the tree, and its exuberant growth is in no way related to the growth cycle of the tree. One informant told me that "the arol lacks the tree's deep roots, just as the pseudoheadman lacks the influence and power of a true headman." I was also told that the arol does not begin its growth where a true tree should. Rather, "it begins its growth in the middle" (*pane pe pangramu*). It is a sort of upstart that has not gone through the necessary or appropriate steps in attaining its position. Of course, these same remarks apply to the pseudoheadman. The final inference of the trope is that what influence the pretender does possess really depends on the power and approval of a true headman. The pretender is parasitic on a true headman as the arol is parasitic on its tree. Thus, perhaps the most subtle idea expressed by the metaphor is that a person who "begins in the middle," who does not go through the long process referred to as "building one's name" might ultimately be dependent upon others, especially leaders.

Metaphors that anthropomorphize speech and allude to the development of social influence by referring to physical development are consistent with proverbs that mention the strong parts of the body in order to allude to personal power and influence. For instance, prominent men and sometimes prominent women are referred to as *itar ino tokwo*, "the backbone of the house"; *itar mugulu*, "the stomach of the house"; *itar momsoine*, "the heart of the house." Elder men are also often referred to as *udiep mugulu*, "the stomach of the men's ceremonial house." These last two metonyms are significant in that they equate strength with the interior of the human body while simultaneously suggesting a quality of depth or profundity. The tropes attribute such qualities to elders. The symbolic equation of the heart with the elders is also significant in that in traditional belief the heart is thought to be the source of the body's strength and also the source of the power of magical speech. Thus, metonyms that equate prominent people with this part of the body suggest that they are perceived to represent the animating forces of Rauto society.

The speech of prominent men and women is also associated with other sacred portions of the body, especially the mouth, as in the metonym *amala mlok palaklak auna*, "speech (of the elders) rests on the mouth of the center post of the men's ceremonial house." In the trope the importance of prominent men is alluded to by a reference to the center post of the men's house, an architectural feature that literally holds the ceremonial house up. Big men are identified with the center post. Their mouths, identified in the trope with the top of the center post, support the structure of the ceremonial house by uttering strong speech. The trope identifies this speech with the roof beam of the ceremonial house, thus suggesting that this speech is, to use one of our own tropes, over the heads of others, especially young people. The main idea expressed by the metonym is that the speech of leaders plays a central role in the affairs of the men's house and thus in the affairs of the hamlet. Appropriately, prominent men are also referred to as *udiep apna* (the head of the men's ceremonial house). The symbolic correlation of firm speech with the mouth in metaphor is particularly significant when one considers the ritual importance that the skulls and jawbones of prominent men and women had, and continue to have in some places in Aroue, in mortuary ceremonies.[2]

After the death and burial of a person and a period of interment, the skull,

2. All the groups of southwest New Britain, from the Aroue islands in the west to Gasmata in the east, refer to themselves as Aroue.

jawbone, and hand bones are unearthed. The remaining pieces of flesh are cleaned from the bones by a ritual specialist. After the period of their preparation by the ritual specialist, the bones are wrapped in sweet-smelling lemon basil and placed in the men's ceremonial house. In the next few days, and also at times during the next few years, a number of different singing and dancing ceremonies are held to honor the bones of the dead. At a ceremony that I attended, the jawbones of two men of renown were placed in the middle of two small pearlshells and covered with the lemon basil. Two dancers, nephews of the deceased, then held the pearlshells in front of them with outstretched arms and began to perform a graceful skipping dance. They danced parallel to one another from one end of the hamlet's dancing ground to the other and back again. As they performed, people attending the ceremony sang the special songs associated with this particular part of the ceremonial song cycle. A few women stood on either side of the dancers' path and waved sweet-smelling herbs and colorful crotons at the bones as a sign of homage to the dead. I was told that the jawbones of the prominent dead were honored in this way because, during life, the voices of these men and women "spoke of giving food to others," "uttered the taro magic" that insured the survival of the hamlet group's members, and "arranged the killing of pigs and the distribution of pork at ceremonial pig kills." The hand bones are unearthed and honored because, in life, prominent men and women are said to have "given many gifts of food to others." The skull is honored because it most powerfully recalls the memory of the dead person and because the eyes of the skull are said to continue to watch over the hamlet, insuring its survival and prosperity, just as, during life, the eyes of headmen and headwomen watched over and supervised the hamlet group and its affairs. Indeed, the skull and bones are thought to continue to contain something of the efficacy or even spirit of the dead. For this reason the dances are called *igle vagna*, "spirit of the jawbone," to indicate the belief that the agency of the deceased never becomes wholly detached from the bones. Thus, while the bones remain in the hamlet, something of the agency of the dead remains permanently attached to the hamlet. For the Rauto the most powerful symbol of the power of human agency is the voice. By memorializing and honoring it in mortuary ceremony, they provide the person with a form of personal immortality at the same time that they celebrate strong speech and the human voice as the foundations of social life.

ADEPDEP AND METAPHORS OF VIOLENCE
AND ANTICOMMUNITY

Violence and the fear of domination once touched the lives of the Rauto in an
immediate and sometimes overwhelming way. Violence, or the prospect of it,
colored the relationships between kin and introduced an element of uncertainty
to the relationship between nonkin. Domination or the threat of it made and
continues to make Rauto people wish to live apart from each other, so that they
can run their lives without the interference of others. From their own accounts,
observations, and metaphors about their past, it is clear that the uncertainty
introduced into their lives by the possibility of violence sometimes made the
Rauto willing to compromise their independence and to curb their anger and
suspicion of others. But anger and suspicion were and still are close to the surface of social life. This remains a fact of daily understanding. Consequently,
the Rauto have ways of talking about this aspect of their society and of their
history. Metaphors of violence, annihilation, sorcery, and suspicion all express
thoughts and feelings about the conflicts and strains of their social life. When
supplemented by actual accounts of violence, these tropes can be seen to represent an intellectual response to the dilemma of having been caught up within
this life while simultaneously professing ideals that were the antithesis of it.
Perhaps the great dilemma of Rauto existence is contained in the fact that the
preeminent symbol of a productive and peaceful social life—the voice of the
adepdep—is perceived as well to represent the antithesis of it, that is, to represent antistructure itself. The following metaphors catch some of the nuances of
ambiguity in thought about the voice of the prominent:

Oduk gel ti moi moi	The crowd of men come
lik osua la ko ma re	together, their shields
amta la rik uiling	resting [on the ground].
uaro ma malanga gerger	His [the adepdep's] eye looks
apna.	over the hundreds of
	spears; they appear to
	be the branches of the
	gerger apna [tree].

The trope describes one of the most ambiguous, emotionally charged, and
potentially violent moments of traditional Rauto social life: the moment when
the dawn begins to break after an all-night song festival. At Rauto song festivals
a hamlet group or village leader invites a great number of men and women in
order that they might either honor one of his children prior to the performance
of a ceremony for them, receive either pork or live pigs from him as a part
of a ceremonial exchange, witness the ceremony surrounding the slaughter of

a tusked pig, and/or sing or perform aurang, so that the pigs and taro of the hamlet group leader and of his kin group will multiply and grow. People are generally invited to a song festival for a combination of these purposes.

The ethnographer J. A. Todd, who worked among the Kaul, a linguistic group located some fifty kilometers east of the Rauto, thought that these festivals were primarily mechanisms for the "redress of wrongs" because during such events long-standing grudges and feuds would frequently find violent public expression (1935). He was perhaps partly correct in this observation. In any case, Aroue song festivals were and remain social dramas that contain political, economic, religious, sexual, and aesthetic elements. The metaphor that I have translated alludes to the relationship between the violent and the political aspects of the song festival.

Throughout the night, men and women invited from different hamlet groups, or perhaps a distant village, dance and sing in a group that is separate from that of the members of the hamlet group that has sponsored the ceremony and on whose ceremonial grounds the song festival takes place. The different groups spend the night alternately competing with each other through song and threatening one another with spears and shields. Men from the different groups sometimes break off from the mass of dancers performing a circle dance called the *agreske,* and form themselves into opposing lines. They hold their shields out in front of them and lean back and point their spears at members of the opposing line. They then advance to the center of the dancing ground to a point at which their spears almost touch those of their adversaries. At this point they usually break off and begin again to dance the agreske, only to continue to repeat this maneuvre throughout the night. Hamlet leaders range among the men exhorting them, according to their inclination, either to peace or violence. Spear fighting most often takes place just as the dawn breaks, after the hostile feelings of the men have been raised to fever pitch by a night of taunts and threats. People told me that they wait for dawn before they begin to fight because at that time they can more clearly distinguish between the faces of their enemies on the one hand, and those of their friends, and quite possibly kin, on the other. In the metaphor, it is during this particular moment that the adepdep admonishes the warriors to stand together, so that he might look over and marvel at the number of spears (i.e., men) that he has drawn to his festival. In the trope the powerful image of the spears of scores of warriors is rendered by invoking the image of a tree (*gerger apna*) that has an extraordinary number of branches—so many, I was told, that even if one stands some distance from it, the tree blocks out the view of the surrounding forest. By halting the fighting of individual men at the end of the song festival by his voice and order, the adepdep symbolically expresses his control over the violence of these men and, as a number of elders suggested, his right to direct this violence himself if he so wishes. The power and drama of this moment of social life is thus usurped by the adepdep. He claims this power by simultaneously showing himself to be a maker of peace and a war leader.

In the next trope the voice of the adepdep is said to prompt the violence of others as they attempt the attack and annihilation of another village or hamlet:

Tir la ko me re	The men appear [and come
ano kaitektek auna	upon the place] as the mouth
langano angan	of the red tide flings the
iri kamut.	the trees upon the shore.

The mouth of the red monsoon tide (auna *kaitektek*) is a metonym for the voice of a leader. In its violence and its ability in some cases literally to bury the shoreline in debris, the *kaitektek* serves as an apt symbol of pure force and destructiveness. Through the use of this analogy, the voice of a leader is equated with annihilation. The trope resembles a number of others in which the Rauto consider the prospect of violence offered by a marauding group of warriors:

Tir la ko pane ko me	The men come upon us as
re langono tir uate	the rain clouds come up
kognas ine pane souro.	above us.

Tir la ko kupiuk me	The men appear and come
tir langano uri	upon us like a waterfall
tir asang.	that overflows [when we
	attempt to catch some of
	its water with an *asang*].

In all these tropes the violence of people is compared to the violence of nature—to rainstorms, crashing ocean waves, and crashing waterfalls. The tropes suggest a kind of violence that cannot be restrained by the usual procedures for the mediation of conflict, such as debate, compensation payment, or dueling. These were and are the accepted Rauto means for the containment of violence within a community. Yet the tropes suggest a kind of violence that leaves no room for rational deliberation. Because they associate violence with the speech of leaders, these tropes provide a vivid contrast to those discussed in the first section of this chapter, which celebrate community and the constructive role of the speech of the adepdep in social life.

A report written in 1949 by the Australian patrol officer S. M. Foley gives us some idea of the way the Rauto prepared for the prospect of concerted violence, of the way that they were forced to deal with the frequent drama of raiding and reprisal common to so many traditional Melanesian societies. The report describes the village of Sabdidi preparing for a "payback" raid expected from the village of Kulawango after a Kulawango man named Kalup had been killed by a group of Sabdidi men:

> Sabidi prepared to repulse Kulwango in this way. On a hillock some fifty feet high, encircling an area of forty yards in diameter an eight foot high palisade was built wherein temporary houses were built and food was stored. At the perimeter of the stockade three trees were left standing. Twenty feet from the base of these trees fighting tops were built which were made accessible by ladders. Two hundred spears were stacked and shields were placed nearby. Several large lumps of limestone completed the armament. From fifty yards out from the base of the hill all bush was felled . . . and another strip leading to water fifty yards wide was cleared.

Elders told me that when a foreign group would attack, the strongest warriors would man the stockade. Young men and women would climb to the fighting platforms and hurl down stones. Women with children would climb to the higher branches of the banyan and hope that their warriors could hold the stockade and prevent the destruction of the hamlet residence, the killing of its men, their own capture and perhaps even murder. The Rauto laid the blame for such violence on their own pride and their inability to tolerate any slight committed against them. Yet they also attributed such violence to the strivings of their leaders, and to the wishes of these men to avenge the slights and wrongs committed against them and their kinsmen and clients. Such thoughts contain subtle recognition that leaders were and remain a cause of the disruption of community.

According to the Rauto, a type of "madness" (rara) descends on people during occasions of violence. During these occasions people give expression to a part of themselves that is not normally tolerated within the bounds of community, as is suggested in the following tropes:

Oduk tipaut a keneng isaru.	The men spear and drown the wallaby.
Oule nakum isa sawoi ko rap a keneng isa. Keneng kanes: pu oule wom oro apkleng omtan osua alingo kano amtugu rara pe nowom. Omrakngong ogo ye soro omtan osua tangan	The dog sniffs out and captures the wallaby. The wallaby speaks thus: You dog have taken your old shield and tricked me, as I could not see you. Now you will kill and eat me. If you had

rema amtagu rikom re	taken your new shield, I
ma.	would have seen it; I
	would have run away.

| Wom isako omngen | You have eaten the wallaby |
| keneng wun ino moro. | along with its blood. |

The first trope, "The men spear and drown the wallaby," invokes a scenario that seems especially striking to the Rauto and that paints a particularly violent picture with words. In this scenario a dog is seen chasing a wallaby (a large marsupial) from its home in the forest and down to a reef just past the shore. Here, a number of men come upon the frightened animal, spear it through, and then dunk it up and down in the ocean in order to drown it. The wallaby is a metaphor for a defeated and helpless warrior. In the trope he appears as prey chased by hunting dogs. The warriors who murder him treat his body as they would that of a prey animal. Similar ideas and associations are expressed in the short fable that I have translated above. Again a wallaby serves as a metaphor for a defeated warrior. Yet in the fable the victorious warrior is himself identified with a cunning dog. He is scolded by his victim for having used stealth to capture his prey. The defeated warrior tells the victor that had he taken a brightly painted new shield, he could not have hid in the forest as easily as he had. Instead, by waiting in ambush for his victim with an old, ruddy colored shield, he escaped detection and was able to spring upon and murder his prey. The last trope suggests a symbolic association between combat and cannibalism; a victorious warrior is said to have "devoured" his opponent.

All of these tropes suggest a close symbolic correlation between the nature of a victorious warrior and that of a hunting dog. These associations appear to be part of a system of discourse about an aspect of human nature and about its relationship to a violent aspect of Rauto life. That the hunting dog serves as a symbol of this relationship is not surprising when we consider how the Rauto speak about dogs and how they use them.

DOGS AND MEN

For the Rauto, hunting dogs are especially important animals for young men, who in traditional times would have made up the bulk of a community's warriors. Dogs seem most intimately associated with that period of a man's youth in which he begins the intensive cultivation of social relationships with people outside of his circle of close kin. During late adolescence, when a man begins to think about acquiring a wife, he is frequently away from his village or hamlet for long periods of time in order to perform the round of social visiting called *songo* or to hunt. Frequently a youth will combine a hunting trip with his dogs with a round of songo. During songo a boy visits the hamlets of distant kin, seeking to be given pearlshells by them so that he can begin to put together a portion of the bride–price needed to take a wife. It is during these social visits that a youth begins to build a network of guest friends and trading partners. The period in a man's life when he begins to make songo should also be the time when he begins to build a reputation as a skillful hunter and provider of game.[3] A young man's dogs are enormously important to him as he begins to build such a reputation. Later, when he chooses a woman (or a woman is chosen for him), his hunting dogs become important to him as he attempts to secure game, which he gives to his future affines in order to establish proper and amicable relations with them.

In short, dogs are an important tool as young men attempt to make their way into full participation in Rauto social life. In this sense the hunting dog is an instrument in the construction of a young man's social identity. Young men seem particularly attached to dogs. If a favorite is killed in a boar hunt, a young hunter sometimes gives up eating pork or some other choice food out of sorrow for the animal.

Despite all this sentimentality about dogs, the Rauto recognize that these animals possess an unruly and sometimes vicious nature. They are also cunning and thieving. Yet not all of these qualities are considered to be undesirable. Before a hunt, for instance, men try to increase the ferocity of their dogs by placing small amounts of charmed ginger and areca nut in their food. These "hot substances" are said to make the dog's stomach "burn with anger." I was told that in prepacification days, young warriors would sit together and would chew areca nut and charmed ginger in order to incite their anger and make them "as quick as dogs" when they went into battle. The metaphor of youth as fighting dog appears to be fairly straightforward here. Elders are especially fond of referring to young men as "dogs" when they leave off their garden work to attend song festivals or songo, or nowadays to take up residence in Rabaul and work as plantation laborers there. This is interesting in that occasionally elders will also refer to wrongdoers as dogs; *oule aroti*, "there goes the dog," is a phrase that they use when they wish to point out such people. Furthermore, people who feel that they have been injured by a person sometimes imply that they will take revenge against them by saying "I will castrate that dog."

The symbolism of the relationship between men and dogs thus appears to be fairly clear. In Rauto discourse, dogs appear as a symbol of the unruly and violent part of a person's nature.[4] The particularly close association of dogs with

3. I observed, however, that the most effective hunters were young married men from twenty-five to thirty-five years of age.

4. Rauto metaphoric discourse about dogs appears to be essentially similar to that of the Homeric Greeks. In both these discourses the dog appears as "a piece of unruly nature next to man

young men, a category of people who, in elders' eyes, have not yet acquired fully settled habits, implies that they also represent a less fully socialized aspect of human behavior. The tropes that describe the nature of men who engage in violent acts by identifying them with dogs now appear to take on a somewhat deeper significance. They imply that this particular aspect of human nature is anathema to a community.[5] We could safely say that in Rauto thought the firm speech of prominent people both regulates this aspect of human nature, thus protecting the community from a strong internal threat, and serves as a symbol for it. The Rauto add yet another caveat to this thought in their traditional metaphors and in their ritual and magical practices. In these metaphors and practices they express their recognition that prominent men and women can pose a serious threat to the internal harmony and productivity of everyday social life. In such practices and thoughts these people appear as symbols of the darker desires and rivalries of everyday social life—the very things that they are thought to control.

LEADERS AND SORCERERS

The Rauto recognize that the powers of the adepdep can amplify what can be called the uncertainty of social life. Sorcerers par excellence, leaders were and are thought to be able to bring sudden death or a long and lingering illness to their enemies and rivals. Believed to guarantee the prosperity of a settlement by performing taro magic, leaders also possess a number of forms of magic that can destroy the taro crop and bring famine to a community. Although they are leaders and organizers of hunting, fishing, and trading endeavors, big men also possess magic to insure the failure of these enterprises and, according to popular conception, are inclined to use it if these affairs are led by rivals and enemies. The point to stress here is that in the Rauto view these exhibitions of power sometimes have little to do with a leader's legitimate interest in social control; they sometimes represent an unjustifiable desire to harm people and to behave in a self-aggrandizing fashion.

In day-to-day life the Rauto spend a good deal of time considering and trying to protect themselves from the ruin that people of rank might cause them. When, for instance, people make their own gardens and perform magic for them, a number of the spells that they chant will be directed to warding off the taro sorcery of powerful men and sometimes prominent women as well.

---

or within him" (Redfield 1975:194). In both Rauto and Greek metaphors the dog is a symbol of the warrior's predatory "instinct" (193). Finally, in both forms of discourse "the dog is the emblem of the imperfectly socialized" (195).

5. I follow Redfield here in speaking of community as a "structure of cooperation" and at least sometimes resolvable conflict (1975: 187).

When people go about performing their daily tasks, they carry with them little bundles of "magical materials" that are meant to ward off the sorcery attacks of men and women of rank. Even a few types of curing magic reveal Rauto concern about the danger presented by the powers of prominent people. A number of the curing spells that I collected represented ritualized attempts to remove the "poison" of a prominent man or woman from the body of an afflicted person. Typically, the spells would end with a litany of the names of well-known sorcerers and leaders. The spells advise them (the leaders) to "be aware of the magic" that is being used to counteract their sorcery.

These ritual precautions and rememdies give one a deeper sense of the meaning of a number of tropes that equate leaders with the unsettling and sometimes destructive effects of sorcery:

Terma makap.	He [sorcerer] kicks sand [upon the place].
Ungup uate parap.	The base of the coconut palm is covered [with dust.]
De pane mlok.	The thought appears and is kept in mind.

The first trope, "The sorcerer kicks sand upon the place," refers to the traditional belief that the sorcery of a headman is powerful enough to destroy a hamlet residence completely. This idea is conveyed through the description of a man completely covering a place or group of men with sand. The second trope, "The base of the coconut palm is covered with dust," expresses the idea that a headman's desire for revenge does not end until someone who has committed an offense against him has been destroyed. The trope was explained to me in the following way. A man commits an offense against a prominent man or woman and expects immediate retribution; however, revenge is not taken immediately. Enough years pass so that the person who has committed the offense begins to believe that the headman has forgotten the incident and has lost his desire for revenge. At this point the offender's understanding of the plans and feelings of the headman have become distorted. The proverb refers to this by the statement that the base of the coconut palm has been covered with dust, the base of the palm being the vision or understanding of a person. While the thought of the future victim of sorcery has become clouded, however, the vision and memory of the headman has remained clear. He has planned to take his revenge at the moment when his adversary least expects him to do so and is least prepared to defend himself against the headman's sorcery attack. The reference to the base of the palm being covered with dust also calls to mind the image of an old and tall coconut palm. The image implies that a great amount of time has passed between the offense and the sorcery attack, a span equivalent to the amount of time needed for a tree to grow old and tall.

This trope resembles a number of others that seem to serve as admonitions to those who would forget their "transgressions" (*amala sulu*) or who would take the power of the headman lightly. For instance the third proverb, "The thought appears and remains," reminds people that they must constantly keep the memory of their transgressions in mind so that they can behave with the proper caution toward those who might have a motive to sorcerize them.

These two tropes express ideas that introduce a good deal of worry into people's lives. The gist of this worry is related to a concern people have with finding friends who will help them dole out compensation payment to someone who has accused them of committing an offense. In interviews and informal conversation about the reasons for this concern, many people spoke of their fear of being sorcerized by their accusers. To this day, the Rauto cultivate friendships and sometimes perform labor for the friend's benefit so that there will be a number of people to turn to when help is needed with compensation payment. I was told that in the past, labor was rendered almost exclusively to those persons from whom one had both the most to fear and the most to gain—people of rank. The logic behind such maneuvering may seem contradictory, but it was and remains perfectly clear to the Rauto. One reduces one's worries about sorcery by becoming a helper or client of a leading person. By working for him, one lessens the possibility that he might seek to harm you. He in turn could offer protection against the depredations of other leading persons, since rivals might think twice about carrying out a sorcery attack on the client of a powerful man. They would fear both the sorcery and the violence of this man.

Here we see that cultivating a reputation as a sorcerer can be beneficial to a person's career. Yet people often expressed dismay to me at how a leader's powers enabled him to control the lives and actions of others. They said that this was even more the case in the past, when the power possessed by prominent men was not held in check by the mission and the law courts. Indeed, the Rauto perceive the exercise of sorcery powers to be morally wrong if these powers are not used to promote what they consider to be legitimate social interests, that is, the punishment of wrongdoers.[6]

Such thoughts highlight some of the moral problems that many Rauto people see in the successful realization of what can be called the ethos of male social/political identity. Being a man of violence, of anger, and of self-aggrandizing

6. The Rauto consider the unjustified exercise of sorcery powers to reflect what they call "bad way," or "bad manner" (*lai sulu*). Although their attitudes about sorcery have obviously been shaped to a degree by mission teaching, the Rauto distinction between the legitimate and the un-

tendencies is considered antithetical to being a peacemaker and a guarantor of justice and solidarity.[7] This antithesis, symbolized by the images of amala arlem amta and often thought to be embodied by the person of a prominent leader, gives a distinctive tone to the life of the Rauto. It does this by creating an implicit understanding that the structure of what I had previously called community is essentially provisional and therefore liable to unravel.

I think it is clear that Rauto metaphors express an ambivalent assessment of the character of the social actions by which men, especially, enhance their power and reputation. In the Rauto view, what we might call social order and social disorder continually give rise to each other as people follow the traditional paths to renown and try "to build their names." That is, the Rauto recognize and live with the dilemma that events that offer the possibility of achievement also sometimes invite violence and/or a general unraveling of the moral underpinning of social life. I would say that this view of life is essentially pessimistic, because it implies that persons often work against themselves and some of the ideals of their society when they attempt to achieve. The most important point to stress here is that the metaphors that express this belief can be considered to constitute an inquiry into the strengths and weaknesses of Rauto culture. That is, the tropes offer a series of evaluations of how some of this culture's ideals of conduct and of person allow either for the continual recreation of or the undermining of community. Because of this evaluative aspect, amala arlem amta cannot be considered to be simply a celebration of dominant ideals and relations of power, nor does it represent a counterpattern of belief that is set against the dominant belief system. It is partly a statement about the nature of the moral problem that the Rauto perceive to arise from their own theories and concepts about the person and about social identity.

---

justified, insidious use of sorcery powers is, as far as I could tell, traditional. Sorcery is considered an important weapon of social control for leaders; it helps them punish thieves, or wrongdoers in general. There is, however, another aspect to the Rauto understanding of the concept. When sorcery is perceived as being practiced for pecuniary gain, or to attain an obvious political advantage over people, or to satisfy a desire for revenge because of a perceived slight, it is referred to as a bad thing (*angan sulu*), a practice which is morally repugnant.

7. The dual aspect of a headman's social persona was forcibly brought home to me when a man conveyed a traditional story to me about the nature and actions of leaders. The story tells of what is alleged to be typical behavior of a leader after someone he has sorcerized has died. It is said that the adepdep will always attend the mortuary ceremony of his victim and show much solicitude to the dead man's kin. Ideally, he should throw himself upon the body and wail and weep until he is exhausted. Afterward, however, he is said to dress up in his best finery: barkcloth, curved pig's-tusks ornament, stone and shell valuables, and dog's-teeth necklaces. He is said to go to a deserted spot in the rainforest and there to rejoice at the death of his victim by dancing up and down and generally whooping it up by himself. This fable conveys a rather cynical view of the nature of leaders.

Sketches of objects given to initiates during the female puberty rite: cordyline leaves (*ulu*); a bunch of betel nut (*uile*); a small pig's-tusk ornament (*paidela*), such as that often worn by a child. Drawings by Coralie Cooper.

Chapter Four

Mythic Images and Objects of Myth in the Female Puberty Ritual

Discourse and objects are not formulas or signs, and even less are they language, but rather tradition, that is, a way of translating the word in its perennity, a manifestation of being in its continuity.

Maurice Leenhardt (1979)

Sculpture of the habitat, prowboard of the canoe, earring, diadem, noisemaker or song, are a person's gesture manifesting some myth from which he draws his life.

Maurice Leenhardt (quoted in Clifford 1982)

During one of the last days of my first field stay with the Rauto, I saw a performance of the ritual that marks a woman's menarche. The ceremony took up one full day, from dawn to dusk, and its poetry and beauty both moved me and helped me understand the type of power that a Rauto woman can draw on to express and construct her identity. The rite also appeared to be a formal celebration of the part Rauto women play in helping to form the social identities of female adolescents, and it demonstrated that Rauto women are considered the producers and possessors of important aspects of their culture's religious imagination.

This last thought brings to mind contrasts between the Rauto ceremonial for female adolescents and the initiation and puberty rites of many of the peoples of Highland New Guinea, the cultural area where most of the recent work on adolescent ceremonies in Melanesia has been conducted (Godelier 1986; Herdt 1982). A number of these authors argue that rites for both male and female adolescents invoke ideas associated with men's interest in the social control of women and youths (e.g., Godelier 1986:50; Hays and Hays 1982:234). There are no indications, however, that women are perceived as disseminators of aspects of the moral tone and aesthetic style and mood of their culture—

what Clifford Geertz (1973:127) has called a culture's "ethos." Nor do we have any examples in the Melanesian literature of women being involved in the creation and elaboration of a people's world view, that is, "its picture of the way things in sheer actuality are," its "concept of nature, of self and society" (Geertz 1973:127). The rites the Rauto perform to mark a woman's menarche, however, appear to provide just such examples.

This ritual has an extremely simple structure. During its performance two senior women (usually the initiates' paternal aunts or women classified with them) who are known for their skill in song magic and respected as women of economic influence present the initiates with a number of objects associated mainly, though not exclusively, with subsistence production and the exchange activities of women. Other objects specifically convey ideas about the power, influence, and privileges of prominent, or "big," women (ilim alang). As they are presented, special magical songs (aurang) are sung by the senior women conducting the ritual and by a rather large number of the adolescents' female matrikin. These songs are said to promote the adolescents' growth and enhance their beauty and health. Their poetry alludes to the uses to which women put the objects presented and represents a celebration of the aesthetic aspect of women's activities. The songs and mimetic acts of the rite also provide allusive encapsulations of some of the different phases or ages of a woman's life, from preadolescence to mature adulthood.

During the rite, the adolescents are also instructed in the names and proper uses of the objects presented, instructions that outline the picture that the Rauto have of women's reality.[1] By manipulating ideas and objects that define the nature of an adult woman—most especially of a socially prominent big woman—aspects of Rauto ethos and world view are drawn into relationship: the aesthetic feel that Rauto women have for their way of life is synthesized with their picture of this life. For the Rauto, then, the ritual construction of gender is a way of expressing ideas about human nature, social and moral life, and power and status (see also M. Strathern 1988).

To say that Rauto women are disseminators of aspects of the moral tone and aesthetic style and mood of their culture is to say that they control an aspect of cultural, or as Leenhardt might say, "mythic" memory. The significance of the acts and images of the puberty rite is that they place the initiates in contact with the cultural and personal memories that are contained by customary objects

1. The reality of subsistence production is a significant aspect of experience for Rauto women. Few leave village life to reside in Rabaul, and even fewer take up work there. Cash-cropping is not well established, and it is not established at all in bush Rauto villages. None of the elder women I knew had been to school, and no younger woman had passed beyond the fifth grade.

and the customary events or scenarios that the rite mimes. The mimesis of the rite demonstrates in part—though only in part—that song, heirloom, necklace, diadem, and menstrual skirt are a woman's "gesture manifesting some myth from which" *she* "draws her life" (Leenhardt 1948: 138; quoted in Clifford 1982:211). These myths are the stories of custom, the stories of collective and personal memory that explain the origins of and the original uses of the objects used during the rite.

In the puberty ritual some of these stories add meaning to the enacted song images, which portray concretely experienced events in the lifeway of a woman. It is not wholly correct, then, to use the terms *symbol* and *symbolic* to describe the objects that are presented to the initiates, nor the acts and images that accompany these presentations. The objects, acts, and images stand for nothing, really. Rather, they appear to embody the moments of experience and action through which the person realizes an aspect of identity and personal authenticity. This last thought implies that each event mimed and sung during the rite and each object given reveal a moment of the initiate's individuation, or attainment of personhood. But such moments differ markedly from Western ideas of the character of the person's spiritual and social development and individuation. This is one of the reasons why the initiates really do not receive formal acknowledgement during the rite that they have come into a completely new stage of social being; neither are new social and sexual responsibilities really taught to or imposed upon them by elders at this time. In fact the initiates sometimes cannot even remember the simple ikit that are taught to them in the ritual. Rather, what is revealed to them is the feeling of what it means to possess the objects of cultural memory, to be introduced to the mythic patterns that give meaning to their use, to know that their use is a powerful gesture of the externalization of self. As I have argued and will now begin to demonstrate, individuation for Rauto can be seen to consist in a series of such moments of feeling; moments that are distinguished by the experience of the emotion that they call *makai*.

While the images and acts of the rite portray moments of immediate experience and feeling that are "scrupulously externalized, clearly outlined, brightly and uniformly illuminated" (Auerbach 1991:3), their seeming naturalism and presentism represent only the most obvious aspects of woman's social identity; they often simply seem to be women's acted or mimed valorizations of their characteristic roles and duties. As Roland Barthes has shown us, however, images and acts often have rounded, elusive, and evanescent meanings and countermeanings, as well as obvious, seemingly naturalistic ones. Countermeanings can be discerned either in images themselves or in the particular contexts that give them meaning. The contexts that provide more rounded meaning and even countermeaning to the images of the puberty rite are the myths that explain the origins and original uses of the objects that elders present to initiates during the ritual. Exploring the full meaning of this ritual, then, and of the ideas of person and gender from which it draws significance, involves viewing the objects and activities of the rite in relationship to these myths. In doing this I will continue to outline and provide an example of the psychological understanding of image and cultural representation that I described in chapters 1 and 2. I will continue to view a form of representation in relation to forms of emotional experience and of transformation.

SOME OBVIOUS SOCIAL MEANINGS AND
FUNCTIONS OF THE RITE

One of the obvious social functions of the rite is "to raise the name," or enhance the social reputation, of the adolescents for whom it is performed. The rite is most often performed for the eldest or most intelligent and socially promising daughters of prominent men and women, and marks the girls for the assumption of a special social status, that of a big woman. It also demonstrates the economic wherewithal of the sponsoring family and ramage, thereby becoming also a social marker for the girl's immediate family and extended kin group. Finally, the ritual provides an opportunity for the senior women who perform it to demonstrate their knowledge of ritual and of song scripts and, through their performance of the various aurang, the power of their voices to promote the girls' growth and health. This expression of self is integrally related to the affirmation of the social and cultural identity of senior women. It is a demonstration that their voices have social, moral, and magical power. This is significant because of the particular importance that voice and song have in this society. As I have noted, song is a social marker for this people.

One of the most interesting aspects of Rauto female puberty ritual is that, by celebrating the role that big women especially play in production and exchange, song serves as a leitmotif of the ideals of female social identity. The songs also allude to the religious aspect of women's economic life—in particular to the important role that song magic plays in their productive activity. Indeed, a few of the aurang sung to promote the growth of female adolescents are also sometimes performed in women's gardening ritual to promote the growth of crops and flowers formally entrusted to women's care during the puberty ceremonies. In both ritual contexts, a woman's social identity is defined and her reputation enhanced partly through her demonstration of productive ability. This being the case, I must preface my analysis of puberty ritual with a brief discussion of the economic activities of Rauto women and men and the relationship of these activities to Rauto ideals of social identity.

PRODUCTION AND IDENTITY

Big, or prominent, men (*oduk alang, adepdep*) and women (*ilim alang*) are intimately involved in the arrangement, supervision, and sponsorship of most of a hamlet's ceremonial activities. Big men also plan and lead almost all of their groups' productive activities. Women, however, are especially associated with powers that promote the growth of crops, and so big women, too, are usually known for their exceptional productive abilities. Indeed, girls who are being groomed for the special status of an ilim alang will be instructed by their parents, brothers, and maternal uncles in some of the ritual techniques and magical songs of taro production—knowledge that is an important expression of political and economic status and is most often passed on to male children. Usually, however, productive life and ritual life have somewhat different entailments for women and men. While men are primarily responsible for the planting and ritual care of taro, the primary food crop, women have primary though not exclusive responsibility for the planting, harvesting, and ritual care of secondary crops, such as sugarcane, amaranth, sweet potato, and yam. Women are also entrusted with planting various crotons, flowers, and herbs that have important symbolic and religious significance.

Women's prominent position in production is important because the Rauto see effective production, rather than the manipulation of networks of debt and credit, as important to success in ceremonial exchange and trade. Women's productive activities and accomplishments thus stand them in good stead if they wish to participate in the exchange system, and in fact big women are often key players, creating wide trade networks and often cosponsoring ceremonial exchange events formally arranged by their husbands or brothers.

Although big women never attain positions equal in power and status to those of big men, the Rauto recognize nonetheless that the power of a big woman approximates that of a big man. Female puberty ritual provides the most cogent formal expression of this notion, although this is not really what is important about the ritual. What is most important is what it does *not* say about woman's power and religious or mythic identity. The ritual elides more often then it elaborates meaning. The meaning that it elides provides a much stronger statement of women's cultural centrality than does the rite.

Kalapua, a Rauto big woman.

THE PRESENTATION OF THE MENSTRUAL SKIRTS

Both male and female initiation among the Rauto are really part of a cycle of ceremonies, most of them achievement ceremonies, that parents arrange for their children a few years before or after puberty. In addition to initiation, for instance, a man may sponsor a feast to celebrate his son's first public performance of taro magic or the lad's investiture with the costume of the spirit being, kamotmot. Parents may also sponsor a feast after their child has journeyed to a place that he or she has not seen before. By the performance of these ceremonies, parents serve notice that their children are becoming ready to invest themselves forcefully in the social relationships and the spiritual and physical tasks of the adult world.

What distinguishes Rauto initiation ritual from these achievement ceremonies is the initiation's aim of celebrating and cultivating the physical attractiveness of adolescents. In fact some informants said that the puberty and initiation ceremonies could be considered forms of "love magic," since one of their primary aims was to make the initiate attractive to members of the opposite sex.

By all accounts, the menarcheal ritual has always been a more central part of Rauto religious life than male initiation. A number of Rauto even said that the menstrual rite was the most important of all their ceremonies. When I asked one of these people to explain what he meant by this statement, he said simply that the ceremony was something that his people "could never give up," however much introduced social change might alter the tenor of life in southwest New Britain. I took this to mean that the rite provided a particularly compelling statement about what it meant to be a Rauto, one that, according to some, could not be dispensed with. The symbolism of the menstrual rite is certainly more complex than that of male initiation. Though the latter ritual is performed in three different stages, which correspond to Van-Gennep's phases of separation, transition and reincorporation, the major act of the rite consists mostly of a simple teeth-blackening ceremony. There are no grades involved in male initiation. Also, there are no rules as to whether the rite should be performed for a group of initiates, or for a single one. Nor does the major aim of this rite appear to be the cultivation of a specifically male gender identity. A number of the elder women I knew had gone through the teeth-blackening ceremony along with their male kinsmen when they were young girls. In short this ritual is in no way as important a gender marker or as spectacular a ritual performance as are the male initiation rites described by ethnographers of Sepik and Highland cultures. In contrast, the female puberty ritual is both an important gender marker and what Singer and Geertz might call a major "cultural performance" (see Geertz 1973:113).

Though the female puberty rite is most often performed for a firstborn or a promising and intelligent daughter, sometimes a family, or coresident families of the same descent group will arrange for two daughters of approximately similar age to go through the ceremony together. In precontact times, the expense of these rites was so onerous that only prominent families could afford to sponsor them. Nowadays, the rites are held more often because the expansion of trade networks following pacification and an influx of cash from plantation labor and cash-cropping permits more people to obtain or commission the traditional valuables required.

The rites cannot begin until the girl's family has amassed sufficient wealth in the form of pigs, taro, and shell valuables to pay for the ritual services that will be provided. On the one hand, therefore, the rites may not take place until several years after a girl's first menses; on the other, they may be performed before the onset of menstruation if the family has accumulated the necessary wealth.[2]

The major part of the ritual is directed by two "sisters" of the girl's father— either his true siblings or parallel cousins—assisted usually by the girl's maternal uncle and a large group of his classificatory female siblings. The night before the ritual proper, these officiants take the girl to a menstrual hut located on the outskirts of the hamlet settlement or, in coastal Rauto villages, on the edge of the sea. Throughout the night, these aunts and cousins bring the girl food and drink and provide her with a special skirt to wear while she sleeps. This skirt, called the *agosgoso,* is made from the colorful leaves of a wild banana. Some of these leaves also are placed between her legs "to absorb her menstrual blood."

The next morning at sunrise, the two aunts (*ado*) remove the skirt from around the girl's waist and throw it into the ocean or, if the ceremony is performed in a bush village, into the forest at the outskirts of the hamlet. The girl or girls then are led into the men's house of their father's ramage, where the two aunts scrape coconut meat and rub the extracted oil onto the girl's breasts, so that her skin will appear shiny and attractive.

At the ritual I attended, the two initiates were rather shy and became embarrassed as their aunts oiled their bodies.[3] This elicited howls of derision from

2. A number of informants said that this was a traditional practice. If this is true, it indicates that the Rauto have always had a rather more relaxed attitude toward menstrual blood than have the neighboring Kaulong (see Goodale 1986:131).

3. One was the daughter of a man who had taught school for a time. Although he was not a big

the assembled women and provided them with their first opportunity to begin clowning. Uttering pseudo war cries and pulling on each other's breasts, they danced around the men's house, bumping into one another and often knocking people down.

When the clowning ended, the two aunts began to paint the girls' bodies. Red ocher (*agiu*) was brushed onto their hair, and their faces were painted with red and white marks called *tinga tinga*. Then the girls were taken to the center of the men's house, where their aunts presented each of them with a second, newly made agosgoso skirt and a skirt the Rauto call *yaoli*. The aunts painted the skirts with red ocher and then informed the girls that the yaoli were "their own grass skirts," which they should wear until the end of their lives. The plants from which they were made, the girls were told, represent their personal finery, which they should use to decorate their bodies whenever they worked in their gardens or attended song festivals. They should cultivate these plants around their taro gardens and houses in order to beautify them. The two aunts then pointed out and individually named each of the plants making up the yaoli. The aromatic scent of the plants and the burning and effervescent quality of their sap are thought to stimulate the girls' skin and thereby promote their physical growth. The plants also have a variety of uses in other Rauto rituals; most, for instance, are used in the performance of taro magic. The implicit message of the aunts' instruction was that these important materials are controlled by women, and that their care and reproduction is a woman's privilege.

The girls were then shown and told the names of important cultivars that they should plant or harvest: these included a taro corm and stalk, two kinds of yam, amaranth, and sugarcane. The youngsters also were shown and told the names of the tobacco plant and the vine on which the betel pepper grows. They were then instructed in the proper way to cut the taro corm from its stalk with a clamshell cutter and told that if a nontraditional object such as a knife were used, the taro stalk would produce no food.

Finally, aurang for the new agosgoso skirts, also known as *lelme*, were performed. Like the agosgoso tossed into the sea, these ceremonial lelme are made predominantly from dark purple, bright red, and yellow wild banana leaves. The two aunts opened one up and then, holding a hemp tie each, brought it up to one of the girls' waists and began to swing it back and forth against her backside as they sang the song for the lelme:

---

man, his family was prominent, and he relied heavily on family members to meet the costs of the ritual. The two senior women who officiated were respected big women.

Lelme, ngapapenwo lelme	Swing the skirt
lelme, lelme,	[back and forth] back
lelme, ngapapenwo lelme	and forth.
Lelme lelme	

After a few minutes of song, the lelme was fastened around the girl's waist, and the act was repeated for the second girl. Then the yaoli were raised up and fastened above the girls' waists, some of the leaves being slipped inside the lelme, between their legs. As this operation was performed, the women all sang the song for the yaoli:

Yaoli a yao a	The yaoli skirt,
yaoli a yao a	yaoli.
a komela aupua.	You put it on thus [it is
	yours now].

The significance of these first few activities in the puberty ritual lies in their relation of a system of aesthetics to notions of physical development and bodily health. Outlining this relationship, which is what I will do here, means outlining the connotations or referents of the mimed actions and activities of the rite. These referents or associations correspond to a conscious ideology, an ideology that makes up only a part of the meaning of the image of the presentation of the menstrual skirts.

Informants told me that painting and anointing the girls' bodies makes them healthy and their skin attractive. The scent of the yaoli plants and the bright colors of the other skirts also are said to promote growth and health because they are pleasing to the senses—they "give joy" to the girls. The same was said of the senior women's singing, but these women told me that the songs also "moved their hearts" and sometimes made them cry by causing them to remember those who had sung the aurang for them when they were young girls. The songs allow elders to remember the poignancy of their own pasts at the very moment that they invest their spiritual power in the next generation.

These statements made it clear to me that these first few rites are meant both to impart physical sensation and to elicit sentiment from the girls and the other ritual participants, and so sensitize and prepare the girls' minds and bodies for the instruction to come. The beautification and painting of the skin also may represent a ritual attempt to cultivate outward physical signs of the development of the self and social identity.

A discussion of color symbolism will help support these points. Red and white, the major colors displayed during the rite, express ideas of health, growth, and personal power. The color red (dimor), which appears as ocher paint on the yaoli and on the girls' bodies, is associated in several contexts with growth. To begin with, red ocher is used to promote the growth of young boys during male initiation and of the taro crop in a number of garden rites. Second, red is associated with beauty and sexual desirability, a connection made most clearly during Rauto song festivals, when young men and women enhance the beauty of their skin by painting their faces and bodies with red dye from *bixa orellana*.[4] Third, red is also the color most frequently used to signal that a person has acquired an important bit of ritual or traditional knowledge. After a child has seen or participated in a ritual for the first time, for example, adults will paint him with a streak of red to signify his right to speak about the ceremony. Finally, red is also placed on children or young men and women when they are in a ritual, or liminal, state—a time when people are, in the Rauto view, in the process of augmenting the self either with knowledge or ritual power.

Red may be associated with increased physical and personal power because, in the Rauto forest environment, red is often the color of things such as fruits or areca nut that are fully developed, or ripe (see Gell 1975:327). Whatever the case, red in the woman's puberty ritual appears to signify that the girls are developing in both body and mind. Together with their anointment with coconut oil, it also suggests a link to the development of their sexual attractiveness, a point I shall develop further in my analysis of the next phase of the ritual. The color white is also used in the puberty ritual. In Rauto culture, white is the preeminent symbol of anger and warfare; thus, before going into battle warriors would smear their faces with lime powder. But white also conveys the idea of privilege: traditionally, for example, the young daughters of big men or women would have lime powder put on their faces during their ritual seclusion prior to marriage. Since the puberty ritual is about the privileges and duties of women, white is therefore a very appropriate color with which to express these ideas.

Notwithstanding the attention given to color, Rauto women told me that the most important part of this first phase of the puberty ritual was the girls' investiture with the "women's skirts." With these presentations, the girls begin to acquire the outward signs of a new status. The skirts, especially the yaoli, signify a woman's acquisition of new duties and privileges. But what was fascinating to me was the way their presentation was related to a complex set of ideas about menstrual blood and the girls' developing power.

Almost all of the plants from which the skirts are made, and in the cultivation of which the girls are instructed, are also used in gardening rituals to

4. Traditionally, men and women would try to bleach their hair and skin red with ocher to give it an attractive cast. Nowadays, store-bought hair coloring is used. Although skin with a reddish hue is considered most attractive, I noticed no attempts by people to bleach their skin.

promote the healthy development of a taro crop. It seems, then, that the grass skirts, most especially the yaoli, are not only meant to make the girls grow well, but are also a visual sign that they are acquiring a greater ability to produce food. In this ritual phase, in other words, the girls become associated with principles and forces that aid the development of food and people. Yet the lelme and yaoli are, at least during the puberty ritual, "menstrual" skirts. They denote the presence of menstrual blood, which paradoxically is usually thought inimical to processes of human, animal, and plant growth and health. A woman should not work in her garden while menstruating, for example, lest "wild pigs smell her menstrual blood," follow the scent to the garden, and eat the growing taro crop. Menstrual pollution (*karauong*) is also thought to harm a developing taro corm if a menstruating woman should step over its stalk. Moreover, a menstruating woman is also thought capable of harming men, pigs, and old women by stepping over them.

A girl's menarche thus marks the fact that she now possesses a dangerous and sometimes destructive power. Yet the Rauto choose to mark this event by celebrating her constructive economic, social, and moral influence. One might argue that this paradox expresses the idea that women are influential partly because they are dangerous, especially to men. But this does not satisfactorily explain why, in the context of the puberty ritual, menstrual blood signifies an increase in a woman's personal power, while in other contexts it is thought to lessen her productive powers and diminish rather than augment her other abilities. I would point out, however, that it is men, not women, who most often voice fears about the polluting power of menstrual blood. Moreover, women certainly do not feel that menstruation places them at the periphery of social and cultural life. Rather, female puberty ritual suggests that the nature of women is partly defined by the fact that they menstruate, and women seize this opportunity to place themselves at the mythic center of Rauto life, and then to draw strength from this center. Yet, the ritual does not reveal the mythic character of the menstrual skirts and indeed of female identity. The myth that tells of the origins of the skirts, of menstruation, of women's objects and activities, indeed of the origins of the female sex, provides a more rounded understanding of the meaning of female identity, and even of female ethos than does the simple presentation described here. The story reveals how woman's possession of the menstrual skirts and of female dress was her first gesture of assertion and of female personhood. The myth reveals that woman had literally to wrest her gender from man.

> Men were not originally men. They followed women's ways. They carried around with them and used all the things that women now have: their oven

stones, their oven tongs, their clamshell cutters for harvesting taro, their taro shell scrapers. They menstruated as women do, and, as women, when they did they left their garden work exclaiming, "Oh! I can't work now. I have my period, I'll have to rest." As women, they would comb the reefs for crustaceans and small fish, and they would also collect fresh water snails. Then one day one of these supposed women came upon a real woman, and this real woman called out, "Hey, you really large woman over there, where are you going?" And she answered, "I'm just going to comb the reefs for some small fish, although I wish I didn't have to do it all by myself. It's just that all my friends have their periods now, and they are all much too exhausted to help me out. Do you see them over there resting on the verandas of their houses?" "Never mind them," said the real woman. "Come over here and let me get a good look at you," she said, eyeing this supposed woman suspiciously. "You know, I don't think you're really a woman." As she said this, she lifted up the other woman's skirt, and after seeing what was hidden by the skirt, exclaimed, "Hey, you're not a woman. Is a woman so big as you? You don't even have breasts. And your genitals are hanging down there. You are a man. Give me my woman's skirt, give me my menstrual skirt, give me my woman's fishing net, my oven stones, my taro scraper, my taro cutter. And give me my menstruation." And then the real woman gathered up the things that were given to her, and she put on her female dress and her menstrual skirts. She then told the man about the objects that rightfully belonged to him, and she pointed them out to him. "There, there are your fishing and hunting nets, and your fishing spears; and there is the men's house. Go there now, and give me my things. And menstruation, that belongs to me, so leave it alone." And so the woman gathered up her things, and the man gathered up his.

We have two images before us then. That evoked by the puberty rite presents a naturalistic scene, and an obvious meaning; it simply pictures the initiates being given their adult women's dress, their menstrual skirts, and a number of objects that this culture associates with women. The images and acts of this opening phase of the rite suggest that women simply and naturally come to possess these objects at the time of their puberty. The mythic narrative belies this suggestion however.

The narrative indicates that woman's first act of authentic personhood consisted in taking her menstruation and her women's objects and dress from men. The moment when she does this portrays her immediate assumption of female identity. We see here a Rauto "myth of identity" (Leenhardt 1979:23). Though this myth seems a living part of the Rauto present, it contains a sense of the past. "It was not always so," it seems to say. Identity had to be won through a gesture of assertion, rather than simply put on, as a menstrual skirt is put on.

The myth expresses this insight as much by its psychological character and humorous tone as by the sequence of events that it outlines. The opening sequences that describe men following woman's lifeway, carrying out woman's everyday tasks, and experiencing the state of menstruation seem to parody female personhood rather than provide an authentic mimesis of it. The "she-males" portrayed here seem grossly effeminate, frivolous, and clumsy as they comb the reefs for food, run from their gardens at the slightest hint of menstrual blood, and collapse exhausted on the verandas of their family houses during their menstruation.

In contrast, the narrator's portrait of the one woman of the myth seems an example of authentic personhood. This character quickly sends the man on his way by pointing him to his own sphere of activity with absolute certainty. She assumes her own identity and asserts her claim to her woman's objects with as much certainty. "These are my things," she seems to say, "I will take them and be what I am."

A portrait of woman and of female ethos begins to emerge in the myth, one that is counterposed to the narrator's weak parody of female personhood. This ethos corresponds to the assertiveness seen in the puberty rite, yet it stands in contrast to the first sublime and simple act of the rite—the presentation of the menstrual skirts. Or rather, the acts and images of the first presentations of the puberty ritual are given meaning by two different, yet simultaneously experienced feelings. The sort of pride (*adang dang*) evident in the women's clowning and assertive if ribald celebration of the sexual parts of their bodies contrasts with the sublime plenitude of remembrance that is evoked by the aurang. The initiates seem to be the objects of these two emotions, and thus they come to objectify two aspects of female ethos: assertive strength and a sort of sublime emotionality. It seems that the initiates come to objectify memory, emotion, and ethos during this ritual. One of the more rounded meanings of the rite appears to be, as we will see, that female and male ethos and pathos are similar, rather than completely different, indeed opposed, in character.

THE PRESENTATION OF ARECA NUT

Following the girls' anointment and painting and the presentation of their skirts, one of the two aunts took a large bunch of ripe areca (betel) nut in one hand and a lime holder in the other. Handing the areca to her helper, she began to rub lime powder on the girls' teeth. Both aunts then turned the girls' shoulders back and forth rhythmically, pulling the areca nut and its branches across the girls' front teeth. As they performed this ritual, they sang the aurang for the areca nut, songs in the language of the neighboring Gimi that all refer to the harvesting and proper use of the areca:

Komsolei wirwiraie komsolei wirwiraei; Komsolei warapmaei o komsolei warapmaei.	Put the areca nut and the lime together; [the areca has fruit.]
Komsolei klokiaei komsolei klokiaei.	Harvest the areca [from its tree].
Komsolei abrumyaei komsolei abrumyaei.	Remove the areca from its stem.

As the following narratives make clear, areca has great mythic and emotional significance for the life of a woman.

I was at a song festival at Giring. When the festival was ending, and the big men had begun to butcher the hogs, the young men and women were playing their games on the outskirts of the dancing ground. A woman from Aukur, my cousin-sister, sat down next to me, and we began to speak to one another. She held my arm tightly as we spoke. Another woman (whom this speaker later married) also came to sit down, and I told her that we really weren't doing anything; that I was just speaking with my little sister. This other woman then gave a pearlshell to my sister from Aukur, and she told her to take the pay as compensation for her desire for me. Then she sat down between us. She took a red areca nut from her basket, chewed it for a moment, and then gave me part of it."

Areca Nut and the Young Girl

A man and his wife left for the Woman's Sea, leaving their young daughter at home. A cannibal spirit then came upon the family's hamlet and spied the areca tree that stood in the plaza of the girl's house. He entered the plaza and climbed the tree to get at the betel; as he was climbing down a single areca nut fell from his hand, hitting the thatch roof of the girl's house, falling through it and then hitting the girl on her head. She picked the nut up and after looking at it intensely, decided to go outside to see if a bird had knocked it down from its tree. She looked up the tree and saw the cannibal spirit climbing down. She shouted at it, "Are you a man or a spirit? Are you going to catch and eat me?"

"No I'm just a man; let's sit down and chew this areca nut together," said the spirit. The girl replied that she did not want any areca. The spirit then made a grab for her, and she jumped away from it and quickly climbed to

the roof of her house. The spirit then pulled out one of its teeth and threw
it at the house, thus destroying its roof, but the girl managed to jump away
onto the trunk of the areca tree. He then extracted another tooth and hurled
it at the areca nut tree, knocking it down; but the girl managed to jump to
the lower branches of the hamlet's ficus tree. The spirit extracted another
tooth, which broke the lower branches of the ficus. She jumped to a higher
branch . . . [scenario is repeated a number of times]. The girl then began
singing for her mother and father. They heard her song and began to rush
back. They arrived back just in the nick of time. The father raised his spear,
his wife her woman's fighting club, and together they dispatched the spirit.

We have three different images or representations of women's use of areca
before us. In the first, evoked by the mimetic acts of the puberty rite, the initiates are simply presented with a bunch of areca and are shown how to use
them to make their teeth glisten. The image uses areca as a metonym. "Here
is your attractiveness," it seems to say." Take it and use it as is your right. See
how beautiful you can be." The image presents the naturalistic meaning of the
use of areca, and clearly celebrates the initiate's developing sexuality. One of
the acts of this phase of the rite also involves the naming of the areca. As the
naming of a person frequently signals a change of a person's status, so in this
example the naming of the areca signals a change in the status of the object. It
becomes and is ritually marked as a manifestation of woman's sexual being.

In the second image, contained in the recounted portion of a man's life history, a woman uses her areca to begin a sexual relationship with a man, as well
as to compete with another woman for the man's sexual attention. This image
draws meaning from the cultural connotations of areca's use and has the quality
of a "coded message" (Barthes 1990:36). That is, the woman's use of betel
in this example alludes to a body of attitudes about the relationship between
courtship, sexuality, and areca. These attitudes can be read from the image like
a code. Among these attitudes are these: (1) If a woman either continually gives
a man betel or requests it from him, she thereby makes an indirect statement
of interest in him. (2) If she forcefully pushes areca into a man's hand or, as in
the above example, into his mouth, she thereby takes a more aggressive sexual
stance.

These facts about areca's use underscore the point that women often take
the lead in courtship. This is described in the life-history account when the
narrator's future wife in effect makes a public announcement of marriage by
offering him the charmed red areca that she had previously put into her mouth.
The narrator, whose name was Brumio, also alludes to this when he mentions
the young men and women "playing" at the hamlet's edge at the conclusion of
a song festival. Such play usually begins when a woman, who is moved by a

man at a song festival, grasps his arm and refuses to let go of it. As "compensation" for the excitement he has caused her, the man is then to give the woman a pearlshell or a meter of shell money. If the man does not wish the woman to loosen her grip, he will not give her the valuable.

The images of the mythic narrative of the cannibal spirit and the young girl seem to deny rather than augment the meanings that we have just discussed. This seems appropriate, because the primary scenes of the myth describe a woman's refusal of rather than her acceptance of a bunch of areca. This is consistent with a number of other ideas and themes developed by the myth.

The most obvious contrast that the myth provides to the puberty rite is seen in its negative treatment and valuation of sexuality. For instance, the woman described in the myth is (like the female initiates) sexually mature. Yet the myth does not celebrate this quality; rather, it seems to be a cautionary tale that outlines the danger that can present itself to women when they come to possess beauty and sexual capacity. On a metaphorical level, one could view the girl's fear of the cannibal spirit as a refusal to acknowledge her sexuality. This in turn seems linked to the fact that the myth does not portray a moment of individuation or development in the lifeway of a woman: it does not allude to any crossing of a social or cultural threshold. We can support this point by juxtaposing an event portrayed by the myth with one of the myth's major themes. The event is the girl's refusal of the areca nut offered her by the cannibal spirit; the mythic theme is that the girl does not separate herself from the parental mantle. At the myth's end, she remains what she was at its beginning: simply her parent's child. Her temporary separation from the parents in the myth is simply a rhetorical device, meant to portray her as being vulnerable to overly aggressive male sexuality and in need of being saved from it.

One detects a number of negative social attitudes about male sexual aggression in the portrait of the cannibal spirit. In the myth his aggression takes the form of a desire for both rape and cannibalism. The spirit's dangerously exaggerated orality, expressed by the image of his jagged and sharp teeth, as well as by his wish to cannibalize the girl, seems a motif that equates sex with destruction—with the wish to harm or even obliterate the other by incorporating her into his own body. The motif seems somewhat similar to the images that are evoked by the tropes of warfare and violence—images that are about the conquest or even obliteration of opponents. Sexuality is indeed often equated with violence in this culture. The association is often made, for instance, if a man, rather than a woman, initiates courtship. The proper male sexual approach is the indirect one, as is seen in the personal narrative of this section.

This culture entertains other, equally negative images about sexuality that are opposed to the naturalistic and positive allusion to it that is represented in the puberty rite. One of these is the notion that excessive sexual activity can lead to lethargy, a general depletion of physical vigor, and even premature death for both men and women. Some of these ideas are related to notions of the polluting power of females, but others are not. The more rounded, fuller meaning of the presentation of the areca in the puberty rite only emerges when we consider these negative valuations. The presentation seems to brush these attitudes aside with a simple gesture. It seems to say, "Here is this areca; it is a belonging of yours that is a blessing and not a curse." That is, the areca is a metonym for the girl's budding sexuality, and in the context of the puberty rite this sexuality is represented as a blessing.

THE PRESENTATION OF FIRE

In the next phase of the puberty ritual, the two girls were taught the proper care of fire, a process involving two rites, each accompanied by a magical song. First, the girls were seated on the floor of the men's house and instructed to sit with their legs crossed at the ankle. This, they were told, was the posture they should assume when tending a fire or simply sitting. The aunts then had them cross their legs at the knees and explained that this was the position assumed by women who knew the myths of Molyo and Alipo, the two culture heroes who originated the posture. Were those ignorant of the myth to adopt this posture, they were told, an elder might shame them by asking if they knew the meaning of their act. As the girls sat in the style of Alipo and Molyo, their aunts rocked their shoulders back and forth and sang one of the songs for fire:

Kamse kon Alipo,	Put your legs like Alipo
kamse kon Alipo.	taught us.
Kamse kon Molyo;	Sit by the fire as Molyo
kamse pe ayi langono	taught us;
tarango Molyo.	as elder brother Molyo.

The aunts then placed a small, smoldering log by the feet of each girl. Then, lifting the logs up again, they knocked some charcoal ash (*asong*) off their smoldering ends, and blew on the embers until they were bright red and ready to burst into flame. They then replaced the logs on the ground and led the women in singing another aurang for fire:

Atrong lomo aii,	Make your fire,
atrong lomo aii.	make your fire.
Imbir, me aii	First the flame
yau me.	comes, then the smoke.

Fire is a sacred symbol throughout the cultures of southwestern New Britain—sacred because of its association with women and domesticity. Thus, a Rauto metaphor states that a wife is the fire of a man. More accurately, a man's wife is the burning charcoal that transforms raw taro into food and provides nourishment for him and his children.[5]

Fire and women are also symbols of peace. Thus, the sister exchanges that frequently concluded hostilities in prepacification days were described as "exchanges of fire," and the completion of the exchange as "the return of the fire". This symbolic equation, fire = women and peace, is illustrated also in women's use of fire to stop men's fist or spear fights at song festivals, for instance. Either she can throw a burning log down between the fighters saying, "The fire flames," or she can let fall her grass skirt, exposing her genitals and shaming the men. Commonly, though, she resorts to synecdoche, taking a piece of her grass skirt or sometimes nowadays a piece of her cloth skirt, and waving it in front of the fighters, who, duly shamed, should cease their fighting.

Another Rauto metaphor identifies fire with menstrual blood. The trope *ilim apai ilo ayi,* "the marriageable woman's fire," refers to a red leaf said to have acquired its color when a nubile, menstruating woman stepped over and bled on it. As the menstrual blood of young women is thought to be particularly powerful and harmful, it is not surprising that this red "women's leaf" is used during taro planting ritual to "burn" insect pests from the ground. In this example, ideas about sexuality, menstrual blood, and power appear to be related and symbolized by fire.

The hearth, cookery, oath taking, menstrual blood, the control of violence by women, growth and nurturance, are only some of the more obvious associations of fire. The image of the rite explicitly refers to none of these things; we read them from the cultural context rather than from the ritual image. All the image appears to say is, "Here is a woman tending her fire," a statement that can be considered a motif of rather than a picturing of the many associations between fire and women. However, it is a motif that appears to assign women to the domestic realm. This seemingly naturalistic assignation seems a natural progression from the earlier ritual images and acts that celebrated the initiates' developing sexuality and the phase of woman's life when she is permitted to

5. Perhaps because of this crucial function, fire is also used in swearing oaths. To convince others of his truthfulness, for example, a man will call out *aii nimbir* ("the fire flames") when he finishes speaking. Should the oath be sworn falsely, it is said, the liar's fire no longer will cook his food properly. Fire has similar symbolic dimensions among the neighboring Kaulong (Goodale 1985:233).

A woman prepares a small stone oven.

adorn, beautify, and generally celebrate her developing body. Two phases of a woman's life are celebrated by the simple ritual motifs of the presentation of areca and of fire, then: young adulthood and the full maturity which follows from the assumption of domestic responsibilities and duties. Some of the following presentations support the social assignment of women to the domestic realm; others represent forms of experience that make woman's domestic role seem a simple adjunct to the cultural or mythic importance that is attached to her person. In some cases these images and presentations seem to be forms of rhetoric that actually counter the strict and apparently natural assignment of women to the domestic realm. They have the character of counternarrative.

PRESENTATION OF THE COCONUT-FROND BASKET AND CORDYLINE

Following the presentation of fire, the officiating aunts took two coconut-frond baskets filled with areca nut, lime powder, tobacco, and other items, and placed them on the girls' heads. As they did this, they turned the girls' shoulders back and forth, placing the girls' hands on top of the baskets to steady them. They then sang the first aurang for the coconut-frond basket:

Nga sun karei	I carry the basket [on my
Lolai karei	head.] I carry the basket
muralmeia, muralmeia.	in my hand.

As the other women joined the refrain, the two aunts removed the baskets from the initiates' heads and showed them how to carry them on their shoulders. Next, they demonstrated how to carry the baskets under the arm cupped in the joint of the elbow. Finally, they showed the girls how to swing the baskets back and forth with their arms. Each of these acts was accompanied by a verse of the woman's basket aurang:

Abungmea, abungmea	A woman, her basket is
asapmea, asapmea	held underneath
karei tir melse wisna.	her arm.
Alungmea, alungmea	Carry the basket [cupped
alungmea, asapmea.	in the elbow joint].
Taptapyoa, taptapyoa	The basket is swung [back
taptapyoa, taptapyoa.	and forth, back and forth].

After this, several species of cordyline (types of crotons) were brought out. The first, called *anamoi,* had a dark red leaf. One of the aunts placed its base on the ground and then began to rock it back and forth as though she were planting or harvesting it. As she did so, she sang its aurang:

Anamoi i wom	The leaf of the red
mela,	cordyline,
Anamoi i wom	The leaf of the red
mela.	cordyline. I show the leaf
Ngasok wom mela	of the cordyline to my
ngasokon aki,	cross-cousin; I ask for a
maieng oa	pig; he, my cross-cousin, is
ino vita. [Nga karpan.]	ashamed. [I am angry.]

To the accompaniment of another aurang, the act was repeated with a species called *ulu,* which had a small green leaf:

Luei ulu luai,	The cordyline's leaf;
keskeska aponmot	cut the small leaf, cut
keskeska, keskeska.	the small cordyline's leaf.

The first act of this ritual sequence, the presentation of the coconut-frond basket, appears to have a straightforward enough, if culturally coded meaning: it alludes to a woman's role as dispenser of food and amenities such as areca and tobacco. Women's baskets are frequently filled with these commodities, which they should give to others. In fact, people often scold those who are not carrying their coconut-frond baskets because it means they wish to take from others and avoid sharing betel and food themselves. Thus, the basket is a symbol of reciprocity and sociality, and its presentation to girls during their puberty ritual is partly a metaphorical or coded statement that, as adult women, they must carry their baskets in order to "give things away."

These obvious meanings are ancillary to more powerful mythic insights about women's creative and social power. The first image of this series of presentations—the image that describes a woman simply carrying her basket as if it had no more significance than any other object of adornment—coexists with a powerful mythic image of the coconut-frond basket as a sort of womb. In a story a woman produces the objects of wealth, status, and political power that are such an important part of Rauto social life from her coconut-frond basket. I will recount this myth and discuss its meaning after describing the middle phase of the puberty ritual—the phase in which the initiates are presented with prestige objects that symbolize social and political influence.

The culturally coded significance of the rites involving the anamoi and ulu cordylines lies in their status as sacred representations of political and social power. In some contexts the use of the anamoi is an expression of anger. When men wish to ask their kin for assistance in a feud, for instance, they send them the red leaf of the anamoi with a knot, or series of knots, in the leaf to indicate the number of days or weeks that must pass before assistance is to be rendered. The song of the anamoi refers to a woman who has asked her male cross-cousin (*vita*) for a gift of a pig. Unfortunately, her cousin is unable to meet her request, a delinquency that can be a serious breach of custom and a denial of sociality. In the song the woman expresses her anger by showing the anamoi to him.

Women have the right to point out this breach of custom because of their moral authority in Rauto society. The presentation of the second croton, the green ulu, is a formal recognition of this authority. This plant is cultivated around the boundaries of the men's ceremonial house, the political and religious center of the hamlet or village residence, and it is a symbol of the political, ritual, and moral authority of the house's leaders. (Perhaps appropriately, *ulu* is also the word for a type of compensation leaders collect from people who transgress moral or ritual rules.)

In religious life, the ulu is also the preeminent symbol of the authority of Varku, a spirit thought to be incarnated in a carved wooden mask that appears during the performance of a special song festival. Varku is the most powerful spirit being honored with song festivals. He is associated especially with adult men, and buttresses their control over the ceremonial production, allocation, and consumption of pigs, one of the major symbols of the big man in southwest

New Britain. Through the ulu, Varku expresses demands for pigs and other resources, and honors those who accede to his request. For instance, a first-born or promising daughter of a man who has honored such a demand will be "adopted" by the spirit as what the Rauto call an *aili*. To mark the adoption, the girl is painted with red ocher and taken into the men's ceremonial house, where she stands before the mask. The man wearing the mask then puts his hand on her shoulder to place her under the protection of Varku, and she is given an ulu leaf to show that she shares in his authority and in the authority of the spirit beings called *kamotmot*. She is now privileged to see the sacred masks of the kamotmot kept in the men's house, and she is allowed to aid men when banana-leaf costumes are made for these masks. No longer can she be struck by her parents nor talked about critically, on pain of compensation to the society of men that controls the masks. The ulu does not just signify the protection of Varku, however; it also allows the girl to request resources and compensation from men, a privilege also accorded prominent or big women. In sum the formal presentation of the ulu at the puberty ceremony marks a girl for a career of social influence and achievement. It is a ritual statement that she is to exercise the moral and political influence of a big woman.

There is a mythic image that makes a much bolder statement of woman's religious and political influence than the presentation of the ulu to the initiates. This image is contained by the myth of the capture of the kamotmot. It is a myth that is revealed to boys and to only a few women—those marked for a career of social influence by events such as the puberty rite. The myth reveals how before their capture the spirit beings had originally helped women with their garden work. It then tells how the kamotmot were originally captured and possessed by women and recounts how men envied the women's new posses-sion and stole it from them. Thus, the myth reveals that the political power and authority that accrued to men because of their possession of the spirit masks was orignally stolen from and thus derived from women.

While the naturalistic image of the presentation of the cordyline simply indi-cates that some women have the right to share with men the political authority that derives from the possession of the masks and of the cordyline, the image of the myth indicates that this is rather inadequate compensation for the power and influence that women lost when men stole the masks from them and used them to buttress their own power. The contained and simple images of the puberty rite elide this meaning rather than state it. This elision itself has mean-ing, however, especially if we consider that some of the big women who direct the puberty ritual know the myth of the spirit masks. The simple presentation of the cordylines—emblems of these masks and their power—seems to say, "You men understand the full meaning of our right to possess and use these emblems—a right that you gave back to us. The sacred or mythic center of our custom is our invention, not yours."

THE PRESENTATION OF COCONUTS

After the presentation of the cordylines, a number of coconuts were brought out, and the initiates were instructed in the names of their various parts, in how to plant them, and in how to bunch them together to carry them. Unlike the earlier rites, however, these instructions were not accompanied by an aurang.

In traditional discourse, ritual, and everyday use, coconuts are another symbol of domesticity and of the nurturing abilities of women. Because of its importance in cookery, for instance, coconut cream is referred to as women's breast milk, and a family's coconut palms usually are planted close to where its women tend their fires and prepare food. Indeed, in the myth explaining the origin of the coconut, a culture hero specifically instructs people to plant their palms near the cooking area, so that women will have an easy time harvesting the nuts for food preparation.

The myth tells of the adventures of a lastborn child who has, like many another a character in Rauto myth, lost his father. Being physically unable to provide as much for his mother as his older brother, he decides to compete with the brother by inventing a long bamboo blowgun. His invention becomes a great success, and everyone wishes to borrow it to shoot birds and fruit bats. The hero keeps the invention hidden on a small island just off the coast. One day a big man persuades the boy to take him to the island and show him the blowgun. The big man steals the invention and leaves the boy stranded on the island. The boy then fashions a small raft made of banana leaves and launches himself toward the shore. As he drifts in, a shark attacks his raft, chewing bits of it off and then chewing off bits of the boy's body. Finally, only his head is left bobbing on the waves and singing for his elder brother. The brother spears the head as it comes close to shore. The head tells his brother to plant him near the plaza of their mother's house, so that the nuts of the coconut palm will fall close to her. Thus could the younger brother continue to provide for his family.

The myth represents the coconut as a woman's child. Both the myth and the puberty rite also represent the coconut as a gift and blessing that is offered to women, and themes of the myth appear to justify aspects of the division of labor in this society. Thus, the boy's invention of the blowgun and the theft of it by adult men squarely assign the labor of hunting to men. The boy's second invention, the coconut—which is really the boy's reinvention of himself—appears to assign women squarely to the domestic realm. This is consistent with the fact that the myth appears to valorize the particular closeness of the mother-child bond, a closeness that is elaborated further by the following series of coded associations.

As the myth suggests, the growth and development of the coconut palm serves as a metaphor for the maturation of children. This is seen most clearly during a brief magical rite that a woman performs at the end of the first year of her child's life. The rite involves the bark cloth used to wrap the head of the newborn child in order to elongate it and make it aesthetically pleasing to the Rauto eye. The child's mother buries the bark cloth underneath a newly sprouted coconut, expressing as she does the wish that the growth of the coconut palm should aid the growth and development of the child—that the child grow tall and strong like a coconut palm. The child's life is thereby juxtaposed to the life of the mythic coconut boy, and the child draws something of its life from this mythic participation.

By entrusting initiates with the care of coconuts in the puberty ceremony, senior women appear to be making an allusion to the girls' future domestic duties, the most important of which will be their care of children. Speaking both mythically and practically, one could say that one of the reasons children grow is that women plant the coconut palm and prepare food with its fruit.

SUMMARY: THE FIRST PHASE OF THE PUBERTY RITUAL

Many of the objects presented in the first phase of the puberty ritual are objects of subsistence production, commodities upon which the physical survival of Rauto society depends. More than this, however, as the material embodiment of mythic experience as well as cultural values, they literally must be propagated and maintained if moral and cultural life is to have a meaning that the Rauto would recognize. Their use in economic, political, and ritual life represents a way of expressing value and of motivating or influencing people, as well as of representing the concrete immediacy of mythic experience. In the puberty rite, girls are formally entrusted with these sacred objects and so, in a sense, become agents for the expression of the core of Rauto cultural and social life. Women thus become formally identified with this cultural core; one could say that the ideas about the nature and activities of women are celebrated by the Rauto mythological and cultural system rather than denigrated, as seems to be the case in some other parts of Melanesia.

What is also noteworthy about the first phase of the rite, and about its mythic associations and counterassociations, is the way that it provides a series of images of different aspects of a woman's life-path. This ritual phase especially refers to the developing sexuality of adolescents and to the domestic duties and privileges of adult women. The next phase of the rite alludes primarily to elder women's political, economic, and religious centrality and involves the presentation of prestige objects to the initiates. The objects convey ideas about the political and social influence of people and their families.

THE PRESENTATION OF WIDOW'S SHELL MONEY AND OTHER PRESTIGE ITEMS

The ceremony continued when two different types of shell-bead valuables were brought out and presented to the initiates. First, about 40 meters of blackish or dark brown shell money called *tili asap* ("the widow's shell money"), was brought out and waved before the girls. With the girls facing them, the two aunts placed the tili around their necks. As they made the presentation, they and the other women sang what is perhaps the most beautiful song of the ceremony, the song for the tili:

O tili a o tili a	The tili,
tili asap, wom ina	oh, mother, the
lom tili asapo o	widow's tili,
tili o asap.	widow's tili.

A red shell-bead valuable, the *tili lua,* was brought out next and waved before the young girls while the women sang:

Tili o tili a tili	Oh, mother, your red tili,
lua wom ina tili lua.	your tili lua.

The girls then were shown two necklaces made from cassowary feather quills, called *musmusu.* As the women sang, the two aunts swung the necklaces rhythmically against the girls' skirts and then placed one around each girl's neck.

Musmusu,	The musmusu, I decorate
rambole ino	myself with the finery of
pamgolgnong.	*rambole* [name of a mythical cassowary].

Dog's-teeth headbands (*ngilngil*) were brought out and placed around each girl's forehead, and they were given woven hemp baskets covered on one side with rows of dog's teeth. Then the aunts outfitted the pair with black tortoise-shell armbands.

At this point, the presentation of precious objects halted for a few minutes as one of the aunts painted the girls' faces with white pigment and their shoulders and backs with white marks called *gegeo.* In this instance, the gegeo serve as a symbol of privilege or rank. The aurang that accompanied this activity was as follows:

Anei ilo itar	She stays in her house
ama kainei	alone (she won't work,
anei.	she won't carry).
Oh, ilim sikonong	Oh, ilim sikonong [see
yo apu o	text] woman,
tarang ama	the garden will wait;
kainei anei.	she stays by herself.

The objects presented to the girls in this phase of the ritual are called *alul,* a word I translate as "heirloom." Alul are the prize possessions of family groups. The oldest and most valuable of these objects are individually named, and these names and the general history are known by most of the elders of southwestern New Britain. Alul are said to represent the history of the ancestors of specific kin groups and are referred to as the "memory of the visage or eye of the ancestors"; in a sense, therefore, they symbolize the social history and identity of their owners' groups. Perhaps because of this, they are said to be also the "backbone" or "strength" of a family group or ramage, a metaphor alluding to the economic and political power they symbolize as well as their political and economic uses.

Valuables like those presented in the puberty ceremony are usually the most important items offered in a bride-price.[6] A mere 2 meters from a famous black shell-bead necklace is said to be enough to "sever" a bride from her natal group; 2 meters of a famous white shell-bead valuable is enough to buy the services of a sorcerer. In the past, they were usually the possessions of prominent men and a few prominent women. Their use in the puberty ceremony formally marks the right of the initiates, who are being prepared for the status of big women, to possess them. Thereby, the initiates are advantaged because they are now entitled to use valuables not only for decoration but also for their own political and economic purposes. Later in their lives, for example, they may contribute some of these items to the bride-price of their sons. I have also heard accounts of big women using high-ranking valuables to buy the services of sorcerers. Because of these advantages, most of the puberty songs about the alul convey the idea that the initiates strongly desire them. The songs for the red and black shell-bead valuables, for example, are meant to conjure an image of

6. Women receive the major portion of the bride-price which is offered for their daughters, but they must redistribute much of this to members of their own cognatic descent group.

a young woman looking with anticipation and delight at her aunt's valuables. Equally important, when the initiates are presented with valuables such as the tili asap, they formally exhibit the wealth of their ramage and family, and thus reassert the identity and power of their group. Thus, through the possession and wearing of alul, big women become guardians and "exemplars" of the social, indeed the mythic identity of groups.

In addition to its other referents, one of the songs that accompanies the presentation of shell valuables also alludes to the traditional expectation that, at a later date, the initiate would become an *ilim sikonong,* a "secluded" or "sleeping woman." In traditional times, when a father considered his daughter marriageable, he had her secluded in a special house that she was not allowed to leave during daylight. She did neither garden nor domestic work, and her food was prepared and brought by a number of female attendants, who also provided her with firewood. When she went to her toilet, these attendants shielded her with a pandanus mat "coat" from the view of men.

An ilim sikonong was almost invariably the first daughter of a big man. Her seclusion signaled that her father now would entertain offers of a suitable bride-price. He and his family would sponsor a round of song festivals, to which suitors from other hamlet groups would come and sing the warrior's chant on a dancing ground or plaza cleared next to the girl's house. The young men would sing from sundown to sunrise, trying to entice the young woman out of her house with their singing. If she emerged, it was thought that she wished to elope with one of the singers. Usually, however, her seclusion did not end until a match had been arranged, when another series of song festivals and a large pig slaughter followed, culminating with her being taken to her new husband's hamlet. The expense of honoring one's daughter as an ilim sikonong was considerable and was more easily met by prominent families. Hence, like the puberty ritual, the practice was a marker of social rank.[7]

The path to ceremonial renown being predicated on access to shell valuables, prominent families were advantaged. This is not to say that ordinary people could not attain renown. Through the production and exchange of taro and pork, the manufacture and sale of desired objects such as bark cloth, the acquisition of magical lore, and perhaps the cultivation of a reputation as a sorcerer, they could begin to acquire alul as well as lower-ranking types of valuables. It is important to note, however, that because of the importance of women and women's ritual in Rauto society, the acquisition of the valuables displayed by women during ceremonial events is still an essential part of the

7. Arranged marriage also was and is a marker of social rank.

successful attainment of high status.[8] I would suggest that it is because women are associated with ideals of cultural and moral life that during important ritual events they serve to exemplify the developing renown of family groups.

The religious significance of this phase of the rite is somewhat more profound or fuller than this however. The songs and the presentation of alul highlight the sacred character of the relationship that links the identity of the Rauto *female* person to important cultural objects. Also, Rauto adult women express and construct an ideal of personhood in presenting the girls with the objects of initiation. As elders sing the names of these objects and present them to initiates, they reveal that the character of the person's nature is contained within a series of "participations" or spiritual relationships. In fact, as some of the objects of initiation can be said to memorialize the identities of past owners, when the initiates have them placed on their persons, their own identities participate in and are augmented by ancestral identities. This is why the sight of the bedecked initiates often allows elders to remember those who performed the rites of initiation for them, and to weep because of the poignancy of these memories. The image of the young initiate becomes for an instant an image of the ancestress—it becomes the face of the dead. During the rite the initiates enter the spatio-temporal domain of the ancestors; simultaneously, they remain in their own time and space and live the moment of their initiation when the elder women who sing the aurang transfer the spiritual power of their song and the material, political power of their objects to them.

The senior women are the subject of this rite; the initiates are the rite's object. The initiates seem transformed by the presentations of the rite into objectifications of the memories of the senior women and into the central objects of the seniors' nostalgic emotions. Only through the memories and feelings of the senior women can the initiates enter the sociomythic domain of the ancestors and thereby take on an augmented social or a sociomythic identity.

The more rounded or full mythic significance of the presentation of the alul is conveyed by one of the central myths of this culture, one that credits women with the production of one of the highest ranking alul: the curved pig's-tusk ornament that the Rauto call the *paidela*. I will discuss the conclusion of this myth after describing the presentation of the paidela. A more extensive analysis of the myth appears in this book's conclusion.

8. Another elaborate ceremony is performed when a firstborn daughter is brought by her parents to the place of her mother's consanguinal kin. As in the rite of female initiation, during the ceremony the girl is bedecked with finery and with "woman's wealth." The daughter of a big man is also bedecked with these items when she is brought to the hamlet of her husband just prior to the exchange of her bride-price.

PRESENTATION OF THE PAIDELA

In the final presentation of the puberty ceremony, each aunt placed the curved pig's-tusk ornament, the paidela, around the neck of one of the girls, raised it to the girl's mouth, and then shifted the ornament to the girl's back. Next, they rhythmically twisted the torso of each girl as they sang the aurang for this object:

Paidela pane	Bring the tusks to your
ya gronso mo	mouth; hold them at
augopme.	their base.
Ya gronso mo	Hold the tusks;
lepesme.	they curve sharply.

Afterwards, the aunts instructed the girls in the names of each of the different parts of the ornament.

The obvious significance of these acts lies in the dual meanings that paidela carry in Rauto culture. On the one hand, to wear paidela is to express anger. Thus, during a song festival or prior to a spear fight, men will challenge each other by putting the paidela to their mouths while brandishing their spears. Likewise, big women don paidela during several ceremonies in which women express anger towards men by chasing them with sticks or spitting chewed betel at them: the ceremony of "routing the men" after the birth of a child, the ritual honoring of children, and the ceremonial passage of a new bride to a distant hamlet.

On the other hand, paidela also symbolize a more constructive aspect of self. Both women and men may produce paidela, but the task is onerous. The valued male pigs with the curved tusks from which paidela are made must be fed and looked after for six to ten years. Difficult ritual work is also involved, for a cycle of special song magic must be performed to hasten the growth of the boars and their tusks. Thus, the paidela reflect people's abilities both to raise and transact with pigs and to sponsor important ceremonial events, which in turn testifies to their ability to form networks of debt and obligation.

In the Rauto view, then, paidela symbolize both the aggressive antisocial aspect of the self as well as its socially constructive network-building capacities. The ritual presentation of paidela during the puberty ceremony is a sign that initiates are acquiring both a personal right and a social duty to cultivate these two aspects of self. Thus, women (at least those who are initiated) are ritually accorded the right to act aggressively, but at the same time an allusion is made to their role as caretakers and producers of pigs, and thus to their role as important transactors of wealth and forgers of social networks. The myth of the origin of the paidela imparts a religious significance to this role. This lengthy story tells of a mother's magical power and of the way she uses it to secure a bride for each of her two sons.

The opening scene recounts how a prominent big man has announced that his daughters are to be offered in marriage to the most worthy suitor that can be found. The great man devises a contest for these suitors; they must scale the giant Tahitian chestnut tree that grows in his hamlet, and then they must harvest it. All fail the challenge save the two boys. Their mother enables them to scale the tree by using her magic to make a nearby areca nut tree grow and extend all the way to the canopy of the great chestnut; the boys then use the areca tree as a bridge to the chestnut. After this task is accomplished, however, the other suitors complain that the boys are simply "rubbish men" who are unable to offer a sufficient bride-price to the great man's family. The boys' mother then takes a squealing piglet from her coconut-frond basket and throws it to the ground, where it promptly transforms itself into a giant tusked pig, a pig with paidela. She does this nine more times in order to amass a great bride-price for her sons.

As the mother produced the boys physically by giving birth to them, so now in the conclusion of this myth she gives birth to their social identity by producing the needed objects of wealth. This particular mythic image provides a stronger statement of woman's relationship to the political and economic centers of Rauto culture than do the songs and activities of the puberty rite. It appears to suggest that women are in a sense the actual producers of the objects that are such valued symbols of male political and economic identity, a point to which I return in this chapter's conclusion.

THE CONCLUSION OF THE WOMEN'S PUBERTY RITUAL

After the presentation of the paidela, the two girls were taken down to the shore and a few steps out onto the reef. Here, their aunts handed them some pronged fishing spears and bade them make a few casts. The implicit message was that young women should spend some of their time fishing and combing the reefs for food for themselves and their families. The two girls also were shown how to bathe away their menstrual blood and how to adjust their fiber skirts if they wished to urinate or defecate. The aunts then made the only *direct* reference to either a woman's sexuality or reproductive capacity that I observed, telling the girls the Rauto words for *vagina* and *breast,* and informing them that after giving birth, they should feed their child with the milk from their breasts. (Nothing was said about the care of menstrual blood or the function of the vagina.)

An initiate being taught the care of her menstrual blood.

The women then formed a procession back to the village, where the aunts conducted the girls around the ceremonial house, naming its external sections. At the entrance to the house, the other women threw down several pandanus mats, while others placed mats over the heads of the girls, shielding them from the view of onlookers as they entered the house. Once inside, the aunts instructed their charges in the names of the inner sections of the structure. This instruction is another example of the privileged status of female initiates, representing one of several claims that prominent women make on the ritual and religious knowledge possessed by big men. Indeed, their "possession" of the ceremonial house for the entire course of the ritual is also a symbolic statement that their ritual activities deserve as important and as central a stage as the ritual activities of men.

CONCLUDING REMARKS ON THE PUBERTY RITE

Geertz has written that religious traditions find their most forceful and dramatic expression during the performance of ritual (1973:113–18). In his view, ritual manages to dramatize and thus empower religious belief by "setting before the eyes" the sense and meaning that a way of life has for a people and by powerfully evoking their moral and aesthetic "feel" for this way of life. In the setting of ritual, ethos is experienced more intensely, and a people's world view is pictured more vividly and completely than in the activities of everyday life. On the one hand, ritual points "beyond the realities of everyday life to wider ones which correct and complete them" (Geertz 1973:42). On the other hand, however, it directs the participants' attention back to the world, enabling them to view it with more profound understanding by revealing the ontology on which their views of the world are based. Among other things then, ritual in Geertz's view is a form of heightened discourse about the world that sanctifies the perceived character of the world by relating this perception to a culturally specific ontology or metaphysic.

We can perceive here how the classic understanding of art as heightened imitation of experience has influenced Geertz's theory of cultural representation. There especially appears to be a relationship between the visual character of Geertz's theory and of the ideas of purification and of heightening that inform classical theories of representation. That is, in Geertz's view ritual appears to complete experience not only by rendering it emotionally comprehensible but by allowing one to view all of its most significant or thematic contours as these are acted out, as it were. But what of *la pensée obscure et confuse* of mythic experience, the allusive and evanescent thoughts, meanings, and countermeanings that may enable us to see further and deeper into the nature of experience by representing it as something more than meets the eye.

The puberty rite does create and valorize a picture of the everyday world by celebrating some of the Rauto world's most common objects and activities in song. But this picture is only the obvious meaning of the rite and of the simple song images that accompany the presentation of objects to the initiates. It is really the more evanescent and obscure meanings and countermeanings of the rite that express something of the ontology and the aesthetic on which Rauto concepts of person and gender are based. This ontology suggests that the world view and the ethos that are given expression by the simple acts and images of the puberty rite are understatements of the extent to which women are associated with creative power of various sorts. It is in the rite's counternarrative, in its elusive and allusive meaning, that we come to understand something of the nature of female personhood.

The picture of the world and of a big woman evoked during the rite is composed of elements and objects that the Rauto associate with both men and women. Thus, during the course of the ritual, we see big women invested with symbols that demonstrate their access to big men's power over special valuables and exchange activities, as well as their access to woman's power over garden production and the reproduction of people. The point to stress is that a big woman's access to both male and female forms of power does not make her an anomalous figure in Rauto society. Rather it is precisely because she possesses both forms of power that she is perceived to embody an ideal of female social identity.

The more rounded mythic images and meanings associated with the objects of the rite suggest, however, that women represent an ideal of human rather than simply female identity. We see this assertion first in the mythic insight that men stole their political power from women and that their political and cultural primacy is therefore derivative and rightfully woman's possession. Perhaps the most subversive or carnivalesque suggestion of the myths associated with the objects and acts of the rite is that there is neither a specifically male nor female gender identity. The myths tell of how women took their sex, their menstruation, and the objects that signify female identity from men. They also tell of how men took their objects of power and their influence from women. Neither possessed a natural gender identity; both simply possessed a mythic identity. As Leenhardt well knew, there are no absolute boundaries or categories, such as male and female, in the domain of mythic experience. There are simply juxtaposed emotions and forms of being.

These mythic insights are noteworthy because in other realms of Rauto ritual life, men have to acquire and demonstrate some of the mythic attributes and powers associated with women. This is seen, most especially, during the performance of song magic for the taro gardens, known as *tarang*. As I show in the following chapter, these rituals have profound political and economic meaning for Rauto society. During their performance, garden magicians (*sanger ino*) express their political and economic leadership (male powers and abilities) as well as their control over forces that the Rauto perceive maintain life and promote growth and health (female powers and abilities). In the rites, the garden magician constructs a large effigy of the taro plant. This is made from a number of special magical plants, many of them the same plants used to make the skirts given to girls during their puberty rite, and it is even given its own banana-leaf skirt. The figure thus represents the productive powers of women. What is significant, however, is that the magician symbolically embodies his magical power in the effigy by naming it after the system of magical knowledge and song he controls. In other words, in possessing and performing this system of magic, the magician realizes an ideal of social identity by showing that he has powers and skills of production at his command that are usually associated with women. What the magician does during the rite, then, is really to blur the distinction between male and female personhood and thereby represent a participation or comingling of male and female forms of power.

The fact that the concept of the person and the views of the world evoked in garden ritual and in the female puberty rite are composed of both male and female symbolic elements demonstrates that the ritual activities of men and women, in this particular society at least, evoke models of the person and the world that are not antithetical, as the work of others might lead us to conclude (see Ardener 1972; Ortner 1974). Neither can these models, as they are evoked during the female puberty ritual, be considered pale reflections of the models presented in male ritual activity. Rather, Rauto ritual and mythic life demonstrates that a particular view of the world and of the person acquires a compelling meaning when male and female symbolic elements, categories, and powers are brought into a complementary relationship. It is not so much the case, then, that Rauto women's "powers are considered innate and natural, while men's power is associated with the practice of 'culture' "—that is, ceremony and ritual (M. Strathern 1980:21). Rather, in defining ideals of personhood through ritual activity, the Rauto express the notion that "neither sex can possibly stand for humanity as against 'nature' " (1980:212). Thus, rather than "defining" woman by demonstrating the way that her nature differs from man's, the female puberty ritual conflates male and female realms and thus indicates that the Rauto ideal of humanity is represented by an amalgam of male and female powers.

Equally important, the rite reveals the sacred character that the concept of the person has for the Rauto. An aspect of this character is contained in the relationship—underscored by the ritual—between the person and important objects of both the natural and the cultural world. In presenting initiates with these objects, and by singing them their names, female song leaders forge a series of participations, or sacred relationships. For instance, since some of the objects stand as tokens for people of both past and present generations, when the initiates have them placed on their persons they participate in the identities of these others. Moreover, as the presented objects and their names constitute an aspect of tradition and of memory, their possession by the initiates signals the incorporation of a concept of cultural memory into the very structure of their social identity. Of course, the presentation of foods, plants, and finery to the initiates also underscores the series of participations or relationships between person and world. For the Rauto, the locus of the sacred is contained within these manifold participations, as well as within the instrument of their creation: the human voice.

Chapter Five

Participation and Individuation in the Rites of Production

The person manifests the relationship between these two elements; it affirms itself between these two poles, that of individuation and that of the human reality where participations originate. It is this communal relationship itself, temporalized and individuated, and it holds in itself the union of these two elements, individuation and communion.

Maurice Leenhardt (1979)

Miru pe oduk ogo	*We gaze at their large*
nadiko tarang la ko	*garden; it appears*
amtami la kesine lang	*to our eyes as does the*
malang	*flat and vast surface of*
	the open sea.

Rauto proverb

Most ethnographers who have carried out fieldwork in rural Melanesia know how important garden work and ritual are to the life of the Melanesian. They have witnessed how major portions of each day are spent either working or socializing in gardens. They have observed how much of village ceremonial life is centered on the production and the distribution of the garden crop. A long line of ethnographers beginning with Malinowski have attested to the rich symbolism that is attached to the activity of gardening. They have shown how the Melanesian garden is often a potent metaphor for central concerns and concepts of existence. If, as is often said, Melanesians "live on the ground"— meaning that they are concerned with practical matters such as gardens and production—the ground that they live and work on, most especially garden land, has an aesthetic and emotional resonance which thinkers as diverse in general outlook as Malinowski and Leenhardt could not help but notice.

Perhaps more than any other spot on the Melanesian landscape, the garden

140

symbolizes the meeting point of human will and natural process. It is a spot where people invest their energy, power, and being in an attempt to forge a relationship between themselves and nature. In this relationship they do not try to dominate nature; they try to coax it, to make it more amenable to their own plans and purposes, to enlist it in their cause.

In Rauto productive life the setting up of this relationship with nature is, as well, a celebration of the aesthetic of space and of the nature of the person. The activities and songs of Rauto productive life create a "lived space" by forging a participatory relationship with the land. This represents as important an experience of personal enrichment and of social intensification as does the investment of personal power in the lives of young men and women during initiation rituals. As we shall see, the more obvious symbolism for gardening ritual is modeled in part on the symbolism for children's rituals. As in initiation rites for children, in garden ritual men father and women mother certain nascent potentialities of themselves and of the objects of their activities. They invest in the garden and its crops some of the same symbols of growth, power, and being that they invest in children during initiation. In the process they create a meaning about themselves and about the space in which they live and work. They create an aesthetic of place and a philosophy of person.

Speech and song create an "experiential landscape" for the Rauto by bringing the person into relationship with others, with space, and "with processes of the natural world" (Clifford 1982:210). Speech and song are, among other things, both the aesthetic experience of participation, and the means to create that experience. Yet, such statements actually say little about what can be called the emotional dimensions of the experience of participation. As in the New Caledonia of Leenhardt's day, the emotional experience evoked by moments of participation has a dual aspect. For instance, as we have just seen in our discussion of the female puberty rite, the initiate attains an aspect of identity when she becomes part of the dual entity that can be called the aunt-niece pair. During the rite, she seems to be the domain of her aunt's memories and, reciprocally, her aunt seems to be an image of what the initiate will become; each becomes the other's habitat (see Leenhardt 1979:102–6); each finds something of herself in the other.

We encounter the experience of *le duel* in many of the aspects of Rauto rites of production. The most obvious of these is seen in the symmetry represented by the two magical effigies of productive ritual, the rain and taro effigies. The taro effigy seems to be an image of the great mother; she is the mother of the garden. She dispenses nourishment to her children the taro corms and, by extension, to Rauto men and women, by suffusing the garden with her magic. In one of the aurang of productive rite this magic is even called *mother's milk*.

The rain effigy and the rites of rain making have a seemingly masculine character. As we will see, this effigy seems to be a great man, powerful, dangerous and, like a great or "big" Melanesian man, possessed of powers that are not always put to positive uses. He seems to be the objectification of the dangerous power of the rain sorcerer, of the magician. Like a powerful Rauto sorcerer or big man he is bedecked with all the traditional objects of power: the paidela, the cassowary tibia weapon called *padingo,* the *mokmok* stones. The forms of magic that are contained by the two effigies are also complementary, part of a pair; there is the magic and nurturance of the earth, as provided by the taro effigy, and there is the fructifying and sustaining power of the rain, as contained and captured by the rain effigy. These parities become parts of an ensemble when we consider the part the magician plays in the rites.

The magician seems to be the effigies' child as he calls on them to provide sustenance to him and to his kin. It is this aspect of the rite that causes the magician to feel the nostalgia of remembrance for his own lost kin. The effigies evoke his and other ritual participants' feelings of loss for those who had nourished and supported them in the past—most especially lost parents and grandparents. Simultaneously, the magician and other ritual participants appear to see and feel something of themselves in both the male and female effigies. Their power is invested in these objects, is contained by them. Such power is orchestrated by the head magician, however. In invoking the power of the objects, he makes a claim to be both father and mother of the garden, of his kin, and of all other ritual participants. As he sings, he appears simultaneously as mother, father, and child to these others.

As we will see, the simple naturalistic imagery of the aurang that accompany these rites is the straightforward confirmation of these thoughts. The images of the songs draw some of their emotional power from the archaic or primary experience of receiving nurturance from one's mother and from feeling the physical power of one's father. If we simply viewed these ideas as constituting the full significance of these rites, there would be no reason, save the ethnographer's duty of description, to discuss the rituals. What is important about the rites is that they, like the female puberty rite, show how participation and individuation are a parity, complementary aspects of the process of attaining identity.

One of the ways the rites accomplish this is by combining ancestor worship, or the honoring of ancestors, with what Leenhardt might have called "worship of the habitat." The rites sacralize and create a sociomythic space by incorporating the ancestral presence into the objects and spaces of the natural world. Again in Leenhardt's terms, the space in which these rites situate the person is as much cosmomorphic as anthropomorphic. The sung word and the ritual manipulations enable the person to blend in the same "flux of life" that inhabits the ancestors and the forces and objects of the natural world. At the same time, the songs and rites project human qualities and characteristics onto the domain of nature. In so doing, they reveal another aspect of the individuation process: this process "carries with it the possibility of the person recognizing in himself a plenitude" (Crapanzano 1979:xxv). In seeing the world as a part of himself, the person begins to individuate himself from it while remaining able to draw upon the power it contains. As we will see, this individuation, and this recognition of plenitude is painful, emotionally wrenching. It evokes memories of personal separation, of the loss of mothers and fathers. The taro and rain effigies are also the objectified memories of these lost others; they are these memories transformed into a plenitude of power and nurturance.

While providing a diffuse center or mythic domain for the person, the rites also celebrate the social dimension of *le duel*. As the rites bring together the maternal and paternal principles in the form of the taro and rain effigies, they also confirm the mythic significance of the relationship between matriline and patriline. The taro and rain-making rites are another continuation on the religious plane of the relationship of mutual regard and exchange of services that should ideally join the matrikin and patrikin of a person in common endeavor. Thus, the growth-promoting songs of the taro and rain sorcerer are usually uttered not only for the benefit of his own cognatic or resident group, but also for an invited group of his actual or classificatory nephews. Because of the norms of restricted exchange and cross-cousin marriage, these children of his sisters are also often his matrikin; they are the one-blood kin of an actual or classificatory mother. These nephews place themselves and their sustenance in the hands of their *atenme*, their mother's brother, and his group.

RITUAL AND WORK

The symbolism and character of Rauto rituals of production are shaped in part by a system of concepts about the nature of work and of person. These concepts are a central part of Rauto moral life. In garden ritual as in initiation ritual, they are expressed in relation to a system of aesthetics and of emotion. The garden, or rather certain types of gardens, called *tarang*, visually represent this relationship. The tarang symbolizes the realization of a moral and aesthetic ideal that is the highest end of physical labor.

A tarang is a large garden that is prepared cooperatively by several different family groups or ramages. The preparation of a tarang is a special event. Usually, a single residential group will work under the direction of a ramage group leader (*adepdep*, or *toro*), who will also almost invariably be a lead garden magician (*sanger ino*). Often a single nuclear family will work by itself to cut a garden in the rain forest. A tarang is a song garden; that is, it is the only type of garden that is prepared by the Rauto along with the singing of the entire corpus of magical songs called *aurang*. The great majority of the procedures of garden ritual are also performed most often only for a tarang. Much less ritual attention is given to smaller gardens. A constellation of ideas about the meaning of cooperative effort and of song magic informs this decision. The son of the major garden magician of Wasum put some of these matters into perspective for me after his father had told me the myth explaining the origins of the magical system of song that is used in taro production:

> Before men were given knowledge of taro magic by the culture hero (*oklo uate*) Tuktuk, they subsisted on bananas and yams and just a few taro. The magical system given to our ancestors enabled them to concentrate their efforts on taro production. It made them able to produce large gardens and to work together to do so. We work together now and eat following behind the lead of the garden magician (*sanger ino*); this is good. See how large and beautiful our gardens are.

As this passage and the Rauto proverb at the beginning of this chapter suggest, the sight of a large garden is extraordinarily impressive to the Rauto eye, and in more than an aesthetic sense; it is also impressive in a moral sense. It is an indication that groups have been able, at least temporarily, to put aside suspicion and factionalism in order to pool their resources of labor under the direction of a leading garden magician. Song magic (*aurang*) and large gardens called *tarang* thus imply and create or reaffirm relationships between groups, between person and space, and between person and what the Rauto refer to as the "children" of their gardens: taro. Small gardens prepared separately and without song magic symbolize fewer and less dramatic relationships. As in initiation ritual, aurang connotes participation in manifold relationships. In this way it marks a moral space between people.

The most spectacular products of aurang—strong young women and men, and flourishing large gardens—are the products of manifold relationships. These relationships, though spiritually established through aurang, are materially reinforced through the exchanges of labor, shells, and foodstuffs that accompany aurang. However, in Rauto thinking, as in our own, relationships can be overbearing and exploitative. It is partly for this reason that the preparation of tarang is an exceptional event. Rauto recognize that the performance of aurang can sometimes be as much an expression of the ambitions of leaders as an expression of an ideal of community.

THE EARLY STAGES OF GARDENING AND IDEAS ABOUT
THE LABOR OF MEN AND WOMEN

Work for the preparation of a tarang, and for the performance of the songs and rituals called *aurang* begins when a leading garden magician—accompanied by several young helpers—marks out a section of forest for cutting and preparation. As the sanger ino walks through the forest, he blows lime powder along the edges of the sections of bush that he has chosen for cutting. The lime serves as a marker by which his hamlet mates discern the area of forest that is to be cut.

The climate of rivalry and suspicion that informs intergroup relations and that can undermine some of the objectives of the performance of aurang is revealed by the first magical act of gardening ritual. The sanger ino's helpers seek out a variety of tree that the Rauto call *aku*. At the base of each aku tree that they come across, they dig two small holes. They spit a spray of ginger into one of the holes and blow a bit of lime powder into the other. It is said that the taro sorcery of rivals is most often performed at the base of the aku tree. The lime and ginger are thought to burn the sorcery from the ground. As an added precaution, the earth that has been excavated from the base of the aku tree is placed in a basket. It is then brought to a stream or, in coastal villages, down to the ocean, where the tide can carry it away and disperse the destructive power that it contains.

A few days after the performance of this initial cleansing rite, the sanger ino directs a number of the unmarried and widowed women of the ramage to go through sections of the bush and thin out some of the undergrowth. This may require a week or more of sustained labor. After the bush is initially thinned out by the groups of women, the ramage's married couples mark out and begin to prepare their own sections of the garden, performing a second cutting of the underbrush. The man of the couple then cuts down the trees that are left standing on his plot.

If a hamlet leader decides to perform aurang on a section of virgin bush, the procedure for clearing the forest can be much more involved and the work much more difficult. In this case all of the adult men of one or more residential groups combine their labor to perform the difficult task of cutting virgin timber. The cutting is one of the most dramatic moments of productive life. The Rauto have a myth that relates how a young woman met her death while cutting virgin forest. As people cut the forest, they sing the genre of mourning song, called *akailes,* that is associated with this myth. They sing to the death of this woman of the forest and to the death of the many generations that have existed during the lifetime of the forest. Men and women sing out of sorrow and remembrance of the past, yet they sing as well for the possibilities of the present—possibilities that are being prepared by their combined efforts. As men and women sing the akailes together, they begin together to carve a garden out of the rainforest. Their combined labor prepares a home for their taro, a plant that Rauto men and women sometimes refer to as a child.

The trees and cut bush are left to dry for a number of weeks, or perhaps months. When they have dried out sufficiently, the sanger ino orders the gardens to be fired. As women work to place the burning vines, leaves, and tree branches into small piles, men use their axes to split and section off the middles of the tree trunks that lie scattered about the garden site. The tree sections serve as markers for the separate garden plots.

GARDENS AND PEOPLE

The Rauto garden and the forms of social action that take place in it embody a number of conflicting ideas and values. The garden is a place where Melanesian ideals of openness and hospitality often clash with fears of personal and social vulnerability.

Gardens are for the most part places of escape for the Rauto. Preparing a garden separately, away from the site of the main garden of one's descent group, guarantees a degree of protection from the view of hamlet or village mates. In such places food can be harvested and prepared secretly and thus need not be shared with others; one can escape for a while the social demands, concerns, and frequent animosity of village or hamlet life. The garden is a place where one can put a degree of physical and emotional distance between oneself and others without resorting to an outright declaration of animosity. I observed that this was one of the major reasons that people spent such inordinate amounts of time in their gardens.[1] (See Jorgensen 1988 for a similar discussion of the significance of Telefol gardens.)

Gardens are also places that actually mark the physical and emotional distance that exists between different residential groups or ramages. People belonging to different residential groups generally avoid visiting each other's garden sites for fear of being accused of working taro sorcery on them. These beliefs about taro sorcery are part and parcel of the general status rivalry that usually marks the relationship between different yet proximate kinship groups in Aroue. As the attractiveness and strength of children are a point of pride for families and are the subject of much ritual attention, so is the health and

---

1. Joel Robbins (1988) provides a perceptive discussion of why Melanesian gardens sometimes symbolize people's deep desire to "keep to themselves."

abundance of a group's taro crop; thus, one of the most effective ways to detract from the reputation of a group is to damage its gardens. Headmen usually spearhead intergroup rivalries, including those of productive life. They are especially feared as taro sorcerers by those who do not belong to the factions that they lead.[2] They are the individuals who are most often accused of working taro sorcery.

These traditional concerns are emphasized all the more by the preparation for the performance of an aurang. One person told me that the aurang could serve as an excellent way for a headman to gain access to the gardens of a rival group and there to sorcerize them.[3] Such thoughts brought into focus for me the fact that Rauto gardens are places where life as it is actually lived confronts powerfully articulated and strongly held ideals about how life should be led. It is a place where intense feelings of relationship between people and between person and land are contrasted with the social and emotional distance that results from distrust and feelings of vulnerability.

In many ways the aurang that are sometimes performed for taro production transcend the oppositions I have been speaking of here by transforming them into the social and religious experience of symmetry, of *le duel*. An aspect of this experience proceeds simply from the fact of two or more groups combining their labor and song to prepare a fertile space for their taro children. The sanger ino Kienget performed the rites that I will describe here for the many children and grandchildren of his three sisters, as well as for his own son and grandchildren. One of these groups of nephews was also classified as Kienget's mother's patrikin.

THE ARRANGEMENT FOR TARO EXCHANGE

Before aurang can be performed, the headman who conducts the ritual must arrange for the ceremonial gifts of taro that accompany the planting phase of the rite. The sanger ino asks one or as many as three or four other headmen if their groups are willing to participate in the ritual and to engage in taro exchange. If the offer or offers are accepted, the sanger ino requests that each family of his group donate a portion of their taro harvest to a family of the visiting group. The visiting family will then do a good deal of the labor of taro

2. Even those belonging to the sanger ino's faction sometimes fear his taro sorcery. This is especially true for those who are not close kin of the sanger ino and have entered into disagreement with him.

3. One of the groups which was supposed to participate in the aurang which I saw in March, 1986, declined at the last moment to take part in the ritual because they feared that their taro would be corcerized by the sanger ino.

planting for the group that has offered them taro. They will also be expected to pay back the gift that is offered to them. If the group that receives the gift lives near the host group they will almost certainly bring some of their taro along to be planted. Thus, they place some of their taro under the ritual care of the sanger ino who sponsors and performs the aurang. Also, if several groups have combined their labor to cut a section of bush, they will almost certainly make their gardens together, and thus place their taro under the care and protection of the sanger ino. During my stay with the Rauto, this had occurred once at the beginning of my field work. A subsequent poor harvest of taro had then led to sorcery accusations being leveled against the head garden magician. After these accusations, the groups involved again made their gardens separately.

Before the exchange the group that provides the gift of taro will stand a series of sticks in the ground. The sticks will be placed in a straight line at intervals of from three to four feet and will usually not stand more than three or four feet high. Harvested taro that represents the actual contribution of separate family groups is heaped carefully between every two sticks. When the heaping of the taro is complete, usually a day or two before the performance of the aurang for the gardens, the song and dance ceremony called the *agreske* will be held. Men and women will dance the *agreske* and the *augosang* in the presence of the harvested taro in order to "honor" it and to acknowledge the importance of the gift that is about to be given.

CONSTRUCTION OF THE TARO EFFIGY

Two days before the aurang is performed, the sanger ino disappears into the forest with his helpers to collect the necessary magical plants and substances that will be used during the rite. The gathering lasts for a full day, as each of the plots of the tarang must be afforded a separate bundle of magical materials. The plants that compose the magical bundles are the basic plants of Rauto ritual and religious life: ginger, coleus, lemon grass, lemon basil, wild banana leaves, and ginger species. Their appearance in the taro ritual is but a first indication of the analogy that the ritual presents with female initiation.

This first impression is confirmed by a subsequent act: the fashioning of a large effigy of the taro plant itself out of some of the materials gathered for the magical bundles. The effigy, which stands about five feet high, is also fashioned from a number of plants and flowers that young women especially use as personal finery. It also contains within itself almost all of the plants and flowers that are used to construct the special skirts that are presented to young women during female initiation. The effigy is even provided with its own banana- and croton-leaf skirt, which is made of the same red- and yellow-streaked banana and croton leaves used to make the adult dress of female initiates. The effigy is, in effect, "the woman" of the garden; that is, it represents, in a rather straight-forward way, the productive powers and abilities associated with women.

The effigy is placed in a small wooden box (*lungio*) that is especially con-structed for it, and it sits enthroned on the edge of the garden until the com-mencement of the ritual proper. All around it are the magical bundles that will be used by the sanger ino the next day.

THE FIRST SERIES OF AURANG

On the morning of the aurang, the men and women of the visiting ramages greet their hosts, and the women of the visiting groups then walk toward the heaps of harvested taro. Each woman separates the taro offered to her from its stalk and puts it in a large food basket, placing the stalks on top of the taro corms. The first act of the aurang then takes place. Two small trees of a variety that the Rauto call *sengaseng* are placed on either side of the entrance to one of the paths leading into the garden, and their tops are lashed together to form an arch. The entrance to the garden is now called its "door" (*ino somta*), and the garden becomes, symbolically, a house. The garden's door is then charmed by the sanger ino as he lets fly a spray of ginger, areca nut, and saliva from his mouth. The arches of the door are then said to present a barrier to any taro sorcery that might adhere to the stalks of taro that are now carried through the door. The women carry the taro stalks through the garden door as they sing the special song for the door.

The stalks are carried to the center of the garden, where the sanger ino and his helpers paint the bottom of each stalk with a mixture of red ocher (mag-nesium oxide), the sap of the areca plant, lemon basil, various ginger species, and a variety of wild banana. As the magician works, he and all the other men and women present sing the various aurang for the painting of the taro stalks and for the preparation of the various herbs:

Awore a wo amote a iamote a e ao.	Let us paint the taro, let us paint the taro.
Pongponge a, wo pongponge a.	Let us paint these enormous stalks of taro.
Le urtong a lele urtong a le le urtong a lele urtong a le uo.	We prepare the basin [to hold the blood of the areca] We wring the areca.

Lugu isin	My taro *akate*
akate na	and its shoots.
evine a wo. Evine	The shoots of my taro.
pe oo ua lugu	My taro *auring*
isin auring na evine.	and its shoots.
Amoli ko mai kupo	We wring the
wo amoli ko mai	blood of the areca
kupo.	palm [and bathe our taro].

Amoli ko mai repo	We place the blood of the
wo amoli amol	areca in the areca bark
kol mai repo.	bowl [and bathe our taro].

Ina risngong a.	My mother bathes me.
Ivo risngong a.	My father bathes me.
Ina risngong a.	My mother bathes me.

The symbolism of this phase of the ritual is clarified by the songs that are sung during it. In the words of one of these songs the sanger ino, his helpers, and indeed all the men and women who take part in the rite are called the fathers and mothers of the taro. Their songs and ritual activities are understood to represent some of the same concern and care that people show for their human children. Specifically, the ritual manipulations and especially the "bathing," or painting, of the taro stalks are thought to bring protection to the taro from the sorcery of others. In the last song of the sequence, the taro stalks are heard to answer the songs and activities of their mothers and fathers by noting how they are being bathed and cared for. Several men and women told me that it was important that the taro felt itself to be well looked after, else the corms might decide at some point "to leave the house of their parents." If this should come to pass (i.e., if there is a poor taro harvest), the sanger ino must try to call his taro children back to their home. He does so with a song that is sung just prior to planting:

Wo la mare	I call to you
siasa ka ko wuwu	[you are gone]. You
lo mare.	must rise and come.

Ouie, isin nukrus la	Alas, the taro is finished.
ngado la mare	I call to it, my debt [to
ngado ouloul lo mare.	other ramages must be
	repaid].

Asokol me	The ember of my fire come,

iau me	the smoke of my fire come,
lugu wiling me	my fighting spear come,
lugu isin me	my taro come.

The song refers to the sadness and anxiety felt by the sanger ino after a poor harvest. The performance of the aurang for planting provides an opportunity for the magician to plead with his taro children to return and thus remind them of the many debts that he and his ramage must repay with taro. The last stanza of the song is a moving statement of the relationship between person and taro. In this stanza some of the most sacred symbols of Rauto culture are mentioned: fire, smoke, and the fighting spear. Fire and smoke are symbols of the hearth, of human habitation, of women, commensality, and conviviality. The fighting spear represents, among other things, the strength needed to protect and perpetuate these values. The song identifies taro with these sacred symbols. Indeed, it expresses the notion that taro is as important as these things and that its existence is inseparable from the existence of the person. The aurang also represents an invitation to the taro of other ramages to leave its own garden and find a new home. It is thus itself also a bit of taro sorcery.

THE AURANG FOR THE TARO EFFIGY

At the conclusion of the painting of the taro stalks, the women gather them together and carry them to the appropriate plots for planting. They then return to the edge of the garden to the site of the taro effigy and wait for the sanger ino, who now walks to each of the garden's plots and places a magically charmed green coconut in a hole near the center of each plot. He then implores the garden to drink of the coconut milk and to provide the taro with more of the liquid as it grows. As he and his helpers finish these minor rites, he signals to the participants to begin the aurang for the taro effigy. The singing commences as he begins to walk toward the effigy, and it is meant to represent the voice of the effigy itself:

Ale more o alu more;	You must come and paint
ale more salamit	me; I must go to the
tarang	tarang;
ale more o ale more,	now, you must
ale more, e woronge.	paint my visage.
Ale more o ale more	You must paint my
ale more.	finery and my banana
O koke nel aumo	leaf skirt. I call to

a la mare   you to come (drink at
o koke nel aumo.   the breast of this
                                             flower).

The sanger ino approaches the effigy and begins to paint it with red ocher.
As he does so, he instructs those who have not seen the ritual before in the
names of the various plants from which the effigy is made. He also informs
them that the effigy has a name, which is sometimes used to refer to the entire
system of taro magic possessed by the garden magician. After the painting of
the effigy, all those who have not seen the ritual performed previously are also
painted with a streak of red ocher.

My informants told me that the figure was the "mother's milk" of taro; indeed, the sap of the varied plants of the figure was actually called "mother's
milk." I was also told that the figure was the "mother" of the taro; in the aurang
the figure calls to its children to come and drink at its breast. The point that is
made here is that the magic of the sanger ino is the sustenance of the taro plant.
Through his magic, he participates in the productive principles and powers that
are most especially associated with women. The taro figure, the embodiment
of the sanger ino's magic, mediates the relationship between person and taro.
In creating this figure, the sanger ino establishes a relationship between person and taro that is modeled on the relationship between mother and child.
The ritual humanization of taro during aurang brings it and nature itself into a
relationship of reciprocity and of affection with people.

THE PLANTING OF THE TARO FIGURE

The effigy and the bundles of magical ingredients that are arranged before it
are then charmed by the garden magician, who may speak as follows:

Kambombo, kambombo   Rise up;
Suwil kambombo,   the river Suwil rise up,
Pulie kambombo,   the river Pulie rise up,
Anu kambombo   the river Anu rise up,
Alinpit kambombo   the river Alinpit rise up,
wun alinpit mukap   the river Alinpit, you,
Anu, mukap mukambombo   and the river Anu rise up
wunie nado isin,   with my taro as the
uri ino la tir,   spring flows upward.
pe oro la ko la   Taro rise in my garden.
ko la ko.   It rises in the garden
La tir pe oro la   as does the fount of a
langono uri ino amta.   spring. The taro *enga*

Eenga pipse	rise, taro rise.
isin pipse	The taro *auring* rise;
Auring pipse	the leaves of the taro
Songom gua, lo uoman	sit (majestically). The
isin tengen ngat.	tuber breaks the ground.
	The taro rises as does
	the sago palm.

The spell's symbolism is itself an expression of Rauto concepts of growth, generation, and health. Time and again in ritual life the symbol of water or of effervescent and fragrant liquid, such as the sap of various ginger species, is invoked and used to promote health and growth. In this particular spell the sanger ino's magical power seems metaphorically akin to the power of these elements. Indeed, the spell makes implicit reference to the magician's control over these elements—elements that constitute part of the taro effigy and whose power is embodied by the effigy. Yet, *its* qualities, characteristics, and potential for promoting growth remain inert until men and women call it, the magical bundles, and the taro of the garden to existence through song and spell.

A number of other objects are also called into existence or consecrated during this phase of the rite. For instance a song is performed for the taro effigy's box, or rather more accurately, its throne. Another is performed for the purple and yellow wild banana leaf (*amoi ari*); the song celebrates and coos over the plant's beautiful spotted purple colors, almost as a mother would coo over a beautiful child. Another song is performed to celebrate and animate the powers of the areca-bark bowl that held the charmed magical waters (areca sap, green coconut water, lemon basil) that Rauto women wash their taro-cutting kina shells in. The waters are thought to rid the taro stalks of any harmful sorcery that may have been performed upon them. The power of the taro planting stick is also celebrated and animated through song, as is the magical effervescence of the lemon basil. Also celebrated and consecrated by song are the sticks that divide each person's taro patch from that of another, and also those where the taro corms were placed before the corms were given to the visiting groups of matrikin. As we can see, all these songs simply recite the names of the objects that are being celebrated.

Oulingse uore	The planting stick;
uo oulinse uore	see it work, see it turn
a oure la eiga o.	the earth.
Uo omoi ari	The beautiful colors of
ia omo o omoi ari,	the wild banana leaf, and of
Uo damlo	the coleus.

iamo iamo iamo amoi ari a keskeso iamo a keskeso.	See the colors of the wild bananas.
Urtong a lei le urtonga; urtong a le le uronga.	We wash our kina shells in the areca-bark basket.
Oo ia oma pugoigoio oo omoi ai omo	Oh, the fragrant lemon basil, and the colored banana leaf.
Isin loiei isin kon ouru ouo isin loyei isin konouru.	We carry the taro to its bed. We place it down.
Ie ouo karangei o me kelia. Oua karengio; ia somme meklungo o meklungo, somme meklungo.	Oh, the purple and yellow wild banana leaf, and the sticks [that divide our plots].

The next act of the ritual consists of the full consecration or "call to existence" of the taro effigy,[4] during which the sanger ino instructs the young men of his ramage to lift the effigy off the ground and to begin to carry it to the center of the garden. Four men are needed to lift the object, two position themselves in front and two in the back of the effigy's litter (lungio), place the tree saplings that protrude from either side of the litter on their shoulders, and then form the head of a procession into the garden. The men of the different ramages sing the series of aurang for planting the figure in deep booming voices as they move into the garden. Women and children meanwhile rush ahead of the procession and dance before the effigy while waving colorful crotons and sweet-smelling herbs at it. A number of pandanus mats are thrown down before it, forming a sort of carpet for the procession. The women and children then answer the singing of the men with their own high-pitched melodies, and the singing becomes polyphonic. Before the procession arrives at the center of the garden, the sanger ino rushes forward with three or four men who have in hand their taro digging sticks. He instructs them to begin to dig the hole for the effigy.

4. This phrase is, of course, from Leenhardt's book *Do Kamo.* It is offered in the context of a discussion of the concept of *parole* (p. 137).

The hamlet leader Asong prepares his group's gift of taro.

The series of aurang that are sung at this point are, in part, an invocation of two spirits whose power is thought to aid the taro in its growth.[5]

When the procession arrives, all crowd around the effigy's hole as it is taken out of its box and held above the hole. The effigy is then swayed back and forth as the aurang invoking the power of the spirits is sung for it at the top of everyone's lungs. The singing of the women becomes the voice of the figure as they sing a song that tells the mothers and fathers of the effigy "not to cry or worry, as it was now firmly entrenched in its house," the garden. When the object is firmly secured, the sanger ino's helpers encircle it. They then raise their hands above the top of the effigy, symbolically pulling it upward; thus, they encourage the growth of the taro that is their, as well as the effigy's, children.

Before the magic of planting was performed, the sanger ino, while still in the presence of the effigy, spoke to all of the participants of the ritual. He told everyone assembled that he had not been responsible for the taro blight that had in the previous year ruined much of their crop. He said that he wished no harm to anyone. He then began to speak of his father and of others who had lived

5. One of these is a spirit of the reef called *uilmuk*. After the planting of the taro, he is said to leave his watery home and enter the garden. Once there, he attempts to promote the growth of the taro. The second spirit is the demigod Tuktuk. In myth he is the originator of Rauto gardening magic.

in times past and who had performed this ritual. He talked of how they had handed down their knowledge of it before they had died. As he uttered these words, he began to weep, as the memory of those whom he had known in the past and who were now dead overwhelmed him. Except for the sound of his weeping, the garden then became completely quiet. The old men and women cast their heads down and seemed to turn inward as they thought back to the past with sorrow and nostalgia. The young too cast their eyes downward as they observed the solemnity of the moment. The sorrowful character of this moment presented a sharp contrast to the exuberance and almost defiant expression of human power that had characterized the preceding phases of the rite. Yet, it seemed to be in keeping with the undertone of caution and pessimism that colors Rauto perceptions of the nature of person and of power. That the sanger ino would himself allude to the ephemeral nature of people in the context of a ritual expression of his own strength implied that he understood this strength and power to be evanescent. By alluding to those who had performed the ritual in the past and who were now dead, the sanger ino also made reference to his own ephemeral nature and to the eventual fate of all those who were present at the ritual.

Yet, through such an allusion, the magician and those who shared his feelings of nostalgia were also expressing a sense of gratitude for the lives and acts of the dead. In so doing, they were memorializing the dead—a thought that was only brought home to me when, years after the performance of this ritual, I asked the taro magician why he wept when the taro effigy, called *lekrek,* took shape before his eyes and in his song. He said,

> My father and mother gave me this thing, and the knowledge of its meaning and power. When I make it, I am reminded of them, and their visages come back to me. I see their faces in this thing, and I cry. Their faces appear before my mind's eye along with this thing.

He went on to speak of his parents' generosity to him, and of the good way (*lai itau*) that they had shown to him when he was a child. For him, and for others, the taro effigy and the taro ceremony memorialized such old feelings, as well as the lost relationships and spiritual participations that had given these feelings meaning. At the same time, the taro ceremony expressed the notion that the past was contained in the present; that the spiritual participation and relationships of the present were products of the relationships of the past.

PLANTING MAGIC AND TARO EXCHANGE

The ritual concluded with the aurang and the magical activities for planting and for taro exchange. In this phase of the rite, the magician proceeded to the center of each garden plot, accompanied by three or four young men and women, who carried the magical bundles. At the center of each plot, he planted one of these charmed bundles. He did this by first sitting on the ground and waving the bundles back and forth just above the hole that had been prepared for it. As he manipulated the bundles, he spit billows of ginger onto them and into the holes in which they were placed. When the bundles were planted, he recited another series of spells over them. In these spells, he exhorted the taro to appear above the surface of the ground, just as a "fish jumps suddenly and spectacularly from the depths of the sea and breaks past the surface." His apprentices then performed a spell that urged the taro stalks to anchor themselves to the ground.

As the sanger ino got up to leave each garden plot and proceed to the next, men from the visiting ramages would walk up to the plot and plant the taro stalks that had been carried there. They planted the stalks in a clockwise movement around the bundle of magical materials. The most prized variety of taro, called *auring,* was planted closest to the magical bundle; those less prized were planted further from it. As the men planted, their women threw a few pearl-shells down as a partial payment for the taro that they would be taking back to their homes. They and their men also sang the series of aurang for planting and for taro exchange:

Kiropo la nakiropo lage kiropo.	The skin of the taro is firm. [We shall fill up our baskets with it.]
Uo gilo le lona lage uog ilo lona.	We have harvested all the taro. [We shall cut it off of its stalks and fill our baskets with it.]
Long long visna, visna wo long long koyo ai.	[You and I work underneath these] (gigantic) leaves of taro.
Ia omo a omo e vinsomo ya omo e vinsomo ya omo a	We have planted the taro effigy [and the magical bundles]. The taro is

A boy is marked with red ocher to signify that he has seen and participated in the taro ritual.

A woman, whose skirt is fashioned from magical plants, dances before and animates the taro effigy with her song.

The planted taro effigy.

The garden magician imagines the faces of the dead in the taro effigy's visage, and weeps.

omo e uindring.

enclosed in the ground and
holds fast.

Ko adeng mese uino
sukil ilit aue ino
deng mele ko adeng
mese uino o sukili
itit aue.

The little girls cry [as
they carry the taro up the
hill called *aue*]. It is so
heavy [it hurts their
heads].

One of the songs alludes to how the sanger ino's magic managed to produce taro corms whose surface was not ruined in any way by insects or by mold. The last song describes a group of young girls struggling to carry their baskets of taro up the side of a hill called *aue* and crying because the taro corms are so large and heavy. The song refers to the ample character of the gift of taro that is offered to the visiting ramages.

After the planting was completed, the women of the visiting ramages carried off the huge baskets of taro to their homes. That night the big men of the village honored the newly planted taro by calling for a song festival of the spirit beings, or kamotmot. Thus were the gardens placed under the tutelary care of these spirits. A prohibition upon visiting the gardens was then called by the sanger ino in order to allow the magic that was performed in the garden to take hold.

REFLECTIONS ON THE RITES

The naturalistic meaning of this series of ritual acts and songs is, as I have said, rather easy to decipher. In these images and acts the garden is represented as a house that is full of children. The house's caretaker, its father and mother, is the magician whose manipulations and songs protect and nurture the crop. Leenhardt would have seen a form of anthropomorphism in these practices and images; by them the person seems to project his own qualities and characteristics onto and into the objects, places, and plants of the natural world, thereby bringing them into his sphere of control. There is, it seems then, an element of magical rationalism to the rites and images. This anthropomorphic rationalism is consistent with the meaning of the primary myth of the origins of taro magic and song. As we have seen, the myth tells of how this magic was passed on from the demigod Tuktuk—a divine man—directly to the human realm.

The images and acts of production and of rain making are counterposed, however, by a series of myths and mythic beliefs that Leenhardt would have called cosmomorphic and totemic. The myths describe how the techniques of production, song, hunting, fishing, and magic, and the knowledge of ikit were taught to people by birds—creatures that serve as the totemic emblems of the cognatic descent groups that the Rauto call *rip*. Two birds were thought particularly helpful in promoting the cultivation and growth of the taro crop. These were the birds Kaudok and Udi.

The myth of Kaudok tells of how people originally only raised and consumed pigs, how the aurang and the agreske were sung only in the presence of these creatures. The bird would always watch the ceremonies that were performed for the pigs as it carried its taro stalks from one planting site to the next and performed magic for them. Taking pity on people because of their foolishness, it showed them the use of its plant and revealed to them the magical manipulations and songs that sustain and nurture the crop. The story expresses the mythic insight of the common identity of the human, plant, and animal kingdoms. It balances the obvious anthropomorphic meaning of the images and songs of taro production with the intuition that human power—even that contained by song—is derived from and is a part of the natural world. This insight *is* consistent, however, with certain aspects of the taro rite. It appears, for instance, to lend meaning to the simple songs that are sung for the plants, objects, and tools of the rite. The songs for the garden's door, the areca-bark container of the magical waters, the lemon basil, the taro-digging stick, the garden-boundary sticks, the effigy's throne, the coleus, and the ginger appear to animate and consecrate the objects and plants of custom both by coaxing the natural power they possess out of them and by infusing them with the same power that inhabits the person's word, song, and heart. This comingling "objectification and outward discharge" of cosmomorphic and anthropomorphic power appears to produce an image of "the momentary deity" (Cassirer 1953:35). As the objects and plants are experienced as having the power to promote the growth of taro, in the immediate moment of their celebration, animation, and consecration in song they appear to convey the concrete experience of divine power. This experience leaves little room for symbolic elaboration, for poetry. In the moment when the aurang are sung, consciousness seems entirely taken up by the concrete and immediate presence of the object; this is one of the reasons that the songs simply name these things. Unlike the serpoua, the aurang is a song genre that has little to do with contemplation.

The effectiveness of the aurang in evoking the concrete experience of the sacred is due in no small part to the simple or rather the archaic nature of the objects that they celebrate. The songs' lack of elaborate imagery corresponds to the simple structure and nature of the magical tools and plants used during the rites. It is the power that these objects and songs contain and convey that is important and not the things themselves. The things themselves have little meaning before they are consecrated and named by song, and their simple character and nature enhances rather than distracts from the immediate experience of their consecration and from the sacred. Each of these songs and consecrations is also a mythic act. It is as if each act of the rite, or "each phase of the total action becomes for a moment the domain of an independent god or daemon" (Cassirer 1953:41). The objects are these daemons.

Contrasting the obvious anthropomorphism of the rite with its cosmomorphic aspects reveals its second symmetry. The third symmetry of the rituals is revealed in the complementary animation and consecration of the taro and rain effigies.

The moment in which the taro effigy is consecrated by song is a moment in which the ancestral presence is first seen in it. The aurang "inaugurates the new status" (Freedberg 1989:82) of the object and image as receptacles for the sacred. At the same time, it creates a sociomythic space. The heart of the garden becomes the focal point of human, ancestral, and natural power. *After* the object's consecration, the ensemble of power and presence it contains is experienced as a subtle emotion by ritual participants. The immediate and concrete feeling of intense participation becomes an aspect of the experience of separation from lost others. As we shall see in much more detail in chapters 7 and 8, this feeling of loss, separation, and participation is a moment of individuation and of understanding. The emotion called *makai* is as much an insight as a feeling; the feeling adds force and resonance to the insight that though the person participates in the presence of the image of the ancestor, in the nature of both matriline and patriline, and in the presences and powers of the natural world, he is simultaneously separated from, individuated from, these presences or this spiritual ensemble. Thus, separation and participation are another of the rite's symmetries, one that is also reflected in the character of the taro ritual's own parity or complement: the rite of rainmaking, which is often an essential part of taro production.

These rites are based on the round and black rainstones whose power is controlled by leading men. Each stone is named, and its name represents a certain type of rain. Thus, the rainstone called *mailong* takes its name from a small bird whose circling flight imitates, or is, the actual form of a type of rain squall. *Mailang menen* (the calm sea) is the name of the stone whose rain leaves the seas sleeping calm after it has fallen. In the event of drought, the stones are brought to certain sacred sites—all small pools of water or small springs—and are then wrapped all around with coconut and banana leaves. These bundles form the base of the rain effigies.

The effigy possessed by the magician Kienget was called Gultul, which is also the name of a vine that is full of watery sap. The list of elements of which the effigy is composed is itself an example of a mythic pattern of thinking, of the way the Rauto see power, purpose, and a unifying force in the common objects and plants of the natural world. They see the black rain clouds called *uaskup* in the soot left by a fire. They see the lightening in the way the coconut frond that is made into Gultul's "lantern" quickly catches fire when lit. They see the gentle rain called *akatei* in the gentle yet continual dripping of water from a stalactite, and so Gultul is provided with this object so that he might bring this gentle rain. The Rauto see the rain's mist in the white gossamer flower that they call *sukum,* and so they give this to the effigy. The effigy is also given a bamboo knife which, when struck, is thought to produce the sound that is the rain's thunder. Gultul's visage is fashioned from sap-filled vines; his stomach is filled with a certain variety of nut (*emiak*) that can be heard to fall continually from its tree during a steady but gentle rain. The effigy's arms are constructed from the large leaves of wild taro, whose shape is said to be the form of the black rain cloud, *uaskup*. Its torso is rounded with bark cloth, and it is given its paidela, its cassowary-tibia weapon, and its coconut-frond basket. Sometimes it is also given the stone valuables called *mokmok*. The effigy's visage is then covered with bark cloth, so that the sun's own visage may be blocked off by rain clouds. During the period of its construction, two aurang will be sung for it. One of these songs invokes the names of famous magicians and sorcerers of the group's past. It implores these ancestors to deliver the rain clouds and the rain and to enter into the effigy and thereby lend their power to it. The aurang thus consecrates the effigy.

The completed effigy is then wrapped with a rope that is garlanded with crotons. The rope's two ends are left extending from either side of the figure. These ends are held by the singers and ritual participants, and each end is pulled in order to turn the effigy from side to side as the aurang are sung. After its consecration and animation, the effigy is placed into its spring or pool; in a sense it is placed into its altar. The figure is then left to stand for a few days in order to give its magic time to take effect. After this period of waiting, the head magician goes alone, bedecked with all his objects of power, to meet the effigy. When he confronts it, he spits a billow of ginger and saliva on it and then informs the presence to place its paidela to its mouth just as he places his paidela to his mouth. He then informs it that he will now accompany it back to the hamlet, that the time has come for the effigy and the sorcerer to reveal their power. The magician then places a number of ritual prohibitions on work and other activities, and names the general period during which the rain is to be expected.

The spatiomythic domain that encompasses the rain and taro effigies— the embodiments of male and female power—that encompasses matriline and patriline, that encompasses the cosmomorphism of nature worship and the anthropomorphism of "ancestor worship," that encompasses and circum- scribes the time of the living and of the dead seems, during these rites, to be the domain of the authentic person. That is, the domain that the person enters during the performance of the rites reflects and promotes relationship, or par- ticipation, and individuation. The experience of *le duel* promoted by the rituals enables the person to perceive the parities of which he is composed by placing him in a domain that is, in a sense, both between and within these parities. It is a space in which the person both makes himself part of a dual unity, and *removes himself* from this unity, in the process forming this sense of separation into the emotion that accompanies loss, the emotion called *makai*. In this way the person comes to know something of himself through his relationship with and his separation from other beings, presences, and objects.

Each of the parities that these rites draw their significance from and invoke are, as we have seen, aspects of the word—especially of the magician's word and song. The word represents, objectifies, and contains the social and mythic relationships that are encompassed or circumscribed by the experience of *le duel*. More specifically, the plurality, yet dual unity of the sacred is evoked by word and song during these rites.

Chapter Six

Images of Time, Person, and Place

For the Melanesian the notion of time and the notion of being are indistinguishable

Maurice Leenhardt (1979)

One of the most important notions of cultural anthropology is the idea that meaning is represented by the objects that people create, by the spaces that they inhabit, and by their perceptions of the nature of time and activity. We know that quite often such perceptions are shaped by central cultural metaphors. Thus, to take but one example from the anthropological record, in Marquesan culture the concept of *tapu* gave form and cogency to discourse about space, time, the person, and activity. Dening writes that tapu was "the fundamental categorizing principle of the physical environment, of personal space, of social class, of events and action, of cultural time. It was the organizing principle which gave everything else meaning and about which there could be no agnosticism. It was not only a map of the space within the Marquesan's world, it also marked the boundaries of their world" (1980:89). Thus, when Europeans came and openly mocked the symbolic division of the world—of space, time, and the body—into the categories of common (*meie*) and tapu, the Marquesans glimpsed the cultural boundary of their world.

Dening represents these categories as the central terms of the Marquesan narrative of identity. This narrative involved the figuration of tapu and meie in ceremony, ritual, myth, political action, and in kin and marriage arrangements, and brought forth the Marquesan experience of being. In Dening's view this narrative created a reality of personal authenticity by placing the person in specific sociotemporal domains that were related only through the ideas of meie and tapu. In this view Marquesan culture was a sort of plot that gave meaning to seemingly unrelated events and moments of social time by informing them with these ideas. The plot of Marquesan culture was an instance of human creativity. It created a novel narrative of identity by bringing forth a "refiguration of the human world" (Schweiker 1990:92). Like a novel metaphor, it predicated an innovation of meaning on the flux of experience.

We again hear echoes of the classical theory of representation in Dening's language. We hear echoes of the idea that cultural form, identity, and the person concept are purifications of experience that render it complete, understandable, and spiritually cogent. In Dening's view Marquesan being consisted in the completeness of understanding and of representation that derived from the systematic application of the ideas of tapu and meie to almost all cultural practice.

Leenhardt's work on Melanesian religious phenomenology is interesting not least because it appears to eschew this classical metaphysic of representation. We see this most especially in the chapters of *Do Kamo* that discuss "mythic time" and the sacred ensemble of places and beings that was Do Neva, the New Caledonian landscape. In these chapters Leenhardt shows how being, or the New Caledonian person's sense of personal authenticity, was a consequence of the person's immersion in manifold spatiotemporal, or spatiomythic domains. No abstract principle or idea gave meaning to the process of participation—only the feeling of a renewed strength. As Leenhardt says of the New Caledonian who needed, for instance, advice from the gods,

> At the altar, in a trance, he goes to find his god, battles with him, is possessed by and possesses him. He will henceforth walk with this new strength in him. Or perhaps his vitality is weak. He moves toward the totem. He makes himself like the totem by painting his body, he identifies himself and he finds comfort in communion with it." "Each time he acts he finds himself transported into all the spatio-temporal domains in which the motives determining his choice of action can be affirmed." (Leenhardt 1979:91)

Leenhardt goes on to describe these spatiotemporal domains as aspects of mythic time, in which "the Melanesian finds himself, finds his personality, and in which, finally, his very existence is determined" (1979:91).

Mythic time, then, has more to do with emotion than with any measurement of time. It is the feeling of emotional fullness or plenitude that lends support to the person. Being is this emotion; the person lives spiritually and *is* because of it. In Leenhardt's view New Caledonian ceremony, ritual, speech making, or any other central cultural act could be meaningful only if it conveyed and derived power from this experience of participation in mythic time. The notion of a narrative of identity constructed over the course of time through action, word, personal sentiment, and concern, seems inappropriate here. In fact Leenhardt's ideas of participation and of mythic time and identity seem at first glance the antithesis of Ricoeur's notion of narrative time, in which the person separates himself from the flux of experience to utter and act out an individual identity that has a past and future as well as an immediate present.

Leenhardt also describes Melanesian time in "geographical terms" as a kind of temporal landscape, one that is pictured or imaged as a series of characteristic events or activities. The experience of the temporal landscape unfolds with the commencement of such activities. The New Caledonian terms that describe blocks of time—for instance, the names of the lunar months—thus retain "an immediately sensuous as well as a spatial coloration" (Cassirer 1955:215). That is, for the Melanesian the experience of time has the concrete sensuous immediacy and character of an interaction with a person.

The images of the Rauto lunar calendar appear, at first glance, to confirm Leenhardt's insight into the character of Melanesian time reckoning. They appear to mark out blocks of time by imaging activities that have a concrete immediacy to the person, because they are the dominant activities of social life. Beyond this, however, Riceour's understanding of the relationship between time and the construction of narrative identity has some relevance here. In fact the blocks of Rauto mythic time are nestled within a conception of narrative time. We see this in the fact that narrative time expresses an aspect of the Rauto understanding of personhood; this is its ethos of consociation, the value it places on being involved, mythically or otherwise, in the existence of other beings. The religious sense of participation in the spatiotemporal domains of other beings (a sense that is an important aspect of mythic identity) is consistent with, though not to be explained entirely in terms of, an ethos of social interaction that holds that the investment of self in other consociates is a high moral value. The ethos colors the qualitative experience of time and place, revealing in the process that mythic identity is not antithetical to narrative identity, but that the two forms of being "are of the same family" (Geertz 1973:401).

I use the word *consociation* here to describe a characteristic Melanesian style of both experiencing the world and acting within it. Geertz writes that "consociates are individuals"—in the Melanesian instance we would prefer the word *being* to *individual*—"who share, however briefly or superficially, not only a community of time but also of space." They are persons, or beings, "having face-to-face relationship more or less continuously and to some enduring purpose" (Geertz 1973:365). The enduring purpose of Rauto social practice is to involve as many people as possible in each person's biography. The portrait of the Melanesian big man or big woman as continually striving to draw people and resources to him or herself, and then dramatically investing his or her religious, economic, even personal *mana* in them draws some of its obvious explanatory power from this ethos of consociation. In fact, our discussion of Rauto understandings of the nature of social life and the person paints a picture of a people who know, sometimes in intimate detail, what their consociates are, have, and owe them. Certainly, personal capabilities are culturally played up, being the main subject of most Rauto metaphors and proverbs. Melanesians, unlike, say, Balinese, do not value anonymity for themselves, and they do not act as if their fellows were anonymous to them. This has a number of consequences for their views and experiences of time and place. One of these, as we will see, is that the idea of dramatic climax and ending is an intimate part of their experience of time. Also, a perception of themselves as perpetually attaining power and strength and then slowly losing this strength and perishing is a central theme of their experience of place, as well as of time.

AGENCY AND THE RAUTO LUNAR CALENDAR

The Months of Preparation: September–November

For the Rauto the year can be said to commence during the time in which people begin to prepare for the end of the rainy season and to plan for the activities of the ceremonial season.[1] The dominant theme of discourse about the three lunar months of this period is the theme of social and economic preparation. In discourse, the months previous to the "time of preparation" are characterized as a time of "no activity", as I discuss shortly.

The first month of preparation is called *aileng,* which is said to mean "prepare your shell money." Aileng is said to be "the time for taking inventory of ones resources." It is also designated as the proper time to make visits to the hamlets of kin who owe shell money and to request that they make good on their debts. Thus, aileng is also marked as the time for "the evening up of debts." A specific image serves as a symbol of this month. This is the image of a person sitting in the plaza by the door of his house stringing and generally preparing shell-bead currency for the trading season that is to come. The man is said also to be waiting the repayment of debts owed him.

Adunglo is the month when the hunting nets and, in coastal Rauto villages, the fishing nets are taken out of the various ceremonial houses and repaired. They will then be magically charmed by the hamlet leader (*adepdep*) whose kin group constructed and owns the nets.

For people of the coastal Rauto villages, however, the image that best characterizes this month describes how the large trading and fishing canoes are taken from their place of storage behind the ceremonial house and are drawn

---

1. In outlining the series of meanings that the Rauto associate with the lunar calendar, I do not mean to imply that this people, especially young and middle-aged Rauto, are unfamiliar with Western forms of time reckoning. The church calendar is especially important to them for instance. Still, old methods of time reckoning remain imbued with religious significance.

down to the shore. A second characteristic image that the Rauto use when speaking about this month describes the celebration that follows the construction of a new canoe. The image describes how, in this celebration, the owner and builder of the canoe is doused with sea water by the women of the hamlet. It also describes how the canoe is then paddled to other hamlets and shown to the people. At every stop of this journey, tobacco, shell money, areca nut, and pandanus mats are heaved into the new canoe by the people of the various hamlet groups.

Auom tir (November) is a month of anticipation as well as preparation. During auom tir the Rauto check the progress of the taro gardens that they planted toward the end of the previous dry season. The voyaging, trading, and social visiting of the dry season are impossible without the produce of the gardens. Indeed, the gardens must bear if trading and visiting friends are to be received properly and if voyagers are to be able to make initial gifts of food to their hosts in return for offers of hospitality. The full commencement or even the planning of ceremonial activity is also impossible without the prospect of an ample and continuous harvest.

The main taro crop will have been planted during what we would call the previous January or February. The main gardens should begin to bear a month or two after auom tir. During auom tir, people will wait with anticipation for a sign that the taro stalks have produced corms. The head garden magicians (*sanger ino*) of the various Rauto hamlet groups are sometimes particularly sullen during this time, as they worry about whether or not their magic was effective enough to secure the formation and growth of the corms. During this month, the sanger ino sometimes instructs the young men and women of his hamlet residence to climb to the middle branches of the trees that surround the taro gardens in order to see if the top of the taro corms are yet protruding from the ground. This will indicate that the corm has formed and that the taro stalks have produced food. Auom tir is thought, as well, to signal the ripening of the nuts of the canarium tree (*ngaul*). In fact, the central image of speech about the month describes young people climbing the canarium tree to knock the nuts down and then gazing toward the taro gardens and seeing the tops of the taro tubers protruding from the ground. If the gardens have produced, people should begin to prepare for ceremonials and trading.

The first of these simple images, the one that describes the main activity of aileng, the first month of preparation, alludes to two major social moments: the initiation of an exchange and the moment of the return. The image seems to say the debt will be repaid, the exchange completed: aileng is the natural time for the exchange's completion. The image says nothing of the sheer effort and social time required to repay or to offer. As I read the image—a man waiting

for what is owed him as he prepares to make return on his own debts—I recall
how much of Rauto social life was taken up by the moment of exchange:

> This shell was given to me by my grandfather. Do you see it still carries the
> blood of his circumcision. And this is mine and it holds my blood. These are
> the shells my father gave to me, which I wore at my own circumcision and
> at all the other ceremonies performed for me. This is the ring of tili that I am
> preparing for my firstborn, this for my second, these for my third, fourth,
> and fifth children. Do you see how it is? If any of my kin sponsor a work
> of custom—a circumcision, the work for a woman's first menstruation, any
> customary work for a firstborn, or if there is a marriage exchange—and if it
> would be my right to be given a shell if I attended, then I have to go to this
> custom work. This is one of the ways that I can collect these valuables for
> my children. Then people will say, "This is a man of substance; see how he
> works for his children."
>
> These are my children's decorative shells, and I acquired them in the
> same way that I acquired the other shells. When I sponsor a ceremony for
> them, I must be prepared to pay the ritual debts to those who attend, and
> whose right it is to be given a shell. And I must remember my brothers
> [patrikin] who helped me sponsor these events. I have to make good on my
> debts to them when it comes time for one of their children to be celebrated
> in ceremony. Few of these articles are really mine. As soon as something
> comes into my hand there is an obligation I must meet with it, or a debt I
> must repay. This is the road of custom, and it is a difficult road to follow.

In my friend Braio's description of how he acquired his children's valuables,
we see how much of his own identity and life are given meaning by journeys of
acquisition and repayment, journeys undertaken to meet obligations to children
and to other kin, journeys made along the road of custom. "Preparing your
shell money" means preparing yourself to meet the obligations and to receive
the rewards of social life. The act of exchange, or of preparing for exchange
marks the beginning of social (Ricoeur would say narrative) identity. The act
constantly brings forth the "refiguration of the world."

The moment of exchange also often marks a social beginning. It is a time
for the person to step forward and make a name, or lose one—a thought that
reminds us how the road of custom is kept open by negative as well as positive
social sanctions. It is a road kept open by shame, fear, and competitiveness as
well as by the desire to do well by one's own children and to be thought well
of. There is an ambiguity to all beginnings, and we sense this both in the image
of aileng—an image that describes a man sitting and waiting to be repaid as he
prepares to meet his own debts—and in the following narrative.

> Many of these things [objects of exchange] once belonged to our grand-
> fathers. They are the visages of our grandfathers. If these things are lent

and not returned, or if something of equal value does not come to take their place, this is considered a grave thing. You must try with all your skill of persuasion to secure the return. You must sometimes try, and wait for years for the return. If it does not come, you must speak with a sorcerer and pay him to murder this man who does not make good on his debts. If you or I do not make good on our debts of things of value, we will surely not live very long. These objects can kill us."

The images of the lunar calendar and of these two narratives form a complete meaning or understanding of the moment of exchange. The images and narratives represent different aspects of this meaning. The images of the calendar represent the naturalistic meaning of this moment, a meaning that evokes the experience of what Stephan Gould would call "time's cycle." Gould notes that a view of time as a cycle can give meaning to a moment in the time of an individual life or to a moment in the life of a society or a world by relating this moment to a tradition (or process) that is constantly recreated as it is evoked (1987:14). When there is only narrative, when each event in the life of a person, a society, or a world is thought to be utterly unique, time can lose much of its meaning because it is undefined by value and process. For the Rauto, time's cycle is mythic time—a time when the activities of the person appear to participate in the irresistible force of the natural cycle. This is why in the similes of the lunar calendar the maturation of the taro and yam crops and the calming of the seas appear naturally linked to the readying of the hunting and fishing nets and to the celebrations surrounding the completed construction of the vehicles of the journeys of exchange, the trading canoes. These images in turn all point to the seeming inevitability of the completion of past exchanges, and to the renewal of ceremonial life that the initiation and completion of the exchange signifies. The images place the moment of exchange within the rhythms of the yearly cycle and within the rhythms of mythic time.

But these images tell us little of the moral character of the exchange. They say nothing at all of why the failure to initiate or complete the exchange can be the cause of a social or, in some instances, of an actual death. They do not say that the moment of exchange is the gist of Melanesian moral life, that moral and social identity is "structured by rhythms of exchange" (Clifford 1982:142). Something of this more rounded, fuller meaning is revealed in the two narratives I have quoted. The narratives reveal how the "time of the exchange" is attached to the social and moral definition of the person, a thought that is further confirmed by this brief list of names for types of exchange and of payment.

Uruon: The payment given to reward an accomplishment, such as the capture of a wild boar, or a person's first performance of taro magic.

Ulu: The compensation paid for a ritual or moral transgression.

Kuru: The portion of bride-price given to members of a woman's cognatic group to compensate them for their loss when the woman marries into another group. A portion of the compensation pay received by a dead person's matrikin at the exchanges of death.

Kuru La Amot: A special category of pay given over to kin whom the Rauto refer to as the true or closest maternal cousins of a dead person during the exchanges for his or her death. The pay is given as acknowledgement of the important role these kin played, or should have played, in the life of the dead person.

Augum: Pay given by husband's patrikin to the one-blood cousins of his new wife when these cousins bring the woman to her husband.

Ke Audigi: The amount of bride-wealth given to the newly married woman's mother.

Asong Amta: The compensation given to the brothers and to the one-blood cousins of a dead man. The pay is given by the man who takes the dead man's wife in marriage in recognition of the brothers' and the cousins' levirate.

Loket: Pay given to the kinsman of a boy who supervises the boy's initiation.

Onngo: The pay given to a sorcerer so that he might either kill or leave off killing a man.

Suong: The live pig given to the firstborn son of a bigman during the final night of a song festival. The debt must be returned at a ceremony or song festival sponsored by the firstborn.

Itar Amto: The compensation given to the immediate family of a man whose wife deserts him either before or shortly after the marriage's consummation.

Kupukungon: The compensation given to those who adopt a family's child for a number of years.

Tili Nakas: The compensation provided to the person who ritually shaves and cuts the hair of a person in mourning. The shaving is one of the acts that is meant to mark the formal end of mourning.

Lel Tandra: The pay given by a person wrongfully accused of a transgression to his accusers. In offering the pay, the accused is said to be lifting the shame from his skin.

Ilim Nondro: The completion of a sister exchange.

As we can see from this incomplete list of types of payment and exchange, the moment of exchange defines the moral space occupied by the person. It invests the person with a social identity by directing the full force of custom and social sanction to him as he begins or completes the exchange. Many acts of involvement in another's joy, pain, or accomplishment require the token of compensation from this other. Social units have their obligations and duties to one another as well. This is why there always seems to be either a social or personal debt to be repaid, or an act of exchange that must be initiated. If tapu and meie were the central Polynesian metaphors, marking the most important moments of social time, then *de nondro*, the "return of the gift" seems to be the central Melanesian one. The reciprocal exchange of an object, an emotion, a person (such as the woman who comes to a man's group as a replacement for his sister), of labor, of ceremony, of song, or the appropriate compensation for the giving of any of these things defines an important aspect of Melanesian social time. Social time is really what Rauto time reckoning is about, as we see also in the similes that describe the ceremonial and the monsoon seasons.

Naulong, naulong akap *("You as well?"): December, January*

The ceremonial season is heralded by the month that the Rauto call *naulong*. In fact, the Rauto designate two consecutive months by this name: December and January.

The metaphoric image that symbolizes these two months can be called the image of the return. It is said that during naulong, people who had been living in small encampments in the forest during the rainy season return to the ceremonial ground of their ramage and congregate in a large settlement. Yet, this image is also a symbol for the general exuberance and activity that are thought to characterize these two months.

The image of the social visit also figures prominently in Rauto descriptions of the character of naulong. People are said to "travel from hamlet to hamlet" and from "house to house" to exchange gossip, news, and plans.

The central idea expressed by descriptions of naulong is that human agency is most efficacious during this time. This is why the Rauto say that human labor brings its greatest return during naulong. This idea has practical consequences, as the period toward the end of naulong is one of the most labor-intensive times of the year. The largest taro gardens are prepared and planted now. Elders told me that naulong was also the best time for hunting and fishing expeditions. They said that since the fish and animals were most active during naulong, they could be spotted and caught with less effort. Naulong is also considered to be the most propitious time to initiate children and to perform the aurang for the taro gardens. Two thoughts lie behind this preference. The first is the idea that children and plants "grow quickly" during naulong. The second thought is that the personal power of people is now at its peak. Rauto elders explained this idea by saying that "people's skins are hot" during this time, and that therefore any activity that they undertake has a good chance of succeeding. Thus, the songs and ritual activities of initiation and of taro production will be particularly effective in prompting the growth of crops and children.

We see, then, how human agency is related to the quality of time in discourse about naulong. In this sense naulong is a metaphor both for the waxing of personal energy and for the revitalization of social life.

The two months that follow naulong are *aiei* (February) and *malenge* (March). The images used to characterize the months refer to the activities of harvesting, food preparation, and food exchange.

Aiei takes its name from a type of yam that is harvested at this time. During aiei people are said "to walk through the gardens" and find that the yams are ready to be taken from the ground. It is said that after people observe the growth of the yams, they will "look toward the taro gardens" and see that it is almost time to begin a second taro harvest. The thought that informs this image is that the maturation of the yam tubers hastens the growth of the taro. During the next month, malenge, the taro will be ready for harvesting. A verbal image used to depict the characteristic activities of this month describes how women peel the taro and prepare the stone ovens to cook the taro corms. A second image describes a ceremonial exchange of taro between two different kin groups. More specifically, the image describes how the women of a visiting kin group walk up to a pile of taro that is offered to them and begin separating the taro stalks from the corms. They then are said to fill their coconut-frond baskets with the corms.

Images of death, sorrow and the frustration of human effort: (asivu) *April,* (anamak alang) *May,* (anamak sadi) *June,* (alo) *July,* (alo sadi) *August*

The return of the rainy season is heralded by the month that the Rauto call *asivu.* This is the time of "high seas." Indeed, during asivu the sea becomes violent, rushing onto the shore and appearing "to consume it" as "fire consumes a burning log." Heavy rains and violent offshore winds also mark this time. Characteristic descriptions of the month tell how the tall trees of the forest are uprooted by the strong winds and land in the middle of the paths that connect the various Rauto hamlets.

In Rauto discourse the following two months, *anamak alang* and *anamak sadi,* symbolize the frustration of human effort. Hamlet leaders told me that any endeavor that they directed their younger kinsmen to undertake during this time was almost bound to fail. Appropriately, anamak marks the end of the communal hunting and fishing expeditions of the dry season. Indeed, it is said that now the forest is empty of game and the sea devoid of fish. It is also said that labor brings little return, that if taro is planted, the corms will be extremely small when harvested. Thus, only small tracts of land are prepared for planting, and gardening work in general begins to slow.

Anamak is also the time when families begin to leave the hamlet settlement to take up more or less permanent residence in their garden houses. During times of famine, they may also take up residence at encampments where they will process sago. Not surprisingly then, images of social dispersal also inform Rauto descriptions of these two months; they are called "the time when people leave."

The final two months of the lunar calendar mark the nadir of the Rauto year. These are the months *alo,* and *alo sadi,* roughly July and August. *Alo* is the word that women keen at mortuary ceremony when they first come to view the body of a dead kinsman. They also cry out alo when they say farewell to a kinsman or friend who is about to leave on a long journey. The word is closest to the English word *alas.*

The Rauto use the phrase "the death of a person" when they refer to alo. Indeed, I remember people telling me that alo was "the time of death" and that many people die during this month. Since the rainy season is sometimes a period of severe food shortage, there is probably a factual basis to the Rauto observation about the character of alo. There is, as well, a general feeling that alo is an unlucky time, that it is, for instance, a period when people are prone to injury. I remember a hamlet leader telling me that during alo he would counsel his followers and helpers not to carry out heavy garden work, since he feared that they would sustain an injury. He went on to say that alo was a time when young men and women acted like old people by sitting close to the cooking fires and rarely venturing out or being active.

The symbolic or obvious meaning of this progression of images is easy enough to decipher. The images that describe the months of preparation for exchange and for journeying seem naturally to culminate in images of the social visiting and celebration that mark the ceremonial season. These images in turn seem naturally to be followed by descriptions of the sort of social death, or at least social estrangement, that characterizes the monsoon season. The images also allude to a series of participations. In them the person is represented as participating in the waxing and waning power and agency of the natural world. This thought takes further meaning from the idea that the person's body undergoes a series of emotional and physical transformations during the ceremonial and monsoon seasons. Bodily idioms that specify that the person's skin is "hot," light, and "open" during naulong are consistent with the fact that the ceremonial season is characterized by the investment of personal agency in others through the singing of the aurang. The idiom that best serves as a leitmotif of the ceremonial season is *tandra plo* (open skin); the idiom's meaning refers to a reciprocal flow of communication and interaction between people and to the positive feelings that result from such interaction. *Tandra tung* (closed skin), is the idiom that best describes the state of the person during the monsoon season. The isolation, pattern of social dispersement, and generally unpropitious nature of this period of time seem consistent with the general emotional estrangement, or "closed skin," that people feel most especially during the time called alo.

Emotional estrangement, social isolation, the absence of ceremonial activity, and the curtailing of garden work on the one hand, and exchange, visiting, ceremony and song, intense labor, and intense social interaction on the other form two separate ensembles of emotions, experiences, and meanings. The importance placed on each of these moments or blocks of social time is judged by the distance it marks between the self and the other. Naulong, the period of the most intense social and mythic interaction between persons, is valorized. Alo, which represents the absence of such relationships, is devalorized by the Rauto ethos of consociation.

The character of the yearly cycle also provides an appropriate medium for the expression of an understanding of the life path of the Melanesian person. Thus the similes that describe the "months of preparation" seem also to be metonyms for the beginning of the person's social career. This is the time of preparation for social achievement, for initiating exchanges, accumulating and satisfying debts, and raising one's name. Naulong seems to be a metonym for actual social achievement, for the culmination of one's efforts, a culmination that is represented by the successful attempt to draw people to one's own person by investing spiritual, economic, and political *mana* in them. In the time called alo, one recognizes the senescence of the person whose heart and skin have cooled, who has passed his personal power on to others, and who has begun to withdraw from full participation in social life. The symbolic death and or estrangement that is represented by alo resonates with and reflects the social death of the headman who, upon realizing that his heart is no longer hot and powerful and that his powers have diminished, moves away from his consociates in the main hamlet residence in order to live alone, or with his wife in the forest.

These fuller, more rounded meanings of the images of the times of preparation, achievement, and senescence have a certain pathos. They express intense feelings of mythic and emotional participation with other beings, as well as feelings of loss and separation from these others. Ultimately they express the emotion called *makai* by the Rauto. The particular character and importance of this emotion will become clearer after we consider Rauto concepts of place and, in later chapters, of mourning, cultural invention, and personal individuation.

TIME, AGENCY, AND ENVIRONMENT

The Rauto also possess a second informal system of time reckoning, which they use most especially to meet the need for allocating appropriate amounts of time and labor to gardening activities. In this second system, time is again characterized by allusion to human agency and to productive activity. The system notes the flowering sequence of a number of trees of the rain forest. The flowering of one of the trees is sometimes correlated with a specific lunar month. Thus, naulong sadi, the second month of the ceremonial season, is sometimes also called *umdum amta alwos* (the buds of the *Evodia* have swelled and flowered). The Rauto do not, however, usually identify a specific month by the flowering of a specific tree. The flowering cycle is more a mark of different agricultural and meteorological seasons than of specific months. The Rauto monthly unit is thus exclusively lunar. The entire flowering cycle is as follows:

Aiuop: Pterocarpus indicus flowers. The period from the end of August to October, when the rainy season is coming to an end. Hamlet leaders direct the cutting of new bush. Garden labor increases in intensity. The period is roughly correlated with the months aileng and adunglo.

Umdum: Evodia ellergana flowers. The ceremonial season, roughly from January to the end of February or the beginning of March. This is the most labor-intensive time of the year, when the largest gardens of the year are prepared for planting. People hurry to finish their taro planting before the flowers of umdum fall to the ground. The flowering of the tree is said to hurry the maturation of previously planted taro. It is also said to hurry the growth of taro planted during this period. Taro planted now will be of an impressive enough size to use for ceremonial exchange upon harvesting.

Vekiau: Erythrina indica begins to shed its leaves, sprout red flowers, and then grow its leaves back as the flower petals fall to the ground. Vekiau is usually the period from June to August. The flowering cycle of the tree and its loss and regrowth of leaves, usually take place during the months called alo and anamak. The taro planted now will be small when harvested. Garden work is now curtailed.[2]

2. Panoff (1969:153–65) writes that the Maenge of East New Britain discuss the yearly cycle, and the months of the cycle, primarily in terms of the flowering sequence of the trees which I list here. Panoff also identifies the flowering sequence of a number of other trees and creepers as marks for the passage of the year.

The period of each flowering cycle both determines and marks the intensity of labor that is carried out within the period. It is not surprising then that in metaphor the environment is spoken about as if it possessed both agency and directing power. Thus, the Rauto say that the flowering of a particular tree either encourages or stops people from working in the gardens. As I have noted above, the Rauto also say that the flowering of a particular species either "hurries" or slows down the maturation of the taro crop and determines the eventual size of the taro corms.

These statements become all the more interesting when we reconsider some of the phrases used to describe the character of the environment during certain months. The propitious months of naulong, for instance, are characterized as a time when the environment is filled with energy and signs of activity. During naulong, the landscape appears to be steeped in an imminence of power and agency. The phrases that describe the unpropitious time of alo and anamak convey a perception that the environment, like the people who live in it, is unproductive and also somehow menacing to people. The environment itself is thus described in terms that take their meaning from ideas about the person. Its energies are thought to wax and wane as do the energies of people; its character is thought to change as it becomes either more or less amenable to the plans and purposes of people. Its own purpose and power are discussed in human terms, in terms that refer to the human capability to work and to produce.[3]

TIME, PLACE, AND AGENCY

The concepts of agency and person that give meaning to Rauto discourse about the yearly cycle are part of a philosophy of time. As we have seen, this philosophy is an expression of a system of concepts that define personhood in terms of the ability to shape the nature of the world through one's productive labor, through ceremonial knowledge and ability, and through acts of exchange. In Rauto understanding, the quality of time during the different phases of the yearly cycle is related to these abilities. Rauto concepts of place also reflect the belief that productive human agency shapes the nature of time. I refer most

---

The Rauto in contrast do not, in their own words, "worry very much" about all the phases in the flowering sequences of these trees and creepers. If they wish to orient their productive activities, it is enough for them to know that one of the trees which I have mentioned here has either flowered, or has begun to lose its flower.

3. The Rauto possess a number of other informal means of marking the passage of time. For instance they use numerous terms to describe different times of the day and of the night. Like the Maenge of East New Britain, they also mark the seasons by the position from which the sun rises and into which it sets during the course of the year.

especially here to the concepts *ano* (place), and *tanu* (ancestral place). Yet, in discourse about these concepts, a different though related aspect of the traditional Rauto understanding of time receives expression. Discourse about place most especially has the character of narrative; it represents a culturally specific understanding of the progress of time, what Gould (1987) calls "time's arrow."

Rauto people use the term *ano* to describe the present or former place of residence of an extended family group (*rip*). *Ano* is also used to describe any place in the landscape that is named. *Tanu*, in contrast, would be glossed most accurately as "ancestral place"; it is used as a term for a spot that was first cleared of forest and on which one's kin group's apical ancestor then resided. A family group may change residences many times during the course of its history, and thus may live in many different ano. Yet a group will usually not claim to have more than one or two tanu.

In discourse, ano and tanu are both frequently metaphors for a community or for the bonds of kinship. Thus, people are often identified with the main place of residence of their kinship group and will be referred to as the people of this place (e.g., *oduk arauai ino*, "those of the place called *arauai*". The "origin spot" of a group will also be referred to as *itar uate*. *Itar* is the word for a "family house" (i.e., the house of a married couple) and is, in this case, a metaphor that expresses the idea of kinship relation. The concept is that all the residents of a place are descendants of "the same house"; they can trace their descent back to an ancestral married pair. *Uate* is the word for both origin and base. The phrase *itar uate* (the base of the house) refers to the place of a group by alluding to both the bond of kinship and to shared residence. We could perhaps better translate the phrase as "the bottom of the country." "That is to say that the entire land originates in this place and is supported by it" (Leenhardt 1979:106).

Goodale (1985:231) notes that the typical activities that are performed at the hamlet residence—forest clearing, house building, planting of food-producing trees, ceremonial exchange—mark the spot as the consummate seat of productive social endeavor for the neighboring Kaulong. The historical memory of the people who created the hamlet and sustained it through productive activity is literally inscribed on the Rauto hamlet grounds and on the topography of the nearby forest. This memory is partly contained in the Rauto's knowledge of the personal names given to the food-bearing trees that grow on and around the outskirts of the residence; many of these trees bear the names of the people who planted them. The landscape is also dotted with trees, usually palms, that can properly be called memorials. These are the Koklong, which have been planted on top of a section of a person's skeleton in order to memorialize his or her life. The names and locations and rights to use the products of these trees are remembered by elders, though the people who planted them may have lived generations before. Besides providing a record of the activities of people and the usufruct rights of groups, the named trees are also a part of the mythic identity of the person and the social group. This is seen most clearly in the significance that attaches most especially to the coconut palm.

Many of the coconut palms of the hamlet and surrounding forest have been planted in order to mark the birth and physical development of children. The planting of a sprouting coconut for a child usually takes place early in the child's second year of life. The coconut is planted along with a section of bark cloth used by the child's mother to wrap its head. The wrapping gives the skull an elongated shape that is considered to be beautiful by the Rauto. The palm that grows from the sprouting coconut (called the child's *ueue*) will subsequently bear the name of the child and, indeed, will be seen to embody something of its strength, or soulstuff. The strength and growth of the palm serve as metaphors for the maturation and later the waxing strength of the person for whom it is named. Years, perhaps even decades later, when the palm has matured, one of its coconuts will be planted by its human namesake to mark the birth and development of one of his or her own children. The names and the descent of the hamlet's coconut palms sometimes serve as well then as a genealogy for the residents of the hamlet. The trees that bear the names of children, or some-times of ancestral planters, and that embody the soulstuff of their namesakes, the tanu that hold the skulls of the dead and that anchor the social group to its territory, the forces that inhabit the places of the land, as well as many of the land's objects, form a single ensemble, a single sociomythic space.

Human or mythic agency is, of course, not exercised solely on the hamlet grounds. Old garden sites and sago camps, former hamlet sites, places in the forest where someone has planted a breadfruit or *Canarium* tree all bear the imprint of human activity. These places are named, and their names provide a record of human movement through the land over time. Elders know hundreds of these place names. As they recounted these names to me, they spoke of the people who had lived on the land before them; sometimes they spoke as well of the events and activities that had given a place its name. As I listened, I realized that this recitation of place names had the quality of a social or histori-cal narrative. The Rauto use an image that is at once a metaphor and part of a memory system to help them to recite the names of the places of the landscape accurately. This image depicts the landscape as a series of paths that lead to and from former or current places of residence or activity. To remember the names of these sites, elders said that they "had to walk" along the various paths. As I sat with the elders in the men's ceremonial house, the sequence of place names was recited to me as if the elders were taking part in a journey or imaginary walk through the many paths of the land. Elders would name a place, tell me its history, and then say that they would now "walk on to the next place," and tell me its history. Later, when I went to view a number of these sites, I found that many had no actual paths leading up to them, although perhaps they had in the past. In any event, the paths mentioned by the elders were part of a mental map of the landscape that was at once a part of geographical and historical knowledge, as well as of a feeling of mythic participation with the forces, the identities, of the land.[4]

There is a relationship between the image that the Rauto use to describe their land and a major theme of expressive life. In expressive culture (e.g., metaphor and mythology), the theme of a journey through the landscape is often a symbol for skillfulness, wisdom, and/or productive accomplishment. In a trope for instance, it is said that the speech of a wise and persuasive person "goes around the landscape, visiting all the named places of the land." As I have mentioned in a previous chapter, the reference to the many places of the landscape is an allusion to the points or thoughts conveyed by a person's speech. Someone whose speech and thought are considered to be neither wise or persuasive is someone who is unable to make either his speech or his thoughts "go around all of the landscape." In other words, this person sees only very few of the many facets of a given subject.

A number of Rauto myths are given a narrative structure by this same metaphor of a journey through the landscape. One sees this most especially in stories that tell of the creative activities of culture heroes (*oklo uate*). Often in these stories a culture hero will travel over the land (always from east to west, thus following the course of the sun), and stop at various places along the route. Each place that the hero visits subsequently becomes associated with one of the creative acts that he or she performs on it or with an event that occurs while he or she visits the place. I have presented one of these myths: the story of the origins of taro magic. In the myth the demigods Tuktuk and his sister walk westward together singing the aurang for taro and planting their magical bundles.

One of the points made by the taro myth especially is that the creative activities of the culture heroes literally inscribe their identities onto the face of the land. Another point made is that the places that are identified with the acts of these beings are themselves symbols of productive accomplishment. In the taro myth the culture heroes travel from place to place, planting their magical

4. These concepts of land and landscape appear similar to those of many other Melanesian groups; see, for instance, Clifford (1982:169), Schieffelin (1976:182), Feld (1982:150) and Rodman (1987:34–40).

bundles of ginger, coleus, and lemon grass on the land of the groups that they favor. The journeying and the ritual activity of the heroes renews the fertility of the land. The knowledge that is given to the two fatherless—hence power-less—boys marks the transmission of ritual and productive ability from the divine to the human realm. The myth suggests that the responsibility to renew the fertility of the land now falls on the shoulders of people. By preparing gardens and performing the proper rites of production on them, people imitate the actions of the culture heroes. This point is made explicit in the myth when the demigod Tuktuk has the young boy take his place as he entrusts his knowledge of taro magic to him. To this day, Rauto garden magicians are thought to be the heirs of the culture hero and his young apprentice. By moving over the land in order to cut the forest and prepare gardens, the people also take part in a journey of productive accomplishment.

For people, the investment of self in the places of the land through productive activity (e.g., the planting and cultivation of trees, the building of a hamlet residence, the preparation of gardens) is (as I have argued) part of a process that establishes an aspect of social and personal identity. The "humanization" and improvement (in terms of productive potential) of the land that results from this process is part of the historical accomplishment of the Rauto people. Indeed, the cumulative effect of people's productive work and of their ritual activities and songs contributes to the preparation of a fertile and thus suitable abode for human life. The anthropomorphic symbolism that attaches to the places of the land marks this historical accomplishment and makes these places sacred sites (*ano kotoptopuong*). Naming the resources of the land, remembering and naming the various tanu of the land, then, seems to be a way of both marking and celebrating productive accomplishment.

Places also relate the narrative of time to the rhythms of human activity and of the human life cycle. In this sense they join time's cycle to time's arrow. I say this because in Rauto understanding the human agency invested in a place by a person has the quality of a recurrent restorative force. Yet places hold an ambivalence of feeling for Rauto. They often evoke feelings of regret and of makai for the dead. Remembering and feeling the force and identity of places seems a way of keeping people—even those who are dead—within the realm of one's consociates. At the same time, it confirms the Melanesian sense of people as continually perishing. Places are the memories of losses. Now and in the next few chapters we will consider what the Rauto try to make of such losses.

ANCESTRAL PLACE, TIME, AND THE RITES OF DEATH

Adult Rauto can name up to six generations of their ancestors. They recognize that others lived before the first of these generations, but they retain no memory of them. The Rauto designate those who lived in the time that exceeds the grasp of historical memory as *ausen*. They refer to the time of ausen—the eternity of the past—by using a metaphor that describes the sea breaking on the shore without end and drawing into itself the memory of those who lived and died, as if they were the sands of the shore. The metaphor is only one of a number of sayings which indicate that this people has a keen perception of mortality. Rauto perceive allusions to their mortality in the gloom and inactivity of the time that they call alo; they perceive an allusion to it in the sight of an abandoned hamlet residence whose dancing plaza is overrun with forest grasses and shrubs.[5] Most of all, however, evidence of mortality is provided by the presence of the dead. To this day the ancestral places (*tanu*) of the bush Rauto, Gimi, and Kaulong house the skulls and bones of the dead. Yet, for the Rauto, the bones of the dead and the tanu that house them symbolize the power of the living as much as that of the dead, and death itself provides another opportunity for this people to celebrate principles that sustain life. The reason I wish to begin to discuss the rites for the dead here is that the rites express the understanding that historical time consists in the continuity of human productive and creative effort. The tanu, or ancestral place, is literally a theatre where this understanding of the nature of time is expressed; indeed, it is performed there.

After the trials and vicissitudes of life, people should ideally be buried in the tanu of their ramage group. When people are buried in their tanu, it is said that they are "returning to their origin place" and are "joining their ancestors." The rites and the pig killings that take place during and just after burial are performed out of remembrance for the newly dead. Yet, they also serve as a form of remembrance for the ancient ancestors. Indeed, the initial rites for the dead are said to be performed before and for "the eyes of the ancestors" (*timulmul pe amtasek*).

Just after a person's death, a number of messengers leave the tanu to spread word of the death. The messengers travel to the residences of kinsmen. When they meet these kinsmen and speak of the death, they take a fathom of shell money from their coconut-frond baskets and hold it out in front of them. The showing of the shell money is said to confirm the truth of the messenger's statement. Its real import, however, is to express the idea that the life of a person has meaning and value. To announce someone's death without showing a valuable

5. The Rauto have a proverb that describes this scene: *Oduk tituk ye likano uipot pe apna* (The people have died, grass begins to grow in the plaza of their hamlet).

is to belittle the life and the death of this person. The Rauto say that the death of a dog or a pig can be announced without an accompanying sign. The death of a person requires something more. Those who receive word of the death will then come to mourn the body of their kinsman.

In Rauto society as in many other Melanesian societies, death initiates an elaborate cycle of ceremonial exchange and ritual activity. The acts of exchange and the rites especially involve the reaffirmation of a relationship between the patrikin and the matrikin of the deceased. Thus, I was often told that the death of a person means, among many other things, that the matrikin must receive their compensation pay (*kuru*). As each group of kin of the matriline arrives, they are given pearlshell valuables and food. These kin then give back a smaller number of valuables to the patrikin, partly to compensate these people for the energy and resources they have expended looking after the deceased just prior to his death, for preparing for the rites of death, and in order to "finish their sorrow." The difference in the amount of gift and countergift, which is the profit realized by the kin of the matriline (*ingen ino*), is what is properly called *kuru*. The *kuru* is offered partly as compensation for the grief that the matrikin feel and demonstrate by crying when they come to view the body. The pay is also a final recognition that the matriline was responsible for giving issue to the deceased.

As the social relationships between the different ramages are invoked through this series of exchanges, some of the resources that the deceased used to form relationships during life are destroyed. Thus, a number of his taro stalks are cut with a knife and ruined; some of his coconut palms are cut down, and sections of the fishing and hunting nets that he used in life are torn. Also, the house that he lived and died in is destroyed. If he is a big man, the men's ceremonial house that was built and presided over by him is taken down. In prepacification days his wife and perhaps, if his family did not wish to look after them, his small children would be put into the grave with him.

While the exchanges of death reaffirm the meaningfulness of time by relating a moment in the individual's life to a recurrent event in the life of a society, the destructive actions that precede burial are an almost vengeful representation of the narrative of time. These acts express the conviction that time is a destroyer. They refer to how time sunders relationships between people, how it destroys many of the things that are a product of the labor of a person, how it appears to obliterate personal history. However, the meaninglessness of the narrative of time is denied for a second time in the rituals of secondary burial. During these events, time is once again given meaning through human action.

TIME, AGENCY, AND THE DANCE FOR THE DEAD

The series of destructive acts that are performed before burial appear as a symbolic attempt to erase the mark that the agency of a person has made on the world. There is also the sense that the things that are destroyed are manifestations of the person's being. Their destruction represents a perception that they draw their power from the life of the individual and that they should perish with that life. Yet most of a person's possessions will survive his death. His shells and heirlooms are taken by his sons or by other close patrikin. Many of his fruit and palm trees—resources that bear his name—remain to be used by both matrikin and patrikin. His children remain "to take his place," and his bones remain to be honored by the individuals who benefit from the resources that were left to them by him, resources that symbolize the power of human agency to sustain life.

The first phase of the rites of death are completed about a week after the burial.[6] In a gathering at the grave site, the patrikin of the deceased exchange baskets of food with his matrikin and with his affines. A small fire is then built on the grave mound, and a piece of pork is thrown into the fire and consumed by it. This is done so that the dead person can smell and savor the aroma of burning pork for a last time. My informants also told me that the fire on the grave serves to dissipate the pollution that emanates from the site. The rite and food exchange will also mark the end of a prohibition on garden work for the close kin of the deceased. Prior to the enactment of the rite the smell (*malmal*) of death is said to cling to the bodies of these kin and is thought to be injurious to the garden crop. A whole series of mourning prohibitions do, however, extend well beyond this time.[7]

There are three main phases to the rites of secondary burial that follow. The first of these follows closely upon the exhumation of the skeleton. The exhumation itself is performed some four to six months after the initial burial. The skull, jawbone, ulna, and hand bones are unearthed by three men who are paid handsomely for their efforts. They clean whatever flesh remains on the skeleton and then bring the bones out of the hamlet and into the forest. The men hang the bones on the forked branches of a tree that the Rauto call *sengaseng*. When the pollution that emanates from the skeleton is thought to have lessened, the

---

6. In prepacification days the body, hair, and face of the corpse were painted with red ocher prior to burial. The paint was said to identify the ghost of the dead person.

7. For instance, close kin should give up eating pork or some other choice food out of remembrance of the deceased. They should refrain from washing, sometimes for as long as a year after the death. They should refrain from going to song festivals, other than those which honor their dead kinsmen. When these prohibitions are lifted, they remove the black paint which serves as a sign of mourning.

bones are brought back into the hamlet and installed in a newly built men's house. A song festival is then held to mark the introduction of the bones into the men's house.

For most of the festival the genre of song called *agreske* is sung and danced. It is only toward the middle of the night that the dance for the dead is performed. The beginning of the dance is signaled when two men walk to the head of the dancing plaza where the bones of the dead are placed, hanging from the branches of the sengaseng. The men take the jaw and the hand bones from the tree. One takes charge of the jaw, the other of the bones of the hand. Each places a bone in the hollow of a pearlshell. They then take the pearlshells into their hands and perform the dance for the dead. The two dance from one end of the plaza to the other while holding the pearlshells and the bones out in front of them. The women of the matriline meanwhile array themselves on either side of the dancers' paths and wave crotons and herbs at the bones as the dancers go past. The dancers stop periodically and return the bones to the branches of the sengaseng. At this point the agreske begins again, and the dancers rest at a spot close to the tree where the bones hang. They repeat the dance for the dead a number of times during the night. As dawn begins to break, the bones are returned to the ceremonial house, and the festival ends as it began, with the warriors' chant, the agreske. The dance for the dead may be repeated a number of times in the coming weeks or years. Whether it is or not greatly depends on the amount of resources that are possessed by the family which sponsors the ceremonial.

The major event of the cycle occurs when the bones are painted with red ocher. This may take place as many as ten or fifteen years after exhumation. Those who paint the bones also put a streak of the red ocher across their chests. A streak of red is also placed on the chests of the men who are chosen to dance with the bones. The paint is said to be suffused with the spirit of the dead. A number of people said that after painting themselves with the ocher, they could feel the spirit of the dead person come upon them.

During the course of the song festival, the painted dancers carry the spirit of the dead person on their bodies and in the bones that they hold. As Leenhardt might say, they participate in the time and the being of the dead. Close kin of the dead will sometimes weep as they think back to the life that is symbolized by and contained in the bones and on the body of the dancers. For a moment the dancer creates an image of the dead person.[8] After this ceremony some of

8. I remember once taking a Polaroid snapshot of a Rauto big man. As the picture began to take shape, one of the daughters of the big man came up to me and grabbed the photo. She said that now that she possessed an image of her father, it would not be necessary to take his bones from the grave after he died. She did not now need to have the dance for the dead to invoke an image of

the matrikin may take the bones back to their own hamlet in order to look after them and to be close to them. They will, however, eventually be returned to the home village or hamlet and reburied in a final ceremony.

The bones of the dead symbolize the past agency of the deceased. Thus, the jawbone is honored because it represents the voice of a person—a voice that spoke taro magic, strong speech, and that once spoke of giving gifts of taro to others. The hands are celebrated because they gave gifts of food to others and because they produced and handled food. The dances for the dead thus celebrate a principle—human agency—that gives the narrative of a person's life meaning for himself and for others. The dances are a denial that time simply destroys ideals of person and agency; they affirm that these ideals endure.

The cycle of ceremonies for the dead also celebrates the social relationships that sustained the individual economically and spiritually in life and that were in turn sustained by the individual's own activity. The dances especially mark the culturally important relationship between a person and his matrikin. The concept of the person as the embodiment of agency that is literally performed during the dance allows the Rauto to grasp the element of value in and the cyclical aspect of what Stephen Gould calls "time's arrow." The concept emphasizes the common accomplishment of different generations. It thus affirms the enduring element of value in the time of an individual's life and death, as well as in the life and death of generations. Yet it also establishes a concept of uniqueness for specific acts and specific lives, especially for the lives of people of productive accomplishment. It mediates the relationship between time's arrow and time's cycle by joining mythic to narrative identity.[9]

In the final chapters of this work I reflect upon the emotional resonance that death has for Rauto people; there I consider the essential link between cultural creativity, mourning, and recovery.

---

her father. The bigman, being both a defender of custom and someone trying to keep up with the times, suggested that the photo be substituted for his bones during the dances.

9. I only witnessed two phases of the mortuary cycle during my period of fieldwork. I saw the rites of death and of burial, and I saw one of the dances for the dead which precedes that held for the painting of the bones.

Since the decline in the frequency of patrols after independence, the rites of secondary burial have begun to be performed more frequently in parts of the Rauto and Gimi bush. No doubt hearing of this, the New Tribes Mission has endeavored to establish itself in many of the linguistic groups of southern West New Britain. The first order of business for this evangelical group is always the disruption of the mortuary cycle.

Chapter Seven

To Remember the Faces of the Dead: Mourning and the Full Sadness of Memory

The religious object is within [the person] and therefore as little forsakes him as his self-consciousness, or his conscience; it is the intimate, the closest object.

Ludwig Feuerbach (1965)

The person, in opposition to the individual, is capable of enriching itself through a more or less indefinite assimilation of exterior elements. It takes its life from the elements it absorbs, in a wealth of communion. The person is capable of superabundance.

Maurice Leenhardt (1979)

On the day of a performance of the mourning and song ceremony that the Rauto call *serpoua,* I had been trying to understand the sense of the emotional pleas being made to me and other members of the hamlet in which I was living by a boy whose father had just died. The boy asked us to allow him to take back some objects that had once been owned by his father or that were associated with him in some other way. The things he was asking about had little monetary value and, it seems, had not been important to his father. He asked, for instance, about an old shirt of his father's, some strings of shell money, and an old picture I had taken of the man some years before, as I recorded and photographed a ceremony. The boy, whose name was Lamu, told me that his feelings of sorrow and grief over his father's death made him want to hold and to view these things. Besides evoking sympathy and compassion for him in me, his words and feelings proved a catalyst for forming my understanding of the meaning and cultural importance of the emotion that the Rauto call *makai* (nostalgia/full sadness/plenitude).

In this chapter I consider the genre of mourning song that was performed for this boy's father as a night-long poem about death, loss, and separation, which takes particular emotional meaning from the desire of bereaved people to possess, to hold, and finally to cast off the objects of the dead. In viewing the serpoua as an expressive form—one long poem about death, memory, and the emotions evoked by death—I also qualify a notion, put forth both by philosophers (de Sousa 1990:182) and interpretive anthropologists (Rosaldo 1984:142; Lutz 1988:211; White 1990:47) that a particular emotional experience is perhaps best understood "with reference to the cultural scenarios and associations it evokes" (Rosaldo 1984:142). That is, people come to learn the vocabulary of emotion by associating certain feelings with prototypical scenes or events in life. Such scenes and events are called "paradigm scenarios" by de Sousa, and he defines their character in this way: (1) as situation types that provide the "characteristic objects of a specific emotion type"; (2) as sets of characteristic or "normal responses to a situation" (de Sousa 1990:182) that are shaped and continually reinforced by the values and beliefs to which people are exposed.

In de Sousa's view, learning emotion involves learning the culturally appropriate response to a situation type. An emotion evoked by a specific occasion can in turn be partly considered as a perception of the situation's or event's character and meaning (de Sousa 1990:188). However, emotions are not so absolutely tied to, nor is their character so directly determined by spontaneously occurring events as de Sousa suggests. They can also acquire meaning in deliberate and reflective acts of cultural construction (e.g., dramatic or ritual performance, artistic expression). During such performative moments, awareness of the life significance of events can be forged through a deliberately created form of emotional experience.

In this chapter I show how the Rauto reflectively add depth and meaning to their experience of death; in so doing I consider some ways in which emotions can be considered as akin to a systematic philosophy or, in Michele Rosaldo's phrase, a system of "embodied or felt thoughts" (1984:143). My argument, simply stated, is that the poetic expression of images of loss in Rauto mourning songs is one important way in which both feeling and death are systematically invested with meaning. In advancing this argument the chapter considers an important question that has been raised, though not yet fully explored, by philosophers or anthropologists: How can a pattern of emotions be considered as a kind of philosophy that "frames, transforms, and makes sense of" problems of existential meaning (de Sousa 1990:4), problems of the sort that my friend Lamu was grappling with as he asked me to give him that picture of his father.

Rauto songs and rites of death define emotional experience through the expression of poems that portray the range of situations or scenarios in which particular emotions are typically experienced. Considered together, the images of the song poetry can be viewed as a series of composite metaphors about the nature of loss and sorrow. It is this particular condensation of metaphoric image, and thus of metaphoric meaning, that both reveals and in part creates the various levels of meaning that give particular emotions their character. The serpoua do not simply reiterate the social scenarios during which specific emotions are usually experienced, thereby simply reproducing the emotions associated with these scenarios. It would be more accurate to say, as I do here, that the songs reflectively create a metaemotion for and a metathought about the character of death and loss.

The serpoua are also instructive in that they tell us something of the link between a specific style of cultural creativity, or invention, and a particular ethos of feeling. Indeed, as I show, aspects of the emotional experience evoked by the performance of the serpoua are an essential part of many Rauto acts of cultural creativity. Like these acts, the singing of mourning songs represents a feeling exercise of remembering and memorializing what the Rauto call the "faces of the dead."

Such acts of remembering are viewed here as imaginative and feeling attempts to recover the spiritual and valued essence of presences that have been lost. Readers will recognize in this idea something of Martin Buber's "Melancholy Ontology," especially his idea that "mourning is characterized by three fused movements: loss, imagination, and recovery" (Steinhoff Smith 1989:326–43). What I find particularly moving and, in this context, useful about Buber's work is his notion that the self and emotion are imaginatively formed and then transformed in the process of mourning.

In Buber's view, the self is created and continually transformed as a person reaches out to establish "a unity of relation" with another, or with a felt perception of another's essential character. That is, self-consciousness is born and reborn out of the recognition that separation exists between the self and another, and out of attempts to bridge that separation (Buber 1958:25–27). Reality, or being, is also created anew as well as contained within each attempt at forging a relational encounter with another (Buber 1958:12). However, the need for relational encounter is often perceived to result from the loss of relationship. Indeed, in Buber's philosophy it is loss that initially prompts the reaching out that leads to self-consciousness and self-transformation. Steinhoff Smith goes so far as to argue that self-consciousness without loss is unthinkable in Buber's ontology (1989:336).

The first, or primal loss, is suffered by the newly born child. Separated from a unity of relation with its mother by the event of birth, the child comes to recognize the distinctiveness of its own body and being as it reaches out for and attempts to recover the sense of unity with its mother (Steinhoff Smith 1989:336). This sense, however, is recovered "as a differentiated union; the reality of distance remains as part of it. The recovery is not a return to the state before loss but includes the loss" (Steinhoff Smith 1989:328).

In mourning, as in birth, the self is taken out of an original sense of plenitude derived from the fact of a previously formed union with another and is forced to confront the emptiness occasioned by loss. After a period of time permits the bereaved to feel a certain emotional distance from the object of loss, he or she can begin to use the moral imagination to fill the emptiness within. Thus, a felt image of the lost relationship and person can be internalized as a memory. In this way the valued essence and human quality of what has been lost ideally becomes part of one's own self and of one's way of acting within the world (Steinhoff Smith 1989:341). In this process of imaginative memory making, the bereaved's feelings of grief and, perhaps, of anger and resentment toward the person who has been lost and toward the world are ideally transformed into a full sadness—a plenitude of accepting sadness, gratitude, and even joy.

Buber's psychology of mourning is a parable about the repair of personal worlds that have been ravaged and tattered by a loss. In this chapter I use his psychology of mourning to show how serpoua can be seen to transform individual feelings, and thus aspects of the self, as it realigns, even repairs, social worlds. More specifically, I show how socially disruptive and frequently destructive forms of grief and anger are transformed into the culturally creative emotion called *makai,* and into quietly borne emotional pain (*kipitngen*). As part of the same rhetorical move, I show how the serpoua provides the bereaved with a memory that is to be created and then evoked time and again as an objectified image of meaning, of human power, and of what could perhaps be called the feeling of plenitude. As I indicate, the evocation and creation of this feeling is the true *telos* of the rites and songs of mourning and of many other creative Rauto acts. This is the metaemotion and the metathought about death and loss that the Rauto continually and reflectively seek to create during the major performances that characterize their culture—the emotion of makai.

As I indicate below, this form of nostalgia reveals something of the relational aspect of Rauto concepts of person, an aspect that, as we have seen, is reflected in a host of beliefs and cultural practices aside from those that inform ceremonial life. Yet the performance of the serpoua especially confirms the point that the emotional life of the Rauto person has a crucial relational dimension "often providing a social rather than an individual idiom, a way of commenting not so much on oneself as on oneself in relation to others"

(Brenneis 1990:113). These songs also seem symbolically to "deconstruct" and then reconstruct persons' social identities. They accomplish this by facilitating the symbolic and actual separation of the dead from those things, people, and objects in which they have invested something of personal spiritual power (*nara*) or essence. In creating this form of separation the serpoua present profound problems of meaning "in emotional terms" (Lutz and White 1986:427). One of these problems is the bereaved's need to recover—by reconstructing in another, imaginative form—something of the valued essence of the presence that has been lost.

THE DEATH VIGIL AND THE EVENTS AND EMOTIONS THAT PRECEDE THE SONG CEREMONY

The days just prior to the death of a sick person are usually marked by the vigil of close kin—an event that has a specific emotional tone that consists of both culturally specific types of anger and sorrow. People's anger could be felt especially in the discussions that took place during the vigil, in which both men and women examined the character of the dying person's social relationships in order to determine who may have had motive to sorcerize and thereby murder the person. Such anger usually remains diffuse and undirected at first, because it has no object until a likely suspect emerges during the course of the review of the dying person's life. Frequently, however, this anger builds as people become convinced that their kinsman is being sorcerized by a particular person. The Rauto call this set and intense anger *apeline negek,* and outbursts of it as well as loudly verbalized accusations sometimes erupt during this stage of the vigil. During one such outburst, the son, W., of a man who lay dying, P., went so far as to accuse one of his affines, B., of attempting to sorcerize his father. Treating an affine this way is a serious breach of custom in this society. The son had heard that the affine had made allusion to how P. was being paid back for having accused members of the affine's family of stealing from him. Afterward W. excused his outburst by explaining that news of his affine's words had caused his gorge to rise as "quickly as lightening." This type of explosive anger and the outbursts it often causes are considered socially disruptive and, thus, elders sometimes council people "to swallow" their anger and their talk during the period of the vigil. Those who manage to do this are considered to have exhibited good character and proper comportment (*lai itau*). This strong moral constraint helps to limit the intensity and number of accusations leveled against others during the period of the vigil. If an accusation is brought, ideally it should be done circumspectly, with the suspected person approached and furtively given a type of compensation pay, called *onguo,* to quiet his anger for the wrong that has been done to him. An acceptance of the pay is an indication that he may leave off sorcerizing his victim.[1]

We see in this time of premourning a recognition that the world is somehow implicated in the suffering of the dying. The rage and resentment thought to be felt by the dying person's imagined or actual enemy is what involves this presence in the person's sickness or death. Yet a similar anger draws the kin of the dying into close involvement with the facts of sickness and death. If we credit Freud's idea that those closest to a dying person often feel responsible for having willed this person's suffering and death, then the offering of the compensation pay called *onguo* can be seen as kin's attempt to cast out or project onto others their own feelings of guilt and responsibility for the suffering or death that they are witnessing.

What seems much more distinctive about this, however, and indeed about all phases and aspects of mortuary rite, is the social and individual longing for recovery that the rites express. In the instance of the vigil, what must be recovered is the relationship between the dying person and those that he has injured in some way. The kin of this person themselves begin to take responsibility for the recovery of this relationship, first by asking the dying person about his transgressions, then by calming their own anger for the injury that is being done to one of their own, and finally by offering the onguo. Considered in this way, the onguo can be seen not primarily as a projection of guilt (indeed, the semantics of the Rauto term that most closely resembles the English term *guilt* indicates that it does not), but as an attempt to incorporate the hated other into the drama and feeling of death in a positive rather than in a socially disruptive way.[2]

Yet, socially disruptive anger and animosity also often distinguish the moments that immediately follow death. Indeed, the series of destructive acts that always accompany death—the rending of sections of the dead's fishing and hunting nets, the destruction of his taro, the cutting down of a number of his fruit trees, the destruction of a number of his pearlshells—are often carried out in a spirit of anger. The particular combination of rage and grief that often prompts the closest kin of the dead to take such action, and that often fills their hearts, has a specific name. It is called *iang iango,* a word I would translate as

1. Though most renowned sorcerers are men, women too are considered capable of bringing about someone's death through sorcery and are sometimes accused of having done so.

2. I have argued that for this people conscience consists, in part, of a proper understanding of the moral dimension of tradition, or custom (*lai*). Guilt is contained in a type of regret, felt perhaps more keenly by some than by others, that one has ignored or violated the spirit of tradition in one's dealings with others. The onguo is an offering whose character is in spirit with the "law" of tradition, or custom, in the sense that it is given in order to heal a social breach.

"blind, raging grief-anger." The expression of this emotion sometimes culmi-
nates in some of the most heart-wrenching forms of mourning behavior to be
seen in southwestern New Britain. My closest Rauto friend experienced this
emotion when one of his children died. His words convey a sense of its power
to bring a person to the brink:

> My young boy Ukes, who was named by my father, was my last born. His
> mother had already sung the *segeingen* for him.[3] She and Kapuk took him to
> Mesalia [place of his mother's kin], and he became sick there. His grand-
> parents sent him and his mother back, but I was not there to see them. I had
> gone to Kandrian. After some time the sickness took a strong hold of him,
> and he died. My daughter and some of her cousins rushed to Kandrian to
> bring me the news. They found me there the next morning, drunk and acting
> like a fool. I was startled when they came and put the shell money across
> my leg; I thought one of my parents, or someone like that had died. They
> told me that Ukes had died. My heart jumped into my throat; many thoughts
> raced through my mind's eye, and I lost my senses. My whole body shook,
> and a great pain stabbed my heart. I was iang iango. I remembered my son,
> and I was iang iango. I couldn't cry because I was iang iango. We found a
> boat to take us back, and we headed straight for home. The elders already
> knew my thoughts, and what I would do when I arrived. They told my par-
> ents and my wife to keep out of sight when I came. They knew that if I had
> seen them just then, I would have tried to kill them. I was really iang iango.
> My heart was so full of this feeling that I thought it would burst. They took
> me to my son and when I saw him I held him and cried. The anger left and
> then I was just sad. When I was calmer, Tapme [his wife] appeared, and we
> embraced. That night we sang the serpoua for him. As the others sang, we
> passed the child from hand to hand and spilled our grief on him.

As the feeling of iang iango was described for me, it seemed to involve a
desperate search to find a way to bring an irreplaceable thing or person that
was irretrievably lost back into one's possession. The incipient realization that
there is no way to do that, that the loss is final, brings on the intense emotion, as in the example described in chapter 2, p. 50. Another person who
had experienced this feeling, and who also knew some English, described it
as an internal "struggle" to find a way to come to terms with a loss. He said

3. The *segeingen* is a playful, humorous category of song that is said to belong to women;
that is, it is performed mostly by them. During its performance, women mix up verses of songs
belonging to other, more serious genres. In so doing they playfully deride the more formal aspects
of ceremonial life, especially those aspects formally controlled by men. Women perform this song
genre during a time when one of their sex is celebrating a major accomplishment; for instance,
after having given birth to a child, or while being honored in a special ceremony performed for
firstborn children, or after having weaned a child.

that the struggle "brings anger," and sometimes "causes people to become violent."

In this struggle we can see the grieving person's desire to continue to experience the sense of plenitude that he or she felt daily in interacting with the lost other. But *we* do not see the reason for violence, for the wish to strike out at others and at objects that were part of the fabric of a lost relationship. One of the reasons that grief occasions violence is that the loss of a treasured person or possession is felt to be an assault upon and a theft of an aspect of the self—one that calls out for retribution (*ngot*). A personal loss can have such meaning for the Rauto because they perceive identity to reside both within the individual person and in the ensemble of participations that join the person to others and to cultural and natural objects. Indeed, when so much of religious life is directed toward the spiritual investment of self in others and in objects, a person's sense of self becomes part of and sharpens his or her sense of possession. This is one of the reasons why treasured possessions and treasured people are said to carry one's name and identity (*anine*).

Typically, when a possession is taken from a Rauto person, he or she will either demand compensation or seek retribution. The emotion (*iang iango*) that is evoked by a serious personal loss itself adds force to the frequently socially disruptive desire for retribution—the impulse to strike out at someone or something who may seem responsible for the loss that the mourner has suffered.

When transgressions are committed against Rauto people, they must receive compensation payment if they are to eschew violence or sorcery. Appropriately, then, one of the ways in which the grief-anger of bereaved kin is lessened is through the exchange of death payments. In the exchanges of death it becomes the duty of the dead's matrikin to attempt to quiet the grief-anger of the dead's close patrikin by providing them with pearlshells. It then becomes the duty of patrikin, or of the members of the dead's resident cognatic group, to quiet in their turn the anger and grief felt by the deceased's matrikin. Thus, there is a reciprocal exchange of valuables after death.

The assertion that these transactions are considered actually to transform or quiet people's grief—at least in some of its more dramatic outward manifestations—is given support by the following illustration. The narrative is an account of a form of mourning behavior that was seen by a middle-aged man upon the death of his grandfather around 1982.

> When my grandfather died, all those from Ipuk (matrikin) came down to mourn him. They came bearing their grief and anger. When they reached our gardens, they speared a number of pigs that were rooting around there. Then

they came down on us, their women rushing ahead of their men and swinging their *rege* (women's fighting sticks) at us, and spitting betel at us. My father knew what they would do if they found him, but he remained sitting by the door of his house. The women spit betel on him, and pounded him with their fists. The men then came and threatened him as well as the rest of us with their spears. When they came to my grandfather's body, Lumbat and Saiko laid down next to it and began to speak to it, as each put one of the corpse's arms around his neck. They didn't cry; they just continued to hold the body and talk to it until we gave them a few pearlshells to finish their grief. Then they wept over the body. After a while they stopped their wailing.

The ceremonial exchanges of shells and of other resources that take place after the death of a person are repeated a number of times, since at least three or four groups of kin will usually come to view the body. While the exchanges are meant to ensure personal acceptance of the fact that one has lost a relation and has received at least token compensation for this loss, they also symbolize a type of social reconciliation. The reciprocal exchange represents tacit acknowledgement that members of none of the kin groups will hold the others responsible for the death in their midst. Thus, after the exchange the respective kin groups should ideally continue to be joined in a relationship of mutual obligation and assistance.

THE MOURNING SONGS

The performance of the serpoua is part of the grieving person's move toward the experience of emotions that are more endurable, though as deeply felt as the emotion called iang iango or other forms of anger. Aspects of this move can be perceived in the emotional tone of the song ceremony, a tone created by the portrayal as well as the actual experience of a particular pattern of emotions. As we shall see, these emotions are a type of sorrow (*momso ulong*), a type of nostalgia (*momso makai*), and quietly borne grief (*kipitngen*). A number of the songs are evocative models for the experience of these emotions and thus for how kin should ideally feel about the loss that they have suffered.

After the last group of kin has viewed the body, and the exchange of valuables has been completed, the men who control the spirit masks, called *kamotmot*, will send these spirit beings to the dead's bier.[4] There they will sit by the dead in a slumped fashion in order to express their sorrow. As they arrive, a hush settles over the hamlet out of respect for the masks and for the moment

4. These masked beings are part of a secret society that is somewhat like the Duk Duk society of the Tolai. One of the major song festivals of Rauto cultural life is also performed for the kamotmot.

of death. The serpoua are sung on the evening that follows this visit, while the ghost (*anine*) of the dead remains close to the corpse.

As the songs are performed for the dead person, it is thought that some are sung by the dead. That is, while the songs express the sorrow and grief of the living, it is thought that during the song festival the ancestral dead sometimes use people's voices to express their own sorrow for the loss of their lives. This thought is reflected in the structure of some of the songs. Often the singers put themselves in the place of the dead by singing, in the first person, of the dead's thoughts and feelings. I was also told that the themes of many serpoua were revealed when ghosts of the dead appeared to people in dreams and told the dreamers, and future composers, of their sorrows.

The singing that takes place during the night is not itself referred to as song, but as weeping. Thus people do not say that they sing serpoua, but that they "weep it" (*ti gripin serpoua*). As the singing begins, the dead's immediate family huddle around the body, touching it and crying over it as the songs of their kinsmen make them think back to the life of the dead person. Most men either try to stifle their tears (*pagum gripinngen*), or they cry in the low and soft tones that the Rauto call *ngitngit*. Women more often weep as they inter-mittently cry out in high-pitched wails (*ti gripin nambri nambri*). They can sometimes keep this up for hours at a time (*ti gripin mulo malkat*). Women of the Rauto bush also sometimes mourn by weeping a tune that is said to imitate the melancholy song of the forest bird *uaik*. This sort of singing is said really to stab at people's hearts and make them spill their grief.

The singing begins at about nine at night, and continues until dawn. At first the songs are sung by the dead's own cognatic or resident group. Toward the middle of the night they are joined by another formally invited group, specifi-cally identified as the matrikin of the dead. During serpoua these two groups of kin join and sing in unison, rather than in competition, as in other Rauto song festivals. Occasionally one or two of the song performers will leave off singing and join the other mourners at the side of the dead. There is not, then, the same absolute distinction between audience and performers that one sees dur-ing the Kaluli performances of *gisalo* (Feld 1982:216). Singers both attempt to move others by their song and, when they briefly become part of the audience, are moved by the song performance themselves. The songs total about forty and, unlike other genres, such as the aurang, are sung in no particular order, although the ceremony always closes with the same two songs.

Like the Kaluli gisalo, the serpoua are allusive in nature. Unlike the gisalo, the serpoua are informed with meaning by a number of different themes. These underlying themes are as follows: (1) the dead are nostalgic for their lives; they regret being separated from the activities and scenes of life. (2) Death makes

The spirit beings (kamotmot) mourn the death of a man.

orphans of the bereaved; it is about separation and abandonment. (3) Death involves the dismantling and transformation of the dead person's social identity.

The Dead Are Nostalgic for Their Lives, and the Living Are Nostalgic for the Dead

A number of serpoua that have the nostalgia of the dead for their lives or the nostalgia of the living for the dead as their themes seem especially poignant when one considers them in relation to the celebratory songs that the Rauto call *agreske*. These songs are about the energy and life that is contained in the things of the world. The agreske enumerate the birds, fish, plants, foods, trees, rivers, and animals of the Rauto world as they celebrate the life energy that these things embody and express in their growth or in their movement. Of particular interest to us here are those agreske that enumerate the foods and plants of southwestern New Britain. One of these songs describes a group of young girls harvesting all the known varieties of taro from a garden. Like all agreske the song is sung with much gusto, to a quick beat, and is a celebration of some of the exertions and energies of life. The first two serpoua that I will discuss use a similar image, yet invert its meaning by investing the image with a completely different emotional tone. Indeed, if the agreske are energy, the serpoua are pathos. The rhythms and musical tones of the serpoua that follow are consistent with images that allude to the loss of energy, movement, and life:

Silo mesa lai mare.	
La tan akate.	She takes the *akate*.
La tan amar.	She takes the *amor*.
La tan apaoot.	She takes the *apaoot*.
La tan oulip.	She takes the *oulip*.
La tan ambula.	She takes the *ambula*.
La tan auring.	She takes the *auring*.
Lai mare.	
Mutan krimbak.	Bring the sweet potato.
Mutan uvul.	Bring the banana.
Mutan auo.	Bring the sugar.
Mutan mamim.	Bring the yam.
Mutan isin.	Bring the taro.

Through the use of allusion, the first of these songs conjures an image of a man lying on his deathbed and dreaming of children working in his garden. In his dream he sees a little girl carry the stalk of the taro called *akate* into his garden and then throw it down before the hole that has been prepared to receive it. In the dream and song sequence an older girl then carries a more prized variety of taro into his garden and throws the stalk down waiting for it to be planted. The song concludes by describing an elder daughter carrying into the garden the stalk of the variety of taro most prized by Rauto, that called *auring*. As the dreamer's mind's eye sees this, he dies, leaving this scene of life behind. The second song uses a similar image; again a dying man dreams of his garden and of all the food that he has planted in it. In his dream he summons his daughters to harvest the various crops, and as the eldest daughter begins to harvest his taro, he dies. The two songs evoke feelings of sorrow by, I was told, alluding to the sense of loss and nostalgia that both the dying men feel for what are some of the most commonplace scenes of their lives.

These next two mourning songs allude to the affection that many people of southwestern New Britain feel toward their homes and toward the places and sites of the landscape:

Gripin,	He cries,
o Malanga,	oh Malanga,
o Puit,	oh Puit,
o Mandol,	oh Mandol,
o Sangru,	oh Sangru,
o Magien,	oh Magien,
evindru,	[I have arrived at] the

konong keneng.   hamlet. He sleeps now.

Nga mlok ko   I rest and wait at
ningiau o,   the old place.
nga mlok nga roro.   Alas, Wasum is the
Alei Wasum o   place of another.
eren ilo.

The first of these songs tells the story of a man named Keneng. The man had fallen sick far from his home, and when it became apparent that he would die, his kin constructed a litter for him and carried him back to his home at Magien, a village located on the island of Aviklo, one of the three islands that guard the entrance to the bay of Kandrian. The song alludes to how he was brought past sites on which he had walked and worked, and how he cried as he passed these sites. Informants told me that Keneng had wept because he knew he would never see the places whose names he called out again. The song concludes by alluding to how he died as he entered his men's house at Magien, after having said how he wished to rest there.

The second song is another composed from the images of a dream. Its composer had dreamt that the shade of his grandfather appeared to him and grieved for the loss of his life and for the loss of his former home, Wasum. The composer told me that the shade felt makai for his place, and that he (the composer) had cried when he learned of his grandfather's sorrow and nostalgia. Rauto beliefs about the afterlife offer insight into the reason why the dead are thought to be nostalgic for their lives. There is an agnostic quality or flavor to this understanding, one that is hinted at in a number of mourning songs:

Ivo sa   My father
tila timare   goes to Andeua.
ei Andeua. La lare   Does he go to
ivo sa?   this place?

La ilauve   He goes to this
la motmot,   mountain, then to this
la ilauve   island. Will he
nakul me?   return again?

The first song alludes to the sense of loss felt by a son for his dead father. The son plaintively asks if his father's spirit will go to one of the places of the dead, Mount Andeua. The son's question is made all the more poignant by his feeling that his father is utterly lost to him. The second song alludes to the journey of a ghost to one of the places of the dead and expresses another speculation about the fate of the dead. It plaintively asks if the ghost will journey to a mountain, or an island—abodes of the dead—and if the ghost will then return.[5]

In the few songs that I have given here, the dead are represented as sharing the nostalgic longing of the living for life as it was. In these and other songs the *topoi,* or places of nostalgia for both the living and the dead, are the recalled activities of life, the places where these activities took place, the possessions of the dead—in short, all manifestations or embodiments of the lost person's being. All these places of feeling are referred to as *amta mune* by the Rauto, a phrase that translates as the "mark or imprint of a person's visage." A less clumsy translation of the phrase would be "the memorial of a person." I found it significant that, try as I might, I could not elicit a more abstract term for memory than *amta mune.* Though I tried, I was always told about remembrances (*amta mune*), tokens of memory that facilitated remembering. The semantic convergence between memory and memorial only began to make sense as I learned more about this people's cultural style of remembering the dead or of remembering living but absent kin or friends.

When people feel the makai (nostalgia/full sorrow/plenitude) of lost relationships, they often express the feeling by speaking of the possessions, places, names, plants, and acts associated with the lost person. Acts of remembrance often seem to be a memorializing of these things, places, names, marks, or acts—a making of them into the visage of a person (*pat ino amta mune*), as in this example taken from my field notes:

> As I watched the masked spirit beings [called Kamotmot] dance during a ceremony, I heard the sound of sobbing coming from my immediate right. I noticed that an old woman was crying, and asked one of my friends why. When he whispered my question to one of the woman's companions, he was told that the woman was weeping because she saw the face of her long dead brother in the design of the dancing spirit mask. The mask had once been owned or controlled by her brother and was, as Rauto say, part of his life (*ino togowong*).

The cultural significance that makai has for this people is difficult to downplay when it is pointed out that many of the things, places, and names of the cultural and natural order are carriers of the memories of people and are thus presences in their own right. Indeed, it is not only important cultural objects

---

5. One of the reasons that the New Tribes Mission objects to the rites and songs of death and secondary burial is that they do not shift mourners' thoughts and gaze toward a consideration of the afterlife. These missionaries tell people that they should not "be too concerned" about losing someone to death, since death is, in their view, the beginning rather than the end of spiritual existence. The emotionalism of these rites is also disturbing to the New Tribes people.

that are associated with personal identities or with the identities of the dead. Food-bearing trees are named for and are thought to embody something of the soulstuff of their planters; former habitation sites often bear the names of past residents; even personal names are thought to carry something of the identities of past and present owners. This makes makai and memorial primary spiritual components of the cultural and natural order. What seems most important, however, is that the sort of nostalgic remembering or memorializing that takes place during the composition and performance of serpoua represents the essential gist of most acts of traditional religious expression and experience. When, for instance, a man cries as he composes a serpoua that alludes to his dead grandfather's makai for his lost life; when a magician weeps as he watches the taro effigy take shape by his order and to his song because, in his words, the thing is the face (amta) and memory of his father; when female ritual leaders see the beautifully bedecked initiate and weep because she reminds them of their own pasts and of those, now dead, who once performed the rite of initiation for them, the creation and expression of cultural forms becomes synonymous with the memorialization of lost and loved people. Remembering by memorializing and experiencing makai are thus inseparably linked to the creation and expression of culture.

What ultimately emerges from this form of cultural expression is, in part, a memorialization of the sense of plenitude that the lost person once contributed to the lives of those left behind to remember. This is one of the reasons why images of the dead are made to appear at moments of participatory custom— moments such as initiation or taro ritual that are about the spiritual joining of different generations. During a moment such as initiation, memorializing the dead and the past becomes a celebration of the possibilities of the present and of the waxing strength of a new generation. The feeling of plenitude that derives from helping to create the emerging identity and strength of a new generation becomes an essential part of remembering the part once played by a dead kinsman in creating one's own identity and life. In this way those who remember a dead friend or kinsman during a time such as initiation are able to enter into a new spiritual relationship by incorporating this loved and lost person into the spiritual acts, objects, and facts of the present. As Steinhoff Smith suggests (1989:343) an act such as this, which represents a creative recovering of or recreation of the lost person "in another, imaginative form," may mark the true completion of mourning.

Death Makes Orphans of the Bereaved and Is about
Separation and Abandonment

| Nga uarei | Alas, she has died. |
| meku la | If she could only |

mekia o	come back [so that
nga uarei	we could walk
nukul me ma lango	together as before].

This song alludes to the grief and nostalgia felt by a widower for his dead wife. It is meant to allude to the feelings of an old man, someone who had lived with his wife for many years and had grown very close to her. One informant, an old man named Ponda, told me that the man alluded to in the song becomes sorrowful as he remembers how he and his wife would walk together to their garden each day, how together they would prepare food, how they would often sit and talk together. He went on to explain that the sorrow felt by a widower for the loss of a wife is like the emotion felt by a child that has lost its mother. That is, the sense of abandonment, loneliness, and helplessness that often overcomes a widower can make him feel as helpless as an orphaned child.

The idea that death makes orphans of the bereaved is allusively expressed by the following serpoua.

Alei, vo	Alas,
ivo la	father Akraiut
Akraiut	has died;
ti gripin.	they cry [his children
	cry].

Atete	Grandfather, I remain
Pa lelei	alone [and grieve for you,
la atete.	who will hear my tears?]

These songs evoke feelings of sorrow and pity (*ulong*) by alluding to how death makes orphans of children, leaving them helpless and weeping; yet their tears are heard by no one who either can or will comfort, protect, and otherwise help them. The theme of the helpless orphan is found in story as well as song and reveals a major emotional concern of Rauto people; indeed many myths describe the plights and adventures of those who are disadvantaged because of the loss of one or both of their parents.[6] The plight of being alone, without parents to provide food and emotional support, to provide compensation payment to others for one's transgressions, and to provide advice connotes loss of power and status. It is a state to be pitied. While the serpoua evoke feelings of sorrow and pity by considering some of the emotional consequences of death for children, they also make the larger point that death makes orphans of those who

6. Another way in which the Rauto mourn is to recite some of these poignant myths during the night before a burial. Men and women gather around the body and take turns telling these "sad stories." The night begins with the telling of relatively brief myths. As the night wears on, longer stories are told, some taking one hour or more to recite.

are left behind to grieve. When hearing these songs, the bereaved feel the same sense of abandonment, sorrow, and helplessness as does an orphaned child.

Usually, however, orphaned children can expect help, nurturance and compassion from others. On the night of the performance of the serpoua, there seems to be no such comfort for the bereaved.

Death Involves Emotional and Physical Separation and Is about the Dismantling and Transformation of the Dead's Social Identity

Crossan (1973:341) writes that a metaphoric image "creates a participation in that which it articulates." In his view the emotional power of effective poetic and religious imagery is contained, in part, in its ability to allow people to experience the emotions and thoughts that such imagery represents. The idea is pertinent here since we have seen in the previous set of songs how images of weeping children and of mourning and helpless widows and widowers draw the bereaved toward a sense of abandonment, sorrow, and helplessness. Yet the full Rauto experience of loss, sorrow, and grief is neither wholly contained within or expressed by any single poetic image or any discrete set of images. The full experience of these emotions is conveyed only through the totality of images that are sung during the course of the night. For instance, the imagery of these next few songs amplifies and deepens the experience of grief by adding a sense of physical and spiritual separation to the sense of helplessness and abandonment that death evokes.

> Ruru, matom sale   The dirt covers your face
> ruru matom sale,   my brother. [As you rest
> lutngong.   with your face turned
>   upward, you must see this.]
>
> Mlok pe ano eren,   He rests in another
> nukur kading e.   place, his face hidden
> Nga gripin.   from my view by this
>   promontory. I weep.

The first of these songs describes a sister's feeling as she witnesses the burial of her brother. She weeps as she sees the dirt that is thrown into his grave begin to cover his face and remarks that his face seems to turn upward to meet the soil that is thrown upon it. The wrenching finality of her loss is confirmed by each handful of dirt that strikes her brother's face and begins physically to separate him from her.

The second serpoua alludes to the sense of loss and separation felt by a widow for her dead husband. I was told that the widow had returned to live in her natal village after her husband's death. The image of the song describes her looking back toward the promontory beyond which lie her husband's native hamlet and grave. In the song's poetics the promontory becomes a condensation of meanings, analogies, and feelings—at once a grave marker, an obstacle keeping the widow separated from her dead husband, and, as well, the physical embodiment of her sorrow and grief. She weeps because of the sense of loss and separation that the object evokes in her. The bereaved who attend the serpoua weep upon hearing this song out of a sense of identification with this woman's feelings.

The Rauto have a word, *nakalang,* for both the distance that separates a person from an absent and longed-for other and for objects, such as the promontory mentioned in this song, that image separation and thereby cause emotional pain. In a more literal usage, a nakalang is simply a stick or leaf that serves as a path marker. Placed at the entrance to one of the trails of a crossroad, it indicates the road that has not been taken by a traveler and thus blocks entry to the path by those who would wish to follow and find the traveler. In another figurative usage, the nakalang is said to prevent these others from seeing the person sought for along this path. The serpoua discussed here uses this conventional metaphor in an unconventional way by poetically expressing the idea that death is a nakalang, an object that separates a person from a loved and lost other.

These next few songs are also about the sense of separation created by things or objects, most especially by the objects of the dead. They evoke the mournful realization that the dead have left the grasp of the living. They express the idea that, when people die, the marks left by their lives are found in those things that they have invested something of themselves in: other people, possessions, the land, the trees, and plants that they have cultivated.

Makai io	I yearn for you
Salemando.	Salemando.
Makai io	I see this
makai io.	Croton [that you have
Tiua Tiua	planted], I yearn for you.
bebe lunga.	
Iaugei	Iaugei [person's name]
serei lunga,	I break these
serei lunga,	crotons of yours,
alei, Iaugei.	alas, Iaugei.
Tili lua	Your *tili*
ua lai marei	remains [I hold it
lai marei	and grieve].
Tili lua	

The first song alludes to a woman who, while working in her garden, sees a croton her husband had planted. As she looks at the plant, she begins to grieve and to be nostalgic for her dead husband. The second song describes a woman destroying the crotons that her dead husband had planted around the borders of her house. She destroys these plants while in a state of extreme anger and grief (*iang iango*).

The last song conjures an image of a person viewing and handling an heirloom (a type of shell money) of a kinsmen or friend who has died. As this person handles the object, his mind's eye begins to want to possess it (*amta sisire*). Yet his desire for the object really represents a longing to see the dead person again—to possess him and hold him in the same way that he now holds this person's heirloom. The tragic emotion that is both portrayed and evoked by the song is contained in the realization that the dead person can never be touched or possessed again in this way, that this person has become separated from his possession, that the possession is now simply a token or object of remembrance. The separation the living feel from the dead is symbolized by such objects of remembrance. Thus it is that the serpoua use images of these things to evoke feelings of loss, sorrow, and nostalgia.

This last song is also interesting because it portrays the set of emotions that Rauto people experience during what they call the "second cry." This second period of grieving takes place only some time after the intense initial shock of death and the feelings of utter hopelessness that accompany it have passed. This serpoua and a number of others sung during the song festival are really, then, as much if not more about the experience of nostalgia as they are about the experience of desperate grief (*iang iango*). Indeed, a number of the songs seem reflective and emotionally distanced from the intense drama and feeling that characterize the days just after death (see Scheff 1977, on the aesthetic distancing of emotions in ritual). The imagery of the songs describes passing, although poignant, moments of reflection upon death, experienced at a time when the loss of a friend, a kinsmen, a wife, or child is no longer the only concern of a person's life.

Admittedly, however, the imagery of other serpoua appears actually to bring the bereaved closer to the raw and wrenching emotionalism that typically accompanies the immediate experience of death. For instance, the image of a helpless and crying infant, or of a sister witnessing her brother's burial, or of a woman angrily destroying the crotons planted by her husband in no way enables the bereaved to draw feeling back from the incident of death.

The two distinct emotional tones evoked by the serpoua represent two conflicting desires entertained by mourners. There is first the desire to draw closer to the brute fact of and experience of death, and thus to continue to share something of the lost person's being. As Redfield remarks, according to this logic, "the most perfect mourning would be suicide" (1975:181). Less drastic forms of drawing close to death are represented by Rauto practices such as touching and holding the putrefying corpse, or covering one's body with the soot of mourning—soot that is referred to as the filth of the dead. In this way the mourner symbolically assumes something of the appearance of death.

The second wish expressed and evoked by the images of the serpoua is the desire to distance oneself from the fact of death and so resume the course of one's own life. Poetic images that both evoke and represent this desire can be seen as a series of cues to the bereaved as to how they should begin to draw their grief back from, to distance themselves from the tragic event that they are enduring. They do this partly by alluding to the nostalgia felt by others who have experienced loss and death. The message is that the bereaved should and will eventually feel as these others have. A final series of ceremonial acts and poetic images are needed, however, to achieve and to represent the symbolic transformation of the bereaved's desire to participate in death. These acts and images conclude the song festival.

The final two songs performed during the ceremony evoke and portray feelings of nostalgia and of separation from death by representing images of the socially "deconstructed" and transformed person. The songs are sung at the same time that some of the personal possessions of the dead person are destroyed by mourners in the final act of the ceremony. The ritual act of destroying these possessions can be seen as an attempt to strip away or attenuate aspects of the deceased's personal and social identity. It symbolizes the forced withdrawal of the dead person's identity and agency from the world and from the bereaved.[7] There is a certain cultural logic to such attempts, since, during initiation, the Rauto ritually attempt to construct or augment the social and personal identities of the young by presenting them with important cultural objects. In initiation, the Rauto use song to celebrate and to effect the spiritual joining of the person to others and to important objects of culture. During mortuary rite, the Rauto use song to effect the separation of the person from objects and from others. Thus, death involves, at least at first, the person's withdrawal from a series of spiritual participations. This seems to be its true tragedy for this people:

O uaiko	Oh, uaik's song
uaiko a,	[When you hear this song
a la la re	think of me.]

7. It is in this sense that the songs can be considered what de Sousa (1990:181–84) calls "paradigm scenarios," or models for the experience of types of emotion.

mo rikngong klik	I am going,
o molmolei.	you will see me no more.
O uaiko o uaiko	Look after [these things
o molmolei.	of mine well].
	Look after [these things
	well.]

Sei mo, akai ko	I leave you now, smoke
sei lemo	rising; these things
lemo le	are yours. [No, they go with
mare. Sei	you.]
lemo igegeo.	

In the image created by the first serpoua, a man's ghost takes the form of the bird called *uaik,* a bird whose song is thought to move the hearts of people by making them nostalgic for lost relationships. The song describes how at dawn, at the conclusion of the song festival, the bird spirit pauses in the tree tops at the edge of the hamlet clearing and begins to sing to those it is about to leave behind. The ghost tells his kin to take possession of and to look after his things.

The last song of the festival can be seen as a response to this request. The song is sung as the dawn begins to break at the conclusion of the song festival, and it alludes to a dialogue carried out between a ghost and his kin. The ghost desires his kin to take possession of his things and to hold them as a remembrance of him. However, his children refuse to take the possessions. The last ritual act of the song festival consists of an enactment of the final allusion of this song. In the song, and in the song festival, the kin first gather up all the objects that have been used during the night: betel-nut skins, crotons, and herbs used to keep the smell of the corpse down, the pandanus mat covering that had been placed upon the corpse. Some of the dead's personal possessions are also gathered up: some of his shell money, his coconut-frond basket, his knife, one of his loincloths. These things are then placed into a large coconut-frond basket and, in beach villages, thrown into the sea. The final refrain of the song alludes to the disposal of these things, since with this act the dead's kin tell the ghost that they are sending his things away with him. And so the basket is thrown into the sea by the singers at dawn. One aspect of the person's social life ends when he is ritually divested of his possessions, along with all the memories, social relationships, ideas and values that these things symbolize.

As this occurs, the mourner ideally becomes "free to turn back from the face of death and to reassert his solidarity with the living." At the same time the serpoua "releases the dead to death, so it also seeks to release the living to life" (Redfield 1975:181). Still, there remain the problem of and the necessity for memory making, or the need to incorporate some aspect of the presence that has been lost into the life of the mourner, and into the cultural life of the Rauto people. In order for this to occur, a specific emotional attitude must be cultivated. As we shall see, the final rites of mourning encourage the expression of this attitude, and thus a transformation of experience.

A few months after the performance of Lamu's father's serpoua, an act similar to the final ceremonial act of the song festival was performed as part of a rite to end the series of mourning prohibitions that were being observed by Lamu's newly widowed mother. During the two months since the serpoua had been performed for her husband, she had been observing the prohibition against bathing, and the mark of mourning (soot) had remained smeared on her face and body. She had also not eaten pork or any other choice food out of remembrance for her husband, and she had carried, wrapped around her neck, one of her husband's loincloths. During the rite one of her affines snuck up behind her, forced a bit of pork into her mouth to end the prohibition on her eating pork, and gave her a meter of shell money in order to "finish her grief." The widow spit the pork out and at first refused to take the shell money, which was placed around her neck, on top of her husband's loincloth. She began to weep and cry out, and obviously did not want to be torn from her grief. The man who had been conducting the ritual removal of the mourning prohibitions from the widow, one of her husband's matrikin, named Ponda, then began to scold her harshly, telling her it was wrong for her to feel as she did so long after her husband's death, and that she was not showing good way (*lai itau*). His speech calmed her a bit, enough so that she permitted her affines to wash the soot from her face, to remove her husband's loincloth from her neck, and to take from her house some things of her husband's that she was holding as keepsakes. These things were given to Ponda. He put them in a basket and gave them to his son, who subsequently placed them on a large fire and burned them.

A few days later I asked Ponda why the widow's behavior during the rite had been "unseemly." His response was part of an explanation of an emotion that Rauto call *kipitngen* (quietly or stoically borne grief or pain). He said that it had become time for this woman "to close her sorrow inside of her, and to keep it to herself." He then described the way the woman was now acting:

> She has this feeling now (kipitngen). If you watch her now you will see her laughing, and talking. Yet in her heart, her sorrow remains. She will no longer express this pain as before. She holds it within (*kipit kano lia*). I bear this pain as well. When I remember my younger brother, and how he died,

> this feeling overcomes me. I just hold this feeling (*Nga kipit*). I don't speak
> of this pain in a clear place. This is something that belongs only to me (*lugu
> angan isa*).

I asked many others about this behavior. All either said or implied that they
would feel shame if, after a passage of time, they were openly to grieve for the
loss of even a most beloved person, even a lost child:

> My firstborn child Molokio died. His *tili,* his pearlshells, his dogs'-teeth
> headband, his cassowary-quill necklace—all these things of his remain for
> me to remember him by. I can never forget. I remember him as well when I
> work in my garden. I keep his memory inside as I work. Though it breaks my
> heart, I go on working. I can never forget. My husband's heart too was cut in
> half by this [the boy's death]. Still, this feeling sleeps inside of me only [I do
> not express it]. When people's children die . . . we [parents] hide our hearts
> from others (*momsoinse re kukop pe nesek*).

This elder woman describes a deep, yet bearable form of grief. She speaks
of it as if it were a private possession that had to be locked away inside of her. It
seemed that the internal space she had created for her grief was an integral part
of her memory and her identity, in the sense that it marked part of the contours
of her self, as did the objects of her dead child that she kept as remembrances.

As I sat and talked with this woman, with Ponda, and my friend Vatetio, I
asked if it was difficult to keep such strong grief and sorrow inside, and why
one should try to. Ponda answered:

> It is hard to keep this feeling inside, yet if you always express it, people will
> talk about you. They will become so tired of hearing you speak about your
> pain. Sometimes if you see an old person who has lost someone sitting in a
> garden house by himself, you know that he is remembering and is letting his
> feeling out. Then you feel pain and sympathy for this person, and you should
> leave him alone.

When a person bears emotional pain in this way, he or she is considered
to have exhibited good character, and proper comportment (*lai itau*). When
she burdens others with her grief too often, she violates a cultural ideal of
behavior. Rauto culture thus provides a moral imperative for people to accept
what initially seems unacceptable and unendurable: the death of someone dear,
someone who bears one's name. The rites and songs of death stress this ethic,
since they are ultimately geared toward transforming grief into nostalgia, so
that the person can endure the unendurable. Their *telos* is the evocation of the
emotions called makai and kipitngen.

In this instance kipitngen is simply the quiet emotional pain that is caused by the memory of a loved and lost person. Yet, the cultivation of this emotional attitude is necessary if a space for cultural memory is to be created within the person. Without a certain distance from the brute fact of death and personal loss, both individual living and the sort of collective nostalgic expression of meaning that is represented by both the poetic and actual construction of images of the dead during religious ceremonial would be impossible.

Besides creating a space for personal and cultural memory, the rites and songs of death also provide a moral imperative for the grieving person to accept certain culturally elaborated thoughts about death: the ideas that death makes orphans of the bereaved, and that the dead feel sorrow for the loss of their lives because the scenes and activities of life are so full of poignancy. It is perhaps partly because of these thoughts about death and loss that so much of traditional Rauto religious practice consists in a celebration of and valorization of human agency, and of the sort of spiritual assertiveness that, for instance, gives meaning to the songs of initiation and production. Yet remembering the dead is an essential part of such forms of spiritual assertiveness. Indeed, the visages of the dead are either made or are seen to appear again and again during such key moments of religious life; for example, during the planting of gardens and the construction of taro effigies, during the celebrations of initiation, and during the rites, songs, and dances for the dead. All these sometimes painful acts of nostalgic remembering and cultural creation are imaginative and feeling attempts to recover something of the presence that has been lost. They represent momentary attempts to integrate an image of this presence back into a living ensemble of spiritual relationships and thus, it seems, to reexperience a lost feeling of plenitude.

For this people the sacred seems the closest, the most intimate object. It is, at least in part, the memory of those whom one has lost, palpably sensed in the ensemble of relationships that constitute one's own identity.

SOME FINAL REMARKS ABOUT THE SONG CEREMONY

In a recent work, de Sousa has argued that "emotions can be said to be like judgments, in the sense that they are what we see the world in terms of" (1990:196). The emotions created and expressed by Rauto mourning songs do indeed appear as judgments about or evaluations of the character of the existential problem that death presents both to the bereaved and to his or her social group. The problem for both is to make something meaningful of loss by moving away from a sense of anger and toward makai, the sense of creative nostalgia and of plenitude. The particular pattern of emotions that appears as an essential part of this move represents a way of knowing the life significance of death. It is in this sense that it can be considered part of an actual philosophy, that is, as an "attempt to organize the understanding [of death] into a coherent vision" (de Sousa 1990:2).

This emotion philosophy reflects wider cultural suppositions about the nature of identity, person, memory, and the spiritual world that encompasses these phenomena. That is, it is embedded in a system of belief. Thus, for instance, the emotion makai draws meaning from a culturally elaborated notion that the person consists of a composite of identities; as Rauto ritual life shows, people embody the spiritual power and the social statuses and identities of others, both living and dead, in their own persons. Nostalgic remembering evokes or reanimates this understanding of the person as it recovers and expresses a form of the feeling of plenitude.

Considered in this sense, the nostalgic feeling that pervades Rauto rites and songs of death can be said to reveal the emotional value that participatory relationship and participatory identity have for this people. As I have shown both here and in previous chapters, cultural creativity or invention essentially means and is directed toward the simultaneous recovery and creation of participatory relationships. This results in the creation and evocation of images of the dead—images that embody something of the essence of a presence that has been lost. For the Rauto, an aspect of cultural invention can thus be considered as a culturally specific form of mourning, one that emphasizes the fact that participatory social relations and religious relations are not substantially different.

Considered in this sense, the emotion makai can be seen to organize and relate perceptions—not only about death, but about meaning and memory—in terms of a culturally specific "configuration of human experience" (de Sousa 1990:201), an experience that is marked by the particularly strong need to recreate, repetitively, powerful moments of interpersonal and social relationship. The emotion makai validates this form of experience by imparting a sense of authenticity or reality to it. In this instance, then, we see how emotion can arrange and embody both the cognitive and the experiential elements of culture.

Rauto mourning songs also arrange and embody the cognitive and the experiential elements of culture by making objectified images or texts of them. At the same time, the objectified images of emotion and meaning that are sung during serpoua draw people closer to the form of emotional experience they portray, and in so doing make it into a sharply defined pattern. As this emotional pattern is created in the discourse of the serpoua and in the rites of death, the personal and social experience of death is transformed as a particular understanding of it is formed. This experience and this understanding seem part of folk models of feeling and meaning that are not completely transparent to the Westerner. Indeed, the cultural elaboration of nostalgia and the crucial relationship between this feeling and the creation of meaning appear especially to distinguish this culture.

Paraphrasing Rosaldo's discussion of the semantics of the Balinese emotion *lek* (1984:142–45), one could say that the emotion makai is no more similar to nostalgia, the English term that most closely approximates it in meaning, than Rauto culture is to American culture. The particular emotional and religious resonance of the experience and understanding of makai gives it a degree of meaning and depth that nostalgia simply lacks. Indeed, in American perception nostalgia seems a passive feeling, one that has overtones of sentimentality—a feeling that is itself often denigrated as superficial. In contrast, the experience of makai is an essential part of the active construction of the cultural forms of Rauto religious discourse and practice. That is, it is associated with the most fundamental dynamics of Rauto cultural and individual expression.

As is apparent, this emotion is a major part of the dialectic of Rauto culture. As this dialectic involves continual loss and imaginative reconstruction, it is not surprising to learn that after a number of the objects of the deceased are destroyed during the period of mourning, the deceased literally becomes an object to be recovered. Thus, after burial and a period of interment, the bones of the dead person are taken up and repossessed as part of the rituals of secondary burial. In memorializing and in celebrating the agency of past lives during these rites and during other major cultural performances, the Rauto continually reanimate the world of their cultural concepts and emotions as they continually make a poem of death. The fundamental principles, human powers, and feelings that sustain life and make it meaningful are creatively and reflectively woven into this poem. Indeed, Rauto people draw life and cultural form from death, as they make a poem of it.

Chapter Eight

Mythic Thought, Religious Expression, and Individuation

The emotions associated with certain stories are also experienced in certain customs, rules and rituals.

Malinowski, quoted in Leenhardt (1979)

The metaphors and songs that seem to be reflections of an "instantaneous, fleeting, emerging and vanishing" (Cassirer 1955:178) emotional and spiritual content, the unending succession of names and marks that embody the human presence, the faces of the dead endlessly retrieved or seen in the midst of major cultural performances—all these are phenomena that present a wry face to attempts at summing up or putting a closure on an ethnography that describes them. Singing, speaking, naming, and remembering the faces of the dead are all gestures of indication—individual and social assertions of human presence and power. They are essential expressions of being that create social traditions and person, relationships with the living, the dead, the land, and with the things of the world. They are gestures that establish the cycles and rhythms of exchange and of time itself. The meaning of these gestures is to be found in the form of experience of which they are a part, and which they objectify into images, or "texts." Indeed, the texts of Rauto life, their metaphors, songs, and names are objectifications of experience.

As I write this I recall the image of a newly circumcised Rauto child crying while men of its matriline and patriline dueled with spear and shield in order to portray, and thus objectify, the child's pain and anger. I also recall the images of grief, anger, and nostalgia that were sung during serpoua, as well as the images of everyday activities and of everyday things that were sung as part of the aurang for initiation. As these images of feeling, of everyday life, of objects

216

and activities were evoked, they seemed to draw people closer to the forms of experience they portrayed, and in so doing they valorized this experience. In this sense these acts could be considered to share something of the character of the religious act of the consecration of images. Like the consecration of images of spiritual beings, the objectification of emotions, names, things, and activities during ceremonials takes a seemingly unshaped or raw material—in this case the flux of experience—and makes it into an object of belief.

Song and word are the vehicles of this form of consecration. They are the means by which experience is objectified into meaningful and moving images. The person's "essential power of manifestation," his or her word and song, is then what creates a meaningful and viable existence; it is what animates or calls to existence images such as the taro effigy, the bedecked initiate, the dancer who holds the bones of the dead, the dancing spirit beings, the scenarios associated with loss and sorrow. Thus, the images expressed in song and discourse do not simply convey and express meaning; they create it as they constitute persons.

Yet, while people and their emotions and experiences are "products" of discourse, they are also the producers of these phenomena. Indeed, religious, social, and emotional realities are created or transformed by *persons* during ritual performances such as the aurang or the serpoua. During these events performers "engender particular kinds of experiences in others" (Brenneis 1990:115) through song and other forms of expression. In the process they "constitute" these others as they extend their own power and presence to them. This seems to be one of the ways in which word and song bring the person to a world that "seems a vast interiority" (Ong 1986:164), a reflection of his being that seems "always of a piece with his life situation" (Ong 1986:33).

Leenhardt would have considered such a perception to be an expression of an aspect of mythic consciousness. Like his teacher and friend Lévy-Bruhl, he felt that this way of knowing established no division of the world into outward, and inward reality. Thus it presented the person's spiritual nature and character as being reflected by and embodied in others. This shared spiritual quality is what, according to Leenhardt, determined the character of religious experience. It is what the person seized in the midst of religious performance and expression.

Yet as Cassirer has suggested in his work on language, and as Kohut and Buber have written in their work on the self, the elementary movement of reaching out for or establishing a relationship with another is simultaneously an act of participation and of individuation. It is a means "by which the perceiving and desiring I removes an object from himself and so forms it into an objective content" (Cassirer 1955:181). Individuation then becomes a way

Two juxtaposed images, the usual form of mythic thought: a sea eagle whose body is the face of a spirit being called Varku; a parrot whose body is that of a lizard. Drawings by Coralie Cooper.

of understanding the object by establishing a relationship to it, as well as a way of expressing one's own being. This seeming paradox lies at the foundation of the forms of reality construction and self-fashioning that one finds in religious practice and thought. Thus it is that the forms of Rauto religious or mythic thought simultaneously establish individuation—which is really a way of understanding oneself in relationship to yet apart from the world—and spiritual participation.

In Leenhardt's language the aurang, the serpoua, and the other verbal genres that have formed the subject of this book would also represent the lived and thus immediately experienced forms of a myth—"the myth of identity" (Leenhardt 1979:191). Or we could say that this myth is lived *before* it is formulated into religious discourse, yet it is also lived *through* Rauto religious discourse and practice. Leenhardt's "mythic thought" has been replaced in the discourse of modern psychological anthropology by "primary process thought." Mythic identity has been more difficult to translate. Freudians sometime imply that the "oceanic feeling" of participation with other beings and with the world— a feeling Leenhardt would have considered to represent an aspect of mythic identity—is derived from a dim memory of a "pre-Oedipal phase" of human

development, a time when the person experienced the unconditional acceptance of the mother and the condition of identity with her. What I believe has
been lost in translation here, besides a certain elegance of language, is Leenhardt's insight that the outward forms and beliefs of the mythic life—what
anthropologists might call symbolic forms—are objectifications of an inward
desire not only for participation but also for self-articulation and even, finally,
for a culturally specific experience of personal authenticity that we might perceive to be an aspect of individuation. What a modern symbolic anthropologist
would call a symbol, or a system of religious symbols, he saw as immediately
experienced moments of this desire. Such moments seemed to him both the
projections of and the pathways of feelings through which the person found an
aspect of his or her identity. Thus, in his understanding mythic thought and
feeling were not simply part of and should not be confined to a specific phase
of the person's moral and spiritual development. They were an essential part of
being and of identity.

In reading through the pages of *Do Kamo* we see that in Leenhardt's perception, moments and events through which the person realized an aspect of
identity held a religious aura for the New Caledonian. Though indicative of
individual psychic process and need, these moments were relational in character: the desire for authentic individual wholeness represented the self's desire
for relationship. This desire bespoke more than a simple wish for positive communal forms of experience, however; it bespoke as well a need to seek the
essence of one's own being in the aesthetic images or forms that, as Bachelard
has written, are situated phenomenologically "at the origins of language, and
at the onset of thought" (quoted in Clifford 1982:210).

Clifford feels that Leenhardt was speaking here first of visual and acoustic
forms—for instance, images of the Melanesian landscape, often represented
in sculptures that expressed the felt rhythms of the cosmomorphic life, a life
which was an expression of the Melanesian's relationship to the natural world
(Clifford 1982:210). These forms also had a psychological component however. They were part of the person's psychic community as they enabled the
Melanesian to sense the continuity between his own nature and the natures of
other beings, persons, and forces. They enabled the Melanesian to feel himself a part of a landscape of presences. On these points Leenhardt's religious
anthropology resonates with Jung's religious psychology. Jung's understanding
of mythic archetypes as both the predicates of the individuation process and as
"the psychologically functional equivalent of communities" (Reiff 1968:131)
immediately comes to mind here, as does his notion that the archetypal forms
are the original basis of perceptions of time, space, and the character of aesthetic forms.

For Jung, psychological integration was made possible in religion—in a fashion at least—by a continual, ritually directed joining of the self with the sociomythic forms that he has called archetypes. These forms contained the germ of personality structure: they were the mythic underpinning of personality. Archetypes such as the anima, the animus, the self, and the mother represented different aspects of the person's soul or nature. Their unfolding in myth, dream, and ritual indicated a need for psychological integration and wholeness. As such, these forms seemed to offer a path toward self-realization and a promise of transcendence. Indeed, both Jung and Leenhardt felt that access to the religious and aesthetic forms of psychic experience made possible what Clifford has termed a renewal of life. However, both writers came to believe that mythic thinking or experience should only lay the foundation and provide the initial impetus for the individuation process. A complete immersion in the "flow of participatory emotions" (Clifford 1982:208) brought forth by the elementary religious and aesthetic forms created the type of psychic adaptation that Leenhardt called the personage.

While neither Leenhardt nor Jung was entirely consistent when drawing distinctions between true personhood and "personagehood," an idea that was common to both was that mythic thought should be yoked to rationality so that a person could bring about a psychologically balanced form of individuation. For Jung, this involved training the person to integrate the life meanings of the archetypal images into the conscious personality, while at the same time cultivating the person's ability to distinguish between the personality and these primary or archetypal forms. The personage was someone who could not make such distinctions and thus faced the danger of ego inflation. In Jung's thought this seemed a form of possession; the personage lost his individual identity through too close an identification with the archetypal forms of the collective unconscious. Jung identified this state as a primary psychological component of "primitive thought." Leenhardt too would have labeled such a form of psychic adaptation "primitive." In speaking of pure forms of mythic thought, he wrote that "primitivity lies here, in this aspect of unilateral thought, which, by depriving man of the balance between two modes of knowledge (the mythic and the "rational"), leads him into aberrations" (1979:194).

While Jung feared that a complete immersion in mythic experience would lead to psychological maladjustment, Leenhardt believed that it would lead to cognitive error; that is, that it would lead to, and had in the past led to, a distorted understanding or picture of the world. Leenhardt felt that the mythic world picture had inhibited the development of rational technique, especially technology and science, yet he believed that mythic thought could provide a spiritual and moral component to technique and to rationality (1979:195).

More specifically, it could bring technology and the materialist world picture into line with fundamental human emotional and moral realities. The person who stripped himself entirely of mythic feeling and thought closed off an aspect of experience that could save him from pursuing "his logical work to exhaustion, disgust, and death" (1979:195). That is, it could save him from the soul-crushing rational materialism of the modern age. Most especially for Leenhardt, the absence of myth meant the person's separation from the word: the immediate expression of, establishment of, and experience of emotional and spiritual relations. The moment of the word, the moment of mythic expression, was also the leitmotif of self-creation. Without it, or rather without the form of experience it represented, there could be no authentic personhood.

As we begin to recharacterize the religious forms and modes of expression described in this ethnography, we must reconsider the idea that Rauto cultural or religious forms can be considered as moments of the word, and thus as key emotional moments of a myth of identity and of individuation. We have seen how these forms are often pictured in vivid, concrete imagery—sensuous, rhythmic imagery that seems appropriate to eliciting and conveying the emotional qualities of the religious experience. We may say then, for example, that the images of everyday things and everyday activities that form the basis of the female puberty rite forcefully convey the emotional value that such activities have for Rauto women by expressing and circumscribing a moment of the individuation process. The "sign language" and expressive actions of this rite seem "aspects of the word as they furnish and express in emotion or fervor figures or formulas circumscribing an event" (Leenhardt 1979:190), the event of feeling oneself to be a "true person". The whole rite, including its obvious and obtuse mythic aspects, can be considered a word, a form of mythic expression, as it establishes a series of emotional ensembles between persons, between person and objects, between the living and the dead, between person and world.

There are ways to lend further support to the understanding that the forms of Rauto mythic or religious expression circumscribe moments of the individuation process. One of these is to consider a sample of the Rauto mythology of identity—fixed stories and legends, the events and characters of which seem but moments in which the person lives spiritually. Here I will point out the way that the themes and "emotions associated with certain stories are also experienced in certain customs, rules and rituals" (Malinowski, quoted in Leenhardt 1979:187). The point that I will bring out is that public cultural forms have a mythic underpinning that reveals the character of the individuation process. Considering these ideas will also involve a further, if brief, exploration of the themes of loss, imaginative reconstruction, and recovery—themes that determine the primary emotional tone of the rites and songs described in the preceding pages.

As we have seen, the religious act of recovery entails a reconstellation of lost emotional ensembles through the person's expression of word and song. The fashioning of self and other that distinguishes Rauto ritual and religious life is as much an act of remembering, then, as of self-realization. The themes of memory and recovery appear as the correlates of self-articulation and creation in Rauto mythology as well, as is especially apparent in the countless stories that begin by recounting the image of an abandoned, orphaned child or of a child left without status by the death of its father.

Myths that describe the abandonment of, the adventures of, and the eventual triumph or death of the orphan are considered to be poignant by the Rauto. They are so not only because they describe the orphan's abandonment, but also because they portray this character's need to reestablish and thus recover the lost relationship to the parents. Yet the tales also often present the orphan as moving or growing toward full independence. This is something that cannot be accomplished without a break from the parents (see Kerenyi 1963:28) and from the original dependent condition of childhood. These two conditions—the need for relatedness and attachment to others and the need for self-articulation and individuation—are, as we have seen, firmly embedded in Rauto cultural structures. The first of these that the actual Rauto child encounters is the cultural structure of childhood. The mythological theme of the abandoned orphan and of the orphan's eventual triumph takes its primary meaning from this cultural structure. A summary description of Rauto concepts of childhood would offer more than simply an insight into the meaning of the mythological theme of the orphan; it would also offer a deeper understanding of Rauto concepts of individuation. Thus, I choose to describe these beliefs before delving into an analysis of the myths of individuation.

CULTURAL AND MYTHIC STRUCTURES

According to Rauto folk concepts, the child enters this world with an attachment to another, unseen world. The beings of this other world include the ghosts or souls of the dead, the spirits of various animals, of various places of the land, and of the sea. Rauto people believe that the child's soul is only partly the child's own possession because of the soul's attachment to the forces and entities of this unseen world. In fact, the soul is thought to wish to rejoin the souls and entities that populate the unseen world, and is thus inclined to leave the child's body. While the child is identified with this other, unseen world, however, it also appears to be essentially a part of its mother. One of the ways that the mother imparts her nature to the child is simply by giving birth to it.

Bathed in its mother's blood by the event of birth, the child must remain with its mother in a separate hut for the first month of its life, lest the polluting blood of birth physically harm the community (especially the community of men). The first event of the child's life then consists of its taking on and being identified with an aspect of the mother's female essence: her menstrual blood.

The child then comes into the world marked by the stain of pollution and with a seeming attachment to another realm, and it appears, at least at first, somewhat dangerous to the community. This fear is a recognition of the danger and power of the place from which the child has come and with which it is identified: the realm of spirit, of the dead, of the unseen world. This realm and these forces appear also as metaphors for the creative power of the child's mother. We could put all this another way: the child seems unearthly, extraordinary, because it carries the mark of the creative power of its mother. The child's condition of identity with its mother seems the basis of the insight that it shares an essential nature with the beings and forces of the unseen world. Its relationship to its mother puts it into contact with the creative power that informs and animates life.

Yet the child's proximity to and kinship with the forces of the unseen world are thought inimical both to the development of its consciousness and to its physical development. Again using Leenhardtian language, we would translate this thought as follows: (1) The child seems immersed in the realm of myth; (2) part of the development of consciousness involves the child's individuation from the forms or forces of the mythic realm, as well as from the parental mantle—especially, as we will see, from the relationship of identity with the mother. These ideas form the essential meaning of a whole series of practices that involve the child, one of these being the prohibition of certain foods. The food prohibitions that I spoke of previously represent an attempt to separate the nonhuman from the human components of its soul or identity (*anine*), that is, to separate consciousness from the mythic forms. The continued possession by the child of these nonhuman qualities is thought to inhibit physical growth and to ensure the onset of childhood sickness. Thus, for example, wallaby is prohibited to prevent the child from becoming possessed by the spirit of this entity and thus crippled or constricted in development, as the wallaby appears to the Rauto eye when it shrinks in fear from a hunting dog. Parrot meat is prohibited lest the child become possessed by the spirit of this entity and begin to screech incessantly like a parrot. Fish is prohibited so that its skin does not turn jaundiced like the seemingly sunbaked yellow dorsal of certain reef fish. Once the child is thought to have developed sufficient consciousness and will, at about three years of age, these restrictions are reduced in recognition of the child's individuation from the realm of spirit, from the unseen world.

Juxtaposed to this long list of food prohibitions are the series of feasts and rites that often mark the increasing individuation of the child from its mother, as well as its increasing strength and growth. The appearance of the child's first teeth, the loss of its baby hair, its weaning (sometimes not until as late as three to four years of age), its naming, for boys the formal separation from the mother that is marked by the introduction to the men's house, and for girls the construction of a small house separate from that of the family—these are all marked by ceremony, feasting, and exchange. These cultural practices appear to push the individuation process forward.

As the child becomes less dependent both physically and psychologically upon the mother, a crucial physical transformation is also thought to take place within its body. The child's body is thought to become less like that of its mother, and more like that of its father. This change is thought to consist in the body becoming harder and dryer as it begins to develop and grow. The bodies of young women and children are thought of as wet and soft; those of adult men and, to a lesser extent, adult (especially elder) women are thought of as hard and dry. We could therefore say that in Rauto perception an aspect of physical growth consists of an increasing masculinization of the body. This idea represents another mythic condensation. The child's body is categorized as wet because of its identity with its mother.

Rauto procreation beliefs add support to these interpretations. The Rauto specify that the woman's biological contribution to her child is "only water," while the man's semen is responsible for the formation of the child's bones, organs, and blood, but they also say that the *infant's* body is "mostly water." The idea that is expressed by this phrase is that the infant's bones, blood, and organs contain more water than essential masculine substance. Thus, the child seems wholly of its mother; it is composed of female essence.

The Rauto mother takes on part of the responsibility for developing and hardening the body of her child. For instance, she will continually sit in the presence of fire with her child while warming her hands over the fire and carefully and continually "smoothing" and sculpting the child's features. People feel that the fire and the mother's warm hands dry the baby's body while straightening and elongating its bones, and believe the practice to allow the child to grow quickly and beautifully.

The way that what Leenhardt would call mythic thought informs the cultural practices and beliefs associated with infancy seems straightforward here. A host of these beliefs and practices are consistent with the mythic insights that (1) the mother-child dyad is somehow identified with the realm of spirit, with the unseen world; (2) the child's continued condition of identity with its mother and with the unseen world would result in soul loss, and thus death; (3) The life path consists, in part, of a culturally assisted individuation from the unseen world and from the condition of identity with the mother. Yet, as we shall now see, the most crucial mythic component of the individuation process consists of the attempt to recapture an aspect of the person's original condition of identity with the mother, and thus to recapture the original unified duality of the person. What is revealed by this process is that all adult Rauto are, in a manner of speaking, orphans. The cultural structures of childhood and the mythic beliefs upon which they are founded may underlie at least some of the feelings of loss and separation that are expressed during religious ceremonial. The separation from the mother that these beliefs and practices enforce may be seen as a part of the person's feelings of mourning for a lost intimate closeness with others. In recovering the feelings and memories associated with these lost presences and relationships, the person recovers an aspect of himself. Or rather he continually rediscovers that his own nature is fashioned from le duel, that it is a unified duality.

The Orphan and His Mother's Relics

There was a young boy whose father and mother died suddenly, leaving him orphaned, abandoned, and having to fend for himself. He would gather small clams and shellfish on the reefs, and would eat his catch along with the taro that he had raised. He carried on in this way from the time he was a child until the time he became a young man. One night, when he was preparing his cooking fire on the beach, a girl, seeing the fire, and being hungry, approached it hoping to be given some food. She came upon the boy, and the two began to speak to each other.

"Where are your people, your family?" she asked.

"My mother and father died, and I live by myself," he answered.

"You grow and prepare your food all by yourself."

"Who else is there," he answered. "I do all my own work."

As he spoke, the girl noticed how handsome he was, and his voice was sweet to her ear. The two spoke for a long time. She was smitten by him, and she asked him if he would come to her hamlet and be her husband. The two talked about this, and then they made love. Meanwhile her kin, her mother and aunts, and her father and uncles began to search for her. They searched from nightfall to dawn and finally found the boy and girl lying together on the beach.

"Look," they said. "These two are already married." The girl's father, uncles, mother, and aunts screamed at the boy.

"You have married the firstborn daughter of a great man; how will you give bride-price for this woman, you who have nothing! Will you buy this woman with the bones of your mother and father? You are truly worthless. You have committed a great wrong." They scolded the boy thus, and then they left. The boy and girl then went into the boy's house, where the girl fell asleep. The boy began to ask himself what he would do. He sat down by the grave of his parents, and unearthed some of their bones. Holding them, he began to sing the names of his parents and of the valuable red shell called *tili lua*. Many fathoms of the valuable shell came forth from the bones and lay in a heap beside them. He then again sang to the bones of his mother asking her for the white *tili*. And there it appeared in a great heap beside him. He then asked her for pearlshells and for both the tusked pigs called *paidela* and for those, which have no tusks, that are called *sokro,* and these animals and objects appeared beside him. The bones of his mother then began to sing to him, telling him that they had given him three times the amount of bride-wealth that he would require for his bride-price, and that he should offer the bride-price to his woman's kin on the following day. The next morning the girl went to fetch her kin, and told them that her boy had amassed a great bride-price. They were amazed when they arrived at the boy's hamlet and saw all his objects of wealth. All the kin then received their portion of the bride-price and happily carried it away.

In this instance the mythic theme of the orphan expresses the essential recognition of separation: the orphan has already left behind the original condition of identity with the parents. The myth specifies that the boy is completely independent, able to gather and prepare his own food and otherwise to provide for himself. At the same time, the child's lowly status as orphan emphasizes the poignancy of the loss that he has suffered. This includes not only the loss of the parents, but of the systems of support provided by the parents that are normally equated with achievement, high social status, and full humanity.

A subsequent portion of the story emphasizes the loss and need for recovery of another aspect of childhood: the belief in the magical charisma of the parents, most especially the idea that the parents are the source of all good, of all creative power. When the orphan is faced with the challenge of obtaining the valuables that will secure his bride, and thus his social personhood, he seeks the magical help of his dead parents, especially the help of his mother. Through the use of magical song, the orphan reestablishes the relationship with his mother. He calls on her relics to provide him with the essential objects of wealth that he needs to secure his social personhood; she responds with the generosity of a loving mother. She gives him three times the amount of goods he asks for and requires. I would argue here that the mythic theme of the orphan's loss and eventual recovery of the parental mantle and the related theme of the orphan's attainment of social personhood express an essential recognition that individuation includes both loss and imaginative reconstruction, or recovery.

This primary mythic insight both informs and is a reflection of the pattern of Rauto cultural forms and religious rites. That is, one of the key themes of both the mythological and cultural systems is the theme of reinvocation. The theme speaks of the reinvocation of the mother-child dyad, as well as of the feelings of plenitude and of participation with the world that seem such important aspects of this relationship. The moments of expression that key the reinvocation of this relationship are forward-looking or prospective as well as regressive in nature. For example, the moments when the aurang and the serpoua are sung contain within them the promise of a new psychological adaptation for the person, and thus the germ of a new personality structure. These moments are about the transformation of self and other.

Such moments also express the creative desire to invent and to live the meaning of culture form. Obeyesekere's view that the "work of culture" involves the transformation of "archaic motivations" and memories through the creation of images and symbols—symbols that transform private experience into public culture—is pertinent here (1992:60). The essential point, however, is that for the Rauto, individuation itself involves the continual creation and expression of images and figurative usages, and that such images possess many levels of meaning and countermeaning. In one context, for instance, an image may appear to have a primarily symbolic character; in another, a naturalistic character; and in yet another, an obscure or "obtuse" mythic one. Yet all these aspects of the mythic image seem to be aspects of the individuation process. It is primarily the symbolic aspect of the image that appears to redirect the nostalgic longing for recovery of and return to the parental mantle outward toward others, while transmuting this sentiment into a new level of response and understanding. The obvious symbolism of the aurang, for instance, can be interpreted as the poetically expressed wish to extend a parental concern for fostering physical and moral development not only to one's own child, but sometimes as well to an entire generation of youth, and further still to the objects and presences of the natural world. The mythic and naturalistic aspects of the aurang and serpoua meanwhile express nostalgia for lost relationships and refocus feeling and personal memory, evoking powerful, concrete, and immediate or primary experiences of loss and of participation. Word, song, and the cultural or mythic forms and images that they animate are not simply public symbolic forms that are purifications or elaborations of archaic experiences. They transform persons, emotion, and experience by combining immediate intuitive experience and emotion on the one hand with understanding and with the human propensity for symbolic elaboration on the other. The person achieves authenticity in religious performance by experiencing, either alternately or simultaneously, these different aspects of the word and of the mythic image.

This point is supported by another and central Rauto rite and image of recovery: the ceremonial complex that gives the practice of secondary burial its singular religious meaning. The complex is a cultural form that seems an analogue and concrete or primary mimesis of, yet at the same time a transformation or spiritual refinement of, a mythic event or image and a prevalent personal longing. The mythic event is that described in the story of the orphan: the orphan's request to the relics of his mother for assistance and support. The personal desire is the wish to recover some element of value from the lost relationship to the parents, especially to the mother. The dances, songs, and rites of secondary burial both re-evoke and transform mythic and personal longing into a culturewide insight about the character of existence. They express the idea that the resources and abilities that make the person's life possible have come as a gift from past generations.

What interests me most about this celebration is the insight it conveys that becoming a person involves a conscious recognition of the part others have played in fostering the development of one's own power and person. This is a theme that we can explore in more depth through a discussion of a second myth of individuation. The following story specifically deals with the spiritual and creative capacities of the Rauto mother, as well as with the role she plays in the individuation of the male child. As will become apparent, the public cultural analogues of the key themes of this myth are certain aspects of the female puberty rite.

The Mother of the Two Turuk Doves

A big man decided that his two eldest daughters were ready for marriage and so, as was the custom, he had them secluded in their house until the time when a good match could be made for them. In the great man's hamlet stood a giant Tahitian chestnut tree that was laden with nuts ready to be picked. The chief wanted to have a competition, and the two men who were victorious would be allowed to marry his daughters. The big man sent for his messenger, the blue bird *auda suwil,* and told him to spread word of the challenge. The men who could scale and harvest the tree would win his daughters. In the following weeks and months, many groups of worthy and wealthy suitors arrived to try their luck at scaling the great tree. They would try and try, but none managed to scale and harvest the tree. One day, as the blue bird was spreading word of the challenge, he stopped to rest at the hamlet of an old widow and her two sons. As the mother gave some water to the enchanted bird, he told her of the challenge. The woman's two boys wished to try to scale the tree and asked their mother how they could do it, when so many others had failed. Their mother said "Don't worry, tomorrow you two will go and harvest the tree."

The next day at the instruction of their mother, the two boys climbed to the top of their hamlet's betel nut tree. While they clung to the tree, she took some red clay and began to rub the tree trunk with it and as she did this the betel began to grow and bend. It stretched and curved until it reached the top branches of the chief's chestnut tree. The boys tied the betel to the chestnut tree and began to harvest it. In the light of dawn it was difficult for the villagers to see who was up in the trees harvesting the nuts. The people called for the boys to reveal themselves, but they would not. The boys filled their baskets with the nuts and then dropped them. The nuts caused a great din when they reached the ground and distracted the people from looking up at the boys. The boys then hopped over to the betel tree, cut the vine that was holding it to the chestnut, and swung back the many miles to their mother's hamlet. Afterward the two girls went with the blue bird to search for the two boys. He took them straight to the old woman's hamlet. They arrived just as the boys were returning from their garden work. The two couples chatted and chewed betel together and got along very well. The girls decided to stay at the hamlet, and they slept in the boys' mother's house. The next morning the girls sent word, via the blue bird, to their father that they were going to marry the two boys and would be remaining at the boys' hamlet.

All the big man's kin and hangers on ran down the two boys saying how they were worthless and poor, how they had no shells, no pigs, no valuables of any kind. The big man answered that he would see about that, and informed the blue bird that he and his kin would arrive at the hamlet of the boy the next morning to collect the bride-price. When the great man and his entourage arrived the next morning, the entourage challenged the poor boys and their old mother to give them at least ten pigs, and loads of shell money. There were ten tiny piglets in the widow's coconut-frond basket. The great man and his wife stood up. They were holding a string of shell money and they threw it to the ground to start the exchange. In response the older son reached into his mother's basket and caught and then threw a squealing and crying piglet to the ground. As it touched the ground his mother's spell transformed it into an enormous tusked pig, whose bellow resounded through the hamlet and surrounding forest. The boy and his mother transformed all ten of the piglets into giant tuskers. The pigs were so enormous there was no room in the hamlet for anyone to move. And the mother took other valuables from her basket and heaped them before the great man. He and his family were loaded down with the bride-price.

The two girls married the two boys and lived on in the hamlet. This is the origin of the two turuk doves, the cream-colored dove called *mangai* and the black dove, *makul*. These are the two doves that always fell the chestnuts and that taught people how to make the *turuk* baskets that people use to collect the nuts.

The myth begins by describing the main challenge that is to be faced by the two fatherless boys. The challenge consists of a seemingly impossible task. The boys will be required to scale and harvest a giant Tahitian chestnut tree if they are to win the daughters of the preeminent man. The great, food-laden tree serves as a metonym for life, fertility, and sexuality—especially because of its association with the two secluded daughters. It also appears as a symbol of the boys' desire for social and sexual maturity, which must be won against great odds. We could also say, then, that the tree and the challenge associated with it represent the wish for individuation, and for full social personhood. As Jung and his followers stress time and again, the wish for individuation often finds expression—in myth and dream—in images of the life force that they call the libido. The condensation of meanings that characterize such images expresses the all-encompassing and transformative nature of this force (see Jung 1976:222). In the language of the Jungian school, the great chestnut tree would be described as a libido symbol, one that resembles the archetypal image that they call the tree of life. This image often represents the mother, however, as well as the libido, and frequently a desire for regression to and thus reunion with the mother. Thus the symbol often unites the longing for individuation with the desire to return to a condition of participation with the mother. This insight is consistent with, if not a reflection of, this story's assertion that it is only through or with the help of their mother that the boys can achieve social personhood. The myth gives support to this point by describing the role played by the mother in helping the boys achieve the requisite social status. This is part of the point of the myth's concern with status and hierarchy.

We first see this concern in the theme of the secluded daughters. As only the daughters of prominent men and women are secluded prior to their marriage, it is clear that if the boys were to marry these women, they would raise their own social status. The myth implies that because the boys are fatherless and poor, they have much more to gain from the marriage than the other suitors, but are the least likely of the suitors to obtain the prize. Part of this prize would be full social recognition, and a triumph over hierarchy. However, this triumph is accomplished more through the power and wisdom of the boys' mother than through their own efforts. Indeed, when word of the challenge comes unexpectedly to the boys' hamlet they immediately discount their chances; it is their mother who gives them the courage to accept the challenge.

While the mythic scene of the scaling of the chestnut tree is a recognition of the mother's role in producing the social personhood of her children, it is also a symbolic expression of the key moment of the boys' separation or individuation from the mother. At the same time, the scene symbolizes the boys' recapture of an aspect of the mother, which seems to be her nurturative power—a point I elaborate shortly. In this mythic instance, as well as in a number of events that follow, the mother also appears to embody male as well as female qualities and capabilities. She appears as a phallic woman—a ubiquitous figure in world mythology—as her power is expressed through the phallus, represented by the betel tree. The major insight expressed by the representation of the mother's phallic capabilities may be that the libido, or life force has both masculine and feminine aspects, since it is identified with and expresses all forms of human power (see Jung 1976:221). Also, this mythic image can be seen to indicate how the boys' sexuality is in a sense closely tied to and perhaps even created by the mother.

Another aspect of the myth that reveals something of the character of the individuation process is seen in its concern with food and feasting. Thus the striving for social personhood, marriage, and accomplishment described in the story is represented, in part, as a desire to obtain the fruit of the great tree. The regressive and progressive aspects of the individuation process are again portrayed here. For instance, the longing of the boys and the other suitors for the secluded women, as well as for social achievement, seems also a longing for physical nourishment. Here individuation appears as an aspect of orality. The desire of the suitors, especially the boys, for achievement seems as well a desire to recapture something of the physical nurturance originally provided by the mother. The food of the great tree, then, may also represent woman's identification with physical nurturance, with food-giving.

The final events and scenes of the myth express the social value that is placed upon the Rauto mother by juxtaposing a series of assertions and counterassertions. The major apparent cultural counterassertion of the myth is the idea that a mother can literally create the physical and social personhood of her child without the help of a husband. The assertion brings to the fore a number of different perceptions and understandings of forms of female influence and power. For instance, one aspect of Rauto ideology holds that widows are statusless and thus unable to provide high social position to their children, because they do not possess husbands. Men, especially, often assert that all the objects of wealth, all the choice food, and all the honor shown to a wife come to her because of her husband and his influence. If he dies, her position and influence are almost always lessened. Indeed, in prepacification days, she could be killed, ideally at her own request, by her own kin. Her murder was viewed as a form of compensation rendered to her husband's kin in return for all the food, objects of wealth, and honor that came to the woman via her husband's labor, economic transactions, and reputation.

Cultural statements such as the conclusion of the myth of the two turuk doves and the female puberty rite articulate a completely different and, it seems, a more powerful view of the nature of female personhood and power. In such statements it appears that women are understood to produce wealth objects, food, and the moral and physical lives of persons through their own forms of power. These ideas are consistent with other, culture wide assertions that wives are responsible for the wealth and influence of their husbands—that a man can only achieve by taking a hard-working, resourceful, and productive wife. Women's close association with the activities of food production and preparation as well as with principles of human and plant fertility form the basis of these assertions, along with their ability and propensity to transact with objects of wealth.

One of the final events of the myth of the two turuk doves is a consummate expression of woman's creative power. The event seems to be a mythic analogue of beliefs and values expressed during the woman's puberty rite, especially those values and beliefs that credit women with autonomous creative power and with the right to possess culturally important objects of wealth. In the myth the mother magically and autonomously produces the objects of wealth that her sons need to secure their wives and thus make a claim for prominent social personhood. As the mother produced the boys physically by giving birth to them, so now, in the conclusion of the myth, she gives birth to their social identity by producing the needed objects of wealth: she produces ten huge tusked pigs from her coconut-frond basket.

Here the mother's basket seems to be the objectified representation of woman's seemingly magical procreative and creative power, and thus perhaps a symbol for the womb and for orality—the full pouring forth of creative power into the world, and the desire to consume the products of this creative force. Of course, this pouring forth of creative power is made possible by the mother's song and spell, by her word. The mother's word appears at once to be a form of creative power, and of her nurturing warmth projected outward toward the world. Indeed, the warmth and concern of the mother toward her sons results in the establishment of social concordance. Amicable relations are created between two family groups through the marriage exchanges that are made possible by the mother's creative act.

The creative expressions of word and song that characterize Rauto religious life have much in common with this mythical mother's creative act. Such moments represent what Nietzsche might call a Dionysian unfolding, or streaming outwards of forms of human power and concern. Yet, as we have seen, such expansive power requires embodiment in some mythic, verbal, or physical image in order to be conveyed to others and thus to have meaning. The *meaning* of Rauto religious experience is conveyed through the construction of images that structure and transform feeling by subjecting it to a perspective that sometimes requires reflection upon feeling. The character of Rauto religious expression provides an example of how feeling and understanding are united in the continual creation and transformation of the person and of experience. As we have seen, producing or transforming persons in the course of ritual performances involves creating certain types of emotions—nostalgia, sadness—in ways that resonate with wider cultural understandings about word and creative, expressive power. Such understandings are formed, expressed by, and derived from mythic images, which frequently picture and thereby circumscribe moments of the individuation process, as well as of immediate participatory experience.

Individuation itself seems nothing more or less than the fullness of experience made possible by the continual unfolding of the emotional power of word and of image—a fullness of experience that is as much about separation and loss as it is of spiritual participation or communion. Its character is defined by moments of insight and of sadness, as when a woman weeps as she perceives the face of her dead brother in the image of a dancing spirit mask, or when an old magician remembers his parents as he joins in singing the aurang for his grandchildren. The emotions and insights that are contained by such moments form the character of this people's customary religious life and experience.

Bibliography

Index

Bibliography

Allen, M. R. 1967. *Male Cults and Secret Initiations in Melanesia.* Melbourne: Melbourne University Press.

Ardener, E. 1972. "Belief and the Problem of Women." In *The Interpretation of Ritual,* ed. J. S. LaFontaine. London: Tavistock.

Auerbach, Erich. [1945] 1991. *Mimesis.* Trans. Willard Trask. Princeton: Princeton University Press.

Barthes, Roland. 1990. *Image, Music, Text.* New York: The Noonday Press.

Barth, F. 1975. *Ritual and Knowledge Among the Baktaman of New Guinea.* New Haven: Yale University Press.

Battaglia, Debbora. 1990. *On The Bones of the Serpent: Person, Memory, and Mortality in Sabarl Island Society.* Chicago: University of Chicago Press.

Black, M. 1962. *Models and Metaphors.* Ithaca, New York: Cornell University Press.

Bourdieu, P. 1986. *Outline of a Theory of Practice.* Trans. Richard Nice. Cambridge: Cambridge University Press.

Bourne, E., and R. Shweder. 1982. "Does the Concept of the Person Vary Cross-Culturally?" In *Cultural Conceptions of Mental Health and Therapy,* ed. A. Marsella and G. White. Boston: D. Reidel, 97–133.

Boyd, D., and L. Newman. 1982. "The Making of Men: Ritual and Meaning in Awa Male Initiation." In *Rituals of Manhood: Male Initiation in Papua New Guinea,* ed. G. Herdt. Berkeley: University of California Press.

Brenneis, Donald. 1990. "Shared and Solitary Sentiments: The Discourse of Friendship, Play and Anger in Bhatgaon." In *Language and the Politics of Emotion,* ed. Catherine A. Lutz and Lila Abu-Lughod. Cambridge: Cambridge University Press.

Buber, Martin. 1958. *I and Thou.* Trans. Ronald Smith. 2d ed. New York: Charles Scribner's Sons.

Cassirer, Ernst. 1953. *Language and Myth.* New York: Dover Publications.

Cassirer, Ernst. 1955. *The Philosophy of Symbolic Forms.* Vol. 1. New Haven and London: Yale University Press.

Chinnery, E. W. P. 1927. "Certain Natives of South New Britain and the Dampier Straits." Royal Anthropological Report No. 3. Melbourne: Melbourne Government Press.

Clifford, J. 1982. *Person and Myth: Maurice Leenhardt in the Melanesian World.* Berkeley: University of California Press.

Clifford, J. 1986. "On Ethnographic Allegory." In *Writing Culture: The Poetics and Politics of Ethnography.* Berkeley: University of California Press, 98–121.

Cohen, A. 1977. "Symbolic Action and the Structure of the Self." In *Symbols and Sentiments,* ed. I. Lewis. New York: Academic Press, 117–28.

Crapanzano, Vincent. 1979. Preface to Leenhardt [1945] 1979, vii–xxv.

Crick, Malcolm. 1976. *Explorations in Language and Meaning: Towards a Semantic Anthropology.* London: Malaby Press.

Crossan, John. 1973. "Parable as Religious and Poetic Experience." *Journal of Religion* 53:330–58.

de Sousa, Ronald. 1990. *The Rationality of Emotion.* Cambridge, Mass.: MIT Press.

de Man, P. 1979. "The Epistemology of Metaphor." In *On Metaphor,* ed. S. Sacks. Chicago: University of Chicago Press, 11–45.

Dening, G. 1980. *Islands and Beaches. Discourse on a Silent Land: Marquesas 1774–1880.* Honolulu: University Press of Hawaii.

Dumont, L. 1985. "A Modified View of Our Origins: The Christian Beginnings of Modern Individualism." In *The Category of the Person,* ed. M. Carrithers, S. Collins, and S. Lukes. Cambridge: Cambridge University Press.

Durkheim, E. 1965. *The Elementary Forms of the Religious Life.* Trans. Joseph Ward Swain. New York: Free Press.

Eco, Umberto. 1986. *Semantics and the Philosophy of Language.* Bloomington: Indiana University Press.

Eliade, Mircea. 1968. *Myth and Reality.* New York: Harper & Row.

Fajans, J. 1985. "The Person in Social Context: The Social Character of Baining Psychology." In *Person, Self and Experience,* Ed. G. White and J. Kirkpatrick. Berkeley: University of California Press, 367–97.

Feld, Steven. 1982. *Sound and Sentiment. Birds, Weeping, Poetics, and Song in Kaluli Expression.* Philadelphia: University of Pennsylvania Press.

Fernandez, J. A. 1974. "The Mission of Metaphor in Expressive Culture." *Current Anthropology* 15, no. 2: 119–33.

Feuerbach, Ludwig. 1965. "The Essence of Christianity." In *Classical and Contemporary Readings in the Philosophy of Religion,* ed. John Hick. Englewood: Prentice-Hall.

Foley, S. M. 1949. Patrol Report, Kandrian files.

Fortune, R. [1932] 1963. *Sorcerers of Dobu.* New York: E. P. Dutton.

Freedberg, David. 1989. *The Power of Images.* Chicago: University of Chicago Press.

Geertz, C. 1973. *The Interpretation of Cultures.* New York: Basic Books.

Geertz, C. 1983. " 'From the Native's Point of View.' On the Nature of Anthropological Understanding." In *Local Knowledge: Further Essays in Interpretive Anthropology.* New York: Basic Books, 55–70.

Gell, A. 1975. *Metamorphosis of the Cassowaries: Umeda Society, Language and Ritual.* London School of Economics Monograph Series on Social Anthropology, No. 51. London: The Athlone Press.

Godelier, M. 1986. *The Making of Great Men: Male Domination and Power Among the New Guinea Baruya.* Cambridge: Cambridge University Press.

Goodale, J. 1980. "Siblings as Spouse: The Reproduction and Replacement of Kaulong Society." In *Siblingship in Oceania,* ed. Mac Marshall. ASAO Monograph no. 8. Ann Arbor: University of Michigan Press.

Goodale, J. 1985. "Pig's Teeth and Skull Cycles: Two Sides of the Face of Humanity."
    American Ethnologist 12, no. 2: 228–44.
Goodale, J. 1986. "Gender, Sexuality and Marriage: A Kaulong Model of Nature and
    Culture." In *Nature, Culture and Gender,* ed. C. MacCormack and M. Strathern.
    Cambridge: Cambridge University Press, 119–42.
Goodman, M. 1968. *Languages of Art.* Indianapolis: Indiana University Press.
Gould, S. J. 1987. *Time's Arrow Time's Cycle. Myth and Metaphor in the Discovery of
    Geological Time.* Cambridge, Mass.: Harvard University Press.
Greenburg, J., and S. Mitchell. 1983. *Object Relations in Psychoanalytic Theory,* Cam-
    bridge, Mass.: Harvard University Press.
Havelock, Eric. 1963. *Preface to Plato.* Cambridge, Mass.: Harvard University Press.
Hays, T., and P. Hays. 1982. "Opposition and Complementarity of the Sexes in Naumba
    Initiation." In *Rituals of Manhood,* ed. G. Herdt. Berkeley: University of California
    Press, 201–36.
Herdt, G., ed. 1982. *Rituals of Manhood: Male Initiation in Papua New Guinea.* Berke-
    ley: University of California Press.
Jorgensen, D. 1988. "Secrecy's Turns: Revelation in Telefol Religion." Paper delivered
    at the American Anthropological Association meetings, Chicago, Ill.
Jung, Carl. 1976. *Symbols of Transformation.* Bollingen Series. Princeton: Princeton
    University Press.
Kahn, M. 1986. *Always Hungry, Never Greedy.* New York: Cambridge University Press.
Kant, E. 1969. *Foundations of the Metaphysics of Morals.* Trans. Lewis Wite Beck; ed.
    R. Wolff. Bobbs Merrill.
Keesing, R. M. 1975. *Kin Groups and Social Structure.* New York: Holt, Rinehart &
    Winston.
Keesing, R. M. 1982a. *Kwaio Religion: The Living and the Dead in a Solomon Island
    Society.* New York: Columbia University Press.
Keesing, R. M. 1982b. "Introduction" to Herdt (1982).
Kerenyi, Karl. 1963. *Introduction to a Science of Mythology.* Bollingen Series. Prince-
    ton: Princeton University Press, Torchbooks.
Kuechler, S. 1987. "Malangan: Art and Memory in a Melanesian Society." *Man*
    22:238–55.
La Fontaine, J. S. 1985. "Person and Individual: Some Anthropological Reflections."
    In *The Category of the Person,* ed. M. Carrithers, S. Collins, and S. Lukes. Cam-
    bridge: Cambridge University Press, 123–40.
Lakoff, G., and M. Johnson. 1980. *Metaphors We Live By.* Chicago: University of
    Chicago Press.
Langer, Susanne. 1985. *Mind: An Essay on Human Feeling.* Vol. 1. Baltimore: John
    Hopkins University Press.
Leenhardt, M. [1947] 1979. *Do Kamo: Person and Myth in the Melanesian World.*
    Chicago: University of Chicago Press.
Leenhardt, M. 1948. *Arts de l'Oceanie, Photographies Prises Par Emmanuel Sougez au
    Musée de l'Homme.* Paris: Collection Arts du Monde.
Levy, Robert. 1973. *Tahitians: Mind and Experience in the Society Islands.* Chicago:
    University of Chicago Press.

Lévy-Bruhl, L. 1928. *The Soul of the Primitive*. New York: Macmillan.

Lewis, A. B. [1910] 1988. "New Britain Notebook." In *The Field Museum of Natural History Bulletin* 59, no. 8: 6–28.

Lewis, G. 1980. *Day of Shining Red: An Essay on Understanding Ritual*. New York: Cambridge University Press.

Lutz, Catherine, and Geoffrey White. 1986. "The Anthropology of Emotions." *Annual Review of Anthropology* 15:405–36.

Lutz, Catherine. 1988. *Unnatural Emotions*. Chicago: University of Chicago Press.

Malinowski, B. [1935] 1978 *Coral Gardens and Their Magic*. New York: Dover Publications.

Marcus, G., and M. J. Fischer. 1986. *Anthropology as Cultural Critique*. Chicago: University of Chicago Press.

Mauss, M. [1938]1985. "A Category of the Human Mind: The Notion of Person; the Notion of Self." In *The Category of the Person*, ed. M. Carrithers, S. Collins, and S. Lukes. Cambridge: Cambridge University Press.

Obeyesekere, G. 1992. *The Work of Culture*. Chicago: University of Chicago Press.

Ong, Walter. 1986. *The Presence of the Word*. Minneapolis: University of Minnesota Press.

Ortner, S. B. 1974. "Is Female to Male as Nature Is to Culture?" In *Women, Culture and Society*, ed. M. Z. Rosaldo and L. Lamphere. Stanford: Stanford University Press.

Panoff, Michel. 1969. "The Notion of Time Among the Maenge People of New Britain." *Ethnology* 8:153–65.

Poole, J. F. P. 1982. "The Ritual Forging of Identity: Aspects of Person and Self in Bimin-Kuskusmin Male Initiation." In *Rituals of Manhood: Male Initiation in Papua New Guinea*, ed. G. Herdt. Berkeley: University of California Press, 99–154.

Read, K. 1955. "Morality and the Concept of the Person Among the Gahuku-Gama." *Oceania* 25:233–82.

Read, K. 1959. "Leadership and Consensus in a New Guinea Society." *American Anthropologist* 61:425–36.

Redfield, J. 1975. *Nature and Culture in the Iliad*. Chicago: University of Chicago Press.

Rieff, Phillip. 1968. *The Triumph of the Therapeutic*. New York: Harper & Row.

Ricoeur, P. 1979. "The Metaphorical Process as Cognition, Imagination, and Feeling." In *On Metaphor*, ed. S. Sacks. Chicago: University of Chicago Press, 141–57.

Rilke, Rainer Maria. 1975. *Rilke on Love and Other Difficulties*. Trans. John Mood. New York: W. W. Norton.

Robbins, J. 1988. "Order/Disorder as Opposed to What? Entailed and Unentailed Action in Papua New Guinea." Paper delivered at the meetings of the American Ethnological Society. St. Louis, Mo.

Rodman, M. 1987. *Masters of Tradition: Consequences of Customary Land Tenure in Longena, Vanuatu*. Vancouver, B.C.: University of British Columbia Press.

Rosaldo, M. 1980. *Knowledge and Passion: Ilongot Notions of Self and Social Life*. Cambridge: Cambridge University Press.

Rosaldo, M. 1984. "Towards an Anthropology of Feeling." In *Culture Theory: Essays on Mind, Self and Emotion,* ed. R. Shweder and R. A. Levine. Cambridge: Cambridge University Press.

Scalletta, N. 1985. *Primogeniture and Primogenitor: Firstborn Child and Mortuary Ceremonies Among the Kabana (Bariai) of West New Britain, Papua New Guinea.* Unpublished Ph.D. diss. McMaster University.

Scheff, T. 1977. "The Distancing of Emotions in Ritual." *Current Anthropology* 18:483–05.

Schieffelin, E. 1976. *The Sorrow of the Lonely and the Burning of the Dancers.* New York: St. Martin's Press.

Schieffelin, E. 1985. "Anger, Grief, and Shame: Toward a Kaluli Ethnopsychology." In *Person, Self and Experience,* ed. G. White and J. Kirkpatrick. Berkeley: University of California Press, 168–82.

Schweiker, William. 1990. *Mimetic Reflections: A Study in Hermeneutics, Theology and Ethics.* New York: Fordham University Press.

Steinhoff Smith, Roy. 1989. "Mourning Becomes Existence: Martin Buber's 'Melancholy' Ontology." *Journal of Religion* 69:326–43.

Strathern, Andrew. 1975. "Why Is Shame on the Skin?" *Ethnology* 14:347–56.

Strathern, M. 1986. "No Nature, No Culture: The Hagen Case." In *Nature, Culture and Gender,* ed. C. MacCormack and M. Strathern. Cambridge: Cambridge University Press, 174–219.

Strathern, M. 1988. *The Gender of the Gift.* Berkeley: University of California Press.

Tambiah, S. 1968. "The Magical Power of Words." *Man* 3:175–206.

Taussig, Michael. 1980. *The Devil and Commodity Fetishism in South America.* Chapel Hill: University of North Carolina Press.

Todd, J. A. 1935. "Redress of Wrongs in Southwest New Britain." *Oceania* 6:401–40.

Turner, V. 1967. *The Forest of Symbols: Aspects of Ndembu Ritual.* Ithaca, N.Y.: Cornell University Press.

Wagner, Roy. 1978. *Lethal Speech: Daribi Myth as Symbolic Obviation.* Ithaca and London: Cornell University Press.

Wagner, Roy. 1981. *The Invention of Culture.* Chicago: University of Chicago Press.

Wagner, Roy. 1986. *Symbols That Stand For Themselves.* Chicago and London: University of Chicago Press.

White, Geoffrey. 1985. "Premises and Purposes in a Solomon Islands Ethnopsychology." In *Person, Self and Experience,* ed. G. White and J. Kirkpatrick. Berkeley and Los Angeles: University of California Press, 328–61.

White, Geoffrey. 1990. "Moral Discourse and the Rhetoric of Emotions." In *Language and the Politics of Emotion,* ed. Catherine A. Lutz and Lila Abu-Lughod. Cambridge: Cambridge University Press.

White, G., and J. Kirkpatrick. 1985. "Introduction." In *Person, Self and Experience,* ed. G. White and J. Kirkpatrick. Berkeley: University of California Press, 3–26.

Williams, F. E. 1940. *Drama of Orokolo.* Oxford: Oxford University Press.

Wittgenstein, L. 1967. "Remarks on Frazer's Golden Bough." *Human World* 1, no. 3:18–41.

New Directions in Anthropological Writing
History, Poetics, Cultural Criticism

GEORGE E. MARCUS
Rice University

JAMES CLIFFORD
University of California, Santa Cruz

GENERAL EDITORS

Nationalism and the Politics of Culture in Quebec
Richard Handler

*The Pastoral Son and the Spirit of Patriarchy: Religion, Society,
and Person among East African Stock Keepers*
Michael E. Meeker

Belonging in America: Reading Between the Lines
Constance Perin

Wombs and Alien Spirits: Women, Men and the Zār *Cult
in Northern Sudan*
Janice Boddy

*People as Subject, People as Object: Selfhood and Peoplehood
in Contemporary Israel*
Virginia R. Domínguez

Sharing the Dance: Contact Improvisation and American Culture
Cynthia J. Novack

Debating Muslims: Cultural Dialogues in Postmodernity and Tradition
Michael M. J. Fischer and Medhi Abedi

*Power and Performance: Ethnographic Explorations through
Proverbial Wisdom and Theater in Shaba, Zaire*
Johannes Fabian

Dialogue at the Margins: Whorf, Bakhtin, and Linguistic Relativity
Emily A. Schultz

*Magical Arrows: The Maori, the Greeks, and the Folklore
of the Universe*
Gregory Schrempp

*To Remember the Faces of the Dead: The Plenitude of Memory
in Southwestern New Britain*
Thomas Maschio